AUDACIOUS PRAYERS

MAKING BOLD REQUESTS. EXPECTING ANSWERS

ALBERT B. K. APPIAH

WITH A FOREWORD BY
BILL FRASNELLI

WESTBOW
PRESS®
A DIVISION OF THOMAS NELSON
& ZONDERVAN

WestBow Press books may be ordered through booksellers or by contacting:

WestBow Press
A Division of Thomas Nelson & Zondervan
1663 Liberty Drive
Bloomington, IN 47403
www.westbowpress.com
844-714-3454

ISBN: 978-1-6642-5552-4 (sc)
ISBN: 978-1-6642-5554-8 (hc)
ISBN: 978-1-6642-5553-1 (e)

Library of Congress Control Number: 2022901815

Print information available on the last page.

WestBow Press rev. date: 2/15/2022

"I have known Rev. Dr. ABK for the last thirty-nine years. I have followed his journey with God and witnessed his progress with amazement at the constant miracles God has wrought in his life. This book is an inspiration to us all and is living proof that the God in whom Rev. Dr. ABK put his faith and trust, and who is no respecter of persons, can do the same for all of us who love Him, believe in Him, and trust in His faithfulness. The book contains accounts of how God pulled ABK and his family through very trying times because he dared to believe God and to pray *audacious prayers*. The book is eloquently written and easy to read. The powerful examples of biblical characters who prayed audacious prayers and were delivered from pain and suffering by the hand of God makes the book a compelling read and reminds the reader of the awesome power of Jehovah to answer effective fervent prayers and to change our life stories. The book is replete with scripture verses that ABK and his wife, Angie, stood on in order to receive divine healing and breakthroughs in so many areas of their lives. It tells of the trials and tribulations experienced by the couple on the journey of healing, of the upsets, the heartbreak, and the victories won in the face of adversity. This book is a living testimony of the goodness and graciousness of God, who will answer prayer if you dare enough to believe He can. This is a handbook about prayer and what prayer can do in your life if only you will not be moved by what you feel and see but dare to believe God and pray bold prayers of faith whether you are in ministry, are a congregation member, or are an unbeliever. There is something in the book for everyone to relate to. ABK points out that God invites us in John 15:7 (NIV), 'If you remain in me and my words remain in you, ask whatever you wish. And it will be done for you.' I recommend this book to everyone who wants to pray bold, audacious prayers to God and expect answers."

—Rev. Sammy Adjepong, managing director,
Alpha Beta Education Centers Ltd., Accra, Ghana

"*Audacious Prayers: Making Bold Requests. Expecting Answers* is exactly the kind of book I would expect from my good friend and brother in the Lord, Albert. When we first discussed that he was writing a book, my first thought was *Surely it must be a book on prayer.* This book has outstanding content. I loved reading Albert's story and seeing the hand of God in his life. This personal story and experience with prayer is exactly what we all need in this season of life. This book contains both the biblical and theological foundation for prayer and challenges us to be better in its practical application. You will experience many emotions reading this book. You may grieve, lament, feel humbled, be excited to read about a God who answers prayers, and feel challenged to pray more. This book is not advocating a 'pie in the sky' faith whereby all your problems are solved in an idyllic fashion. Rather, it will help you make prayer a sincere pursuit—following the One who hears us, wants the best for us, and is with us in our hour of need. My friend has set the example of what he writes in the final chapter. 'Cry out audaciously to Him, and watch Him answer beyond your expectations!'"

—Rev. Richard Smallie, Live Dead Silk Road, Granite City, Illinois

"In *Audacious Prayers*, Albert Appiah compellingly shares his life story and the breakthroughs God has given him in over twenty-five years of ministry. Woven throughout the book are lessons about prayer and the God who answered over and over again. *Audacious Prayers* will encourage your prayer life and challenge you to a new level of seeking God."

—Dr. Nick Robertson, director, Antioch Initiative, Minneapolis, Minnesota

"Prayer is a biblical practice many engage in without adequate knowledge to be effective. The disciples asked Jesus, 'Teach us how to pray as John the Baptist taught his followers' (Luke 11:1 NIV). It was then a norm that religious leaders taught their followers some unique way to pray. Prayer comes in several forms, and each has its own rules of engagement. Teaching on prayer is therefore essential to obtain the desired results. I know of no better teacher than Rev. ABK Appiah, who is equipped by precept and example to teach on this great topic of prayer. I highly recommend this insightful book to you."

—Rev. Robert Ampiah-Kwofi, Global Revival Ministries, Accra, Ghana

"A few pages into this book, I began to wonder if ABK—my mate from Adisadel College, Cape Coast, Ghana, a top-class boarding secondary school for boys—was being faithful to the title of the book as I was not sure if this was a love story, an autobiography, or an exegesis about prayer. It did not take me long to conclude, to my sheer delight, that it was a combination of all three. How brilliantly and beautifully these three cords are entwined and interwoven throughout the narrative.

"Is it a book about love? Yes! ABK's wife, Angie, comes into the picture in almost every chapter; their love blossomed and has remained undiminished with the passing of the years. The book lives up to its title because some of the prayer requests from ABK were, simply put, audacious! And of course, they became more so as challenges multiplied. Yet with the loving support of Angie and their combined prayers, they pulled through. It is also a love story of ABK and Angie's love for God and God's love for them; this shines through on every page.

"Is it a book about prayer? It is, and an excellent one too. Just read all the audacious prayers and be impressed! The book discusses in detail why this wonderful privilege should not be taken for granted and seen for the loving provision it is from the God who first loved us.

"Is it an autobiography? No question—with warts and all, with triumphs and the occasional despair, and with honesty and genuine struggles—this is an audacious book, audaciously titled, and an audacious attempt at an audacious autobiography interwoven with love and infused with prayer. It is an excellent book that should take pride of place in any home."

—Dr. Paul Mensah, MBChB, FRCOG, senior consultant,
clinical director, Department of Obstetrics and Gynecology,
National Health Service, Scotland, UK

"Ministry to the soul takes place in many ways, and God is so faithful to strengthen our hearts with rich fellowship in the body of Christ. It was my honor to advise Dr. Appiah through his doctoral program in seminary many years ago, and now, years later, to edit this book for him. Truly, the insights and stories on each page ministered to my spirit! The power not only of exemplary love for God and others but also of remarkable faith, perseverance, patience, wisdom, and joy in serving Jesus—no matter what—invigorated my heart as I carefully read each word. May God enrich your soul with the testimonies in this book as He did mine!"

—Rev. Dr. Lois E. Olena, freelance editor, associate professor
of Jewish studies and practical theology (ret.), Assemblies of
God Theological Seminary, Springfield, Missouri

"Influenced by the teaching of God's Word and intensified by his own testimony, Pastor Appiah has given us a book to strengthen our faith and practice a key Christian discipline: prayer. His writing will encourage and embolden your desire to *pray* diligently, powerfully, and more intimately to the Lord."

—Rev. Ariel Rainey, missionary, Madrid, Spain

"'Audacious prayers were uttered amidst great odds' (p. 236). Over the years, I have observed and admired the faith of Dr. Albert and Angie Appiah. Years ago, Albert and I also traveled throughout Northern India to encourage and pray for pastors. Albert and Angie are passionate about the things of God and have persevered under tremendous adversity. After reading *Audacious Prayers*, I now know how they have stayed strong in life and ministry: they know how to touch the throne of God. Their eyes are fixed on Jesus. This book is a prayer textbook that comes from lives who have experienced answered prayers. It is filled with personal stories of hope that remind us that God is still in control."

—Dr. Keith G. Edwards, lead pastor, Centerpointe Church, Fairfax, Virginia

"Isaiah 40:31 talks about renewed strength for those who wait on the Lord. For Rev. Dr. Albert B. K. Appiah, *waiting* literally means *fulfilling God's will and calling*—like a waiter—forsaking all for His glory, hoping against hope like Abraham, contending in prayer like Jacob, interceding like Christ, and awakening the attention of heaven to impact earth.

"What you hold in your hand is not just another theological book on prayer. This is a living epistle of a servant-leader with the mind of Christ, acquainted with His suffering, dedicated to the knowledge of Christ, and therefore with the audacity to experience the power of His resurrection. Audacious prayers are not just *loud* prayers but *fervent* prayers made by people like the writer who have cultivated the friendship of God through obedience and total submission. People like Reverend Appiah know their God and have the audacity to believe His Word, pray audaciously, and always activate that tremendous power that produces miracles signs and wonders.

"The testimonies shared are greatly inspiring, and the principles taught will change the trajectory of your life as you learn to pray audaciously and receive your own spectacular answers. I am truly humbled yet greatly delighted to recommend and endorse this book by my dearly beloved friend, Rev. Dr. ABK Appiah.

"Your prayer life will never be the same!"

—Dr. Nada Owusu, MD, FAAP, author, Danville, Virginia

This book is dedicated to my wife and best friend, Angela, and our twins, Sam and Sara.

Angela invited me to church when we first met. We were friends for five years before I proposed to her. Her strength, intelligence, integrity, love, and support have made all the difference in my life. Her unflinching support and encouragement were indispensable in the writing of this book.

Our twins are a tremendous source of joy to our lives. I am fortunate to be blessed with such a supportive wife and lovely children.

CONTENTS

FOREWORD

Many books have been written on the subject of prayer. Most authors distill the subject down to a formula concerning how to receive from God.

Although we do find what seems to be certain ingredients to effective prayer, such as praying in Jesus's name, Dr. Appiah does not here write a "silver bullet," nor does he prescribe a "do this to get what you want" approach in prayer.

My good friend and ministry colleague brings a balance to the subject of prayer—a balance rarely found on bookshelves today. Albert's honesty and clarity answer many questions people have about prayer being answered as they had hoped and when God's ways are, as He has revealed, "higher than ours"; and the future turns out a little different from expected.

I can personally attest to the power of prayer. I have had the privilege of sharing in prayers of agreement with Dr. Appiah that have yielded miraculous results.

It is therefore my pleasure and privilege to recommend this book. From the story concerning Albert's mother being a great intercessor and example of biblical faith to Albert's prayer for the readers to offer *audacious* prayers, we find encouragement from God's word and the author's personal encounters with God in prayer.

Pastor Bill Frasnelli, lead pastor of Jubilee Christian Center Fairfax, Virginia.

PREFACE

Several years ago, a friend asked me to pick up a missionary arriving at Baltimore Airport from West Africa. Since my friend lived all the way in Danville, Virginia, we hosted the missionary until she could pick her up a few days later. The missionary liked our house and asked me to give her a tour. That was fifteen years ago at the time of writing this book.

Upon entering my study in the basement, she paused and said, "The Holy Spirit is saying that there are books you will be writing." She pulled out two $100 bills from her purse and gave them to me. She said it was a "seed" into the books the Lord wanted me to write. I kept those two $100 bills in a safe deposit box and decided to use it toward the expense of publishing when the time came for writing. Thirteen years later, I exchanged those bills for newly issued ones to prevent them from becoming obsolete.

I enjoy reading and writing and have always harbored a desire to write extensively at some point; however, I always felt incomplete and rather unprepared. I never wanted to write just for the sake of writing. Somehow, I have always felt that I must write when I believe God has matured me and graced me with a story to tell. I believe a book will impact lives only if the writer has been deeply impacted by what he or she has to share. We are only impacted as we experience the issues of life in a way that would encourage and motivate others. Such an impact happens with the passage of time. I believe divine timing is imperative if God is to use a book to touch others. Many friends and well-meaning people have pressured me to write, but I never felt the time was right. Somehow, I feel the writing of this book is timely. It is now time to write. Let me explain why.

On our thirty-first wedding anniversary, my wife and I planned to celebrate with a getaway to Virginia Beach, one of our favorite places. I enjoy the ocean—the peace and serenity it gives, the story it tells about the vast powers of the Mighty Creator who spoke it into being—and I particularly enjoy walking and praying on the beach in the mornings. I can easily spend a couple of hours doing that. I was excited we were going to one of my most favorite places on earth and that I was going with my best friend and wife of thirty-one years. The plan was to leave after service on a Sunday. All arrangements had been made. A gracious and wonderful family friend was coming over to stay with the children in our absence. I had it all figured out that I would spend as much time as I could to start writing this book.

We were all set to go. Somehow, on Wednesday, my wife said, "Honey, I think you should go by yourself and focus on writing." I tried to convince her to come along, but it was to no avail. She would not budge. Finally, I said, "Well, in all things, God works together for the good, so it's OK."

Sunday's service was a special one. It was our "Pastor Appreciation" service done once a year to honor us for our service as pastors. I did not have to preach. It was a time to sit back, relax, and have the church tease us in good fun and express appreciation.

Something interesting happened that day. As the guest speaker began speaking, he suddenly paused and said, "Dr. Albert, there are books in you that have to come out. You need to carve out time to write them. The church must give you some extended time away periodically to write." That was an interesting divine confirmation that it was truly time to begin writing. That guest speaker had absolutely no idea of my writing desires. He had no idea that I was actually on my way to Virginia Beach to spend some time in writing. I tell that story to make the point that I strongly believe this book is meant to impact many lives. The circumstances surrounding its timing so convince me.

The title of this book was originally *Hindrances to Prayer*, but several months after I had begun writing, it became clear that *Audacious Prayers* captured the thoughts in the book better. The latter title gives us the impetus to press on with audacity, knowing that our prayers can come boldly before God's gracious throne to be heard.

Webster's Dictionary defines *audacious* as "taking or willing to take risk, bold, unrestrained by convention or propriety, insolent."[1] Audacious prayers, therefore, involve praying bold prayers—praying without restraint, unrestrained by the conventional fear that we might be asking for too much from God. The Bible encourages us with these words: "So let us come *boldly* to the throne of our gracious God. There we will receive His mercy, and we will find grace to help us when we need it most" (Hebrews 4:16 NLT; emphasis added).[2] I believe that understanding the nature of praying boldly helps believers increase their effectiveness in prayer.

This book is the result of much prayer and meditation, standing as an attestation to the prayer-answering power of the living God. It is woven through with many personal stories that God has graciously allowed us to experience—many challenges we got through only because of the power of prayer.

It is my prayer that you will be challenged and blessed as you make your way through the book. May the Spirit of God open the eyes of your understanding in this vital area of your Christian journey.

Prayer: Lord, I ask that You impact the life of every reader with that which is needed in their lives as they read. Amen.

ACKNOWLEDGMENTS

I am grateful to God for giving me the opportunity to write this book and connecting me with people who made this possible.

In the journey of life, our paths are destined to cross with individuals who can be described as destiny helpers.

This book is the result of the hard work and prayer support of some cherished individuals.

I wish to acknowledge Cheryl Smith for her love, support, and prayers over the years. She prayed fervently and encouraged me throughout the writing of this book. She surprised me one day when she gave me a very generous gift toward the publishing of this book. She is a great family friend and ministry partner.

I also wish to acknowledge Ivy Tettegah, who worked tirelessly behind the scenes to organize and make things easy for me to write. I call her the Amazing Woman. She spent countless hours helping to organize the material for this book. She also designed the cover of this book. I am just grateful for her life.

I am also indebted to Alicia Adams, who took my picture for the cover as well as the board and congregation of Renewal Christian Center who have been a part of our journey for years. Finally, I am very grateful to Dr. Lois Olena, my editor. She worked speedily on the manuscript and helped make this dream a reality.

INTRODUCTION

Prayer is a vital part of the Christian journey. The importance of prayer is underscored by the fact that Jesus spent a tremendous amount of time seeking the face of His heavenly Father in prayer. I believe the prayer life of Jesus kept Him on track to accomplish the purpose for which the Father sent Him. It is significant that after the disciples had paid close attention to the prayer life of Jesus, they came to Him and said, "Lord, teach us to pray" (Luke 11:1 NIV). That is when Jesus taught them the Lord's Prayer.

Prayer is a must for success in the Christian journey. The Bible is full of examples of how God answers prayer. It also has numerous calls for God's children to pray.

This book is about praying bold prayers and believing God to answer them. It is about petitioning God audaciously and expecting answers. It draws on many examples from the Bible to underscore the fact that God does answer prayer—even the most audacious of prayers. It is also woven through with personal examples from the writer's own life about some rather bold petitions that God granted. It talks about the basis of audacious prayers and offers an encouraging challenge for every Christian to pray audaciously and believe God to answer.

CHAPTER 1

THE GENESIS OF IT ALL

I WAS BORN AND RAISED in Ghana, West Africa, and I vividly remember the altar my mother had in their bedroom. My father never went to church when we were growing up. He only became a Christian after his retirement. My mother was different. She was very active in her faith, constantly fasting and praying for her family. I remember my oldest brother once complaining about Mom spending so much time in fasting and prayer, but Mom understood something in her spirit that we were not privy to. We would go with her to church, but I definitely had no clue what it meant to be a Christian. I am utterly convinced that Mom's fasting and prayer are what protected and preserved her ten children through the years. I grew up watching an intercessor in the person of my mother. I spent my teenage years in boarding school and only saw my family during our long vacations. Those times were rather brief because I spent most of my vacation time with an uncle in another city. That was my regimen all through my high school and college years.

After college, I spent some time in London with my college roommate, who was also my closest friend. He came from town one day and said he wanted me to meet a good family friend from back home in Ghana. That was my introduction to my future wife. Of course, I did not know it at the time. The first thing she did was to invite me to church. I was not a Christian and was not particularly interested in church. I knew I was basically a good person and did not think I needed formal religion to live a good and moral life. Somehow I consented though and found myself taking the train every Sunday to join her for church. It was a rather interesting experience for me. The pastor was a former police officer who responded to a call into ministry and ended up planting a church on the outskirts of London. I always looked forward to meeting my new friend, Angela, at the train station and riding with her to the services. I would have my notepad in hand and take copious notes as the pastor preached. I could not relate to the excitement and enthusiasm of the people though; it did not make sense to me. They were a contented group of people who somehow had found peace with God. It was meaningless to me. God could not be that personal, real, or intricately involved in the lives of humans.

After almost every service, I would confront the pastor with my notes and ask why he thought the way he did. Once I said to him that the church's desire to set up a Christian school was not the right thing to do. I said it was simply going to shield the children from experiencing the broader worldview that they were rightly entitled to if they attended regular public schools. I saw Christianity as a way of isolating people from the reality of broader social norms and behavior.

Little did I know that I was in total darkness. I had absolutely no clue of the dangers involved in living without a relationship with one's Creator.

I had always been a smart student and prided myself on my reasoning abilities. Little did I know that I was in total darkness. I had absolutely no clue of the dangers involved in living without a relationship with one's Creator. Pastor Mike was always kind and gracious. He would invite Angie and me to their home for lunch almost every Sunday since we typically also stayed for the evening service before taking the long train ride back to the city. Those times together were my opportunity for endless questions and arguments about the teachings of Christianity. I was searching for the truth, and my young mind would not settle until I was convinced Christianity was worth it. I simply could not come to terms with all the time they invested in church and various undertakings in the community. Pastor Mike was never offended by my numerous questions. He must have found my restless mind rather interesting. I also believe they must have been praying for my soul. Strangely enough, Angie was always understanding and never felt embarrassed by my numerous questions and unbelieving stance. She never pressured me into accepting Christ. She simply kept inviting me back to church with her.

One day during a prayer service, I was in a corner of the sanctuary just trying to relate to everything around me. Angie did not attend that service with me as I had decided to go by myself. I had been attending the church for several months but still was unconnected with what was going on spiritually. That night was different. I sat quietly in the sanctuary as everyone prayed. Suddenly, I felt an intimation within me that it was time to give my life to Christ. The urge was persistent and rather irresistible. I simply got up, went to the pastor, and told him exactly what I was feeling. He was very happy for me. I gave my life to Christ and got baptized the next Sunday. Suddenly, it was almost as if scales had fallen from my eyes. I could now relate to what was going on. The darkness had been cleared. Christ had extended His grace to one more lost soul. The kingdom of darkness had become depopulated by one soul, and God's kingdom had been populated by one more child.

I had never read the Bible or owned one. Angie was so excited for me. Her friend had finally surrendered to Christ. She quickly got me a Bible, which I still have in my study. I was excited and devoured the entire Bible in a rather short span of time. I made copious notes as I read.

After reading from Genesis to Revelation, I came back to the front leaflet and wrote these words: "Life without God is a hopeless end; life with God is an endless hope." I had crossed over from the darkness of the enemy's grip into the liberating life of Jesus. I had a newfound freedom and joy. I could now relate to what was happening around me spiritually. My heart was at rest. I was so grateful. I immediately began processing everything through my newfound Christian worldview.

Shortly after my conversion experience, it was time to leave London and go back home to Ghana. The Lord was not entirely done with me. He had another surprise in store. The church was holding some special services, and I attended every night.

At the last evening service before I was to leave London, the pastor asked the elders to gather around and pray over me. As he began praying, he uttered some rather strange words that I found scary and confusing. I was a new Christian and knew nothing about how the Spirit of God could speak a prophetic word through God's children. The pastor said something to this effect:

> Many things are stirring in your heart. Your desire is to change people through the political arena, but God has something different for you. It is not through politics. A seed has been sown in your heart that is yet to germinate. God has a different plan for your life. There is a light that has been lit in you. It will burn brighter and brighter.

He then closed by praying, "Lord, let every seed dry up except the seed of life." I still remember those words today. They were deeply lodged in my spirit. I felt afraid and confused.

Why should every seed in my life dry out except the seed of life? I was particularly stunned by the fact that he seemed to have revealed the deepest longings of my heart. Deep down in my spirit, I yearned to make a difference in society through politics. After my first degree in economics and political science, my plan was to get a law degree and pursue a career in politics. I saw the political arena as the most feasible means of impacting lives and making a difference in society. How could Pastor Mike emphatically say in his prayers that God had a plan for my life that was totally different from my agenda in politics? He and I had not discussed that. I was even more confused now.

Pastor Mike asked the media crew to give me a copy of the tapes from the service and the prayers he prayed over me. He handed them over to me before the congregation and said, "Albert, take these with you. You would need them someday." As you can imagine, my curiosity and confusion only intensified. How could this man be so sure of himself about what God had told him about me to the point of giving me a recording of it? God was giving me a future point of reference. The Lord did not want me to forget the genesis of my call. I carried those tapes with me wherever I went and whenever I traveled.

A few years after leaving London, Angie and I met back in the United States and got married.

> The Lord did not want me to forget the genesis of my call.

Angie and I had been friends for five years. I was the introvert when we met, and she was the extrovert. I had always admired her integrity, strength of character, intellect, outgoing nature, love for God, and sheer strength to endure adversity. Angie is a gifted administrator and planner. She has an uncommon knack of executing the most complex activities with class and excellence. She researches everything until she comes up with the best solution. Her organizational skills are par excellence.

I could not have been blessed with a greater gift of a wife. I am the visionary, and she is the manager of the family. Our skill sets complement each other. We love each other dearly, and our children know that. I often tease her that I was her divine reward for inviting me to church to give my life to Christ.

We felt blessed and happy. I was working and pursuing an MBA degree. She was working in malaria research. We had a beautiful, new home. We were deeply involved in a newly planted church (one-year-old when we began attending) that worshipped in a school facility. I served as an elder and board member of the church, and Angie was in charge of Sunday school. Angie was already attending that church when we got married, and we were the first couple to be married there. Our wedding was performed in the school cafeteria. I remember my conversation with the pastor as Angie and I were getting ready to drive off for our honeymoon. I said to him, "We will do God's work with our entire being." Those words turned out to be rather prophetic. We labored vigorously to help establish the church. We worked with the youth ministry, which kept us both very busy. Being in a school, there was always a lot of work to do in terms of setting up for services. I vividly remember carrying our personal television set from home to church every Sunday to set it up for the youth. We used our house for all kinds of youth activities since the church had no place to meet outside of the school.

In our personal lives, we felt very blessed as well. Marrying a friend made our relationship especially close. She knew my likes and dislikes, and we had done various things together as friends before I asked her to marry me. We were financially blessed. Life was simply good. We enjoyed traveling and vacationing. We could go wherever we wanted and do whatever we wanted. We had no children then. We could go and come as we pleased. We were great friends and loved each other dearly. We still do after three decades of marriage!

A few years after getting married, I began to feel a stirring that God was calling me into full-time ministry. I could not shake the thought from my spirit. I kept it away from Angie for a while because I was not sure how she would react to the news. I also remembered those old tapes from years back in London. I looked for them and listened to the message. It was true. Those prophetic words were coming to pass. All I could think of was doing what pleased God, but how was I going to break the news to Angie? How was she going to take it? What would the implications be for our lives and marriage?

Finally, I mustered enough courage to tell her. I had it all figured out. I would take her out to dinner and break the good news to her that the Lord was calling me into full-time ministry. Somehow, I felt confident that she would rejoice that God had called me to serve Him in ministry. I quite remember the evening when I informed her. We both enjoy Mexican food, so I took her to a nice Mexican restaurant to break the good but scary news to her. Angie was most unamused. She immediately registered her opposition. She made it clear that she did not sign up to marry a pastor. She was worried about the financial implications of my resigning from my job and pursuing a degree in divinity to prepare for ministry. I remember her response so vividly. "Please let's sell the house. I will go back to Africa and stay with my dad. When you finish your studies, I will come back and join you."

Obviously, the Mexican restaurant had not done the trick. I knew something had to change. The solution was prayer. Prayer works. Prayer changes everything. I began seeking the face of the Lord in earnest prayer. I was determined that I would not compel her to do what she was not convinced about. Only God had the power to touch her heart and convince her about the call into ministry.

Angie's resistance became a turning point in my prayer life. It made me develop a passion for intercession. I started learning to pray audaciously. We lived in a beautiful four-bedroom house, and no one else was with us. I used one of the rooms as my prayer closet. Every morning, I would diligently pray from five to seven without fail before leaving for work. I prayed for God to touch Angie's heart so she could respond to the call and allow me to pursue ministerial training. I also prayed to get closer to the Lord. I spent lots of time on my face and in the scriptures seeking the Lord. I also asked God to make a way for us financially. We had sold our old house and bought a new one. We had lived in our brand-new home for only two years. How were we going to afford the mortgage if I resigned from my job? Those were real questions that needed answers. Those answers could only be received through audacious prayers and audacious faith.

One day, I felt I had waited enough for Angie to come along. I told her it was time to respond to the call. I said to her that we would never be happy if we failed to respond to the call of God upon our lives. We could not hold it off forever. I applied to do a master's in divinity and had to move to Missouri for my seminary education. Angie was still very resistant, but I knew it had to be done. We sat down and did our budget without my salary. Needless to say, it did not balance. I assured her that I was going to trust the Lord to take care of our mortgage every month. I asked her not to worry about that. She simply responded, "You are the economist in this house; tell me how the finances are going to work out under these circumstances."

She also reminded me that the Lord admonishes us in the Word to count the cost before we build. Her question was "Have you counted the cost of what you are asking us to do?" Again, my response was to seek an answer from the Lord. I spent a lot of time in prayer that night, and I heard a word from the Lord. It was from the book of Mark. This was the instance when Peter said to Jesus, "We have left everything to follow you" (Mark 10:28 NIV). Peter was concerned about whether following Jesus was really worth it. He had left his fishing business to follow Jesus. Others like Matthew had left a lucrative tax-collection business to follow Jesus. Was it worth it at all?

Jesus's response was straight to the point.

> No one who has left home or brothers or sisters or mother or father or children or fields for me and the Gospel will fail to receive a hundred times as much in this present age: homes, brothers, sisters, mothers, children and fields—along with persecutions—and in the age to come eternal life. (Mark 10:28–30 NIV)

The next day, I confidently said to Angie that I had a word from God. I informed her of how the Lord answered my prayer with the passage from Mark. However, my spirit was troubled because somehow the words "with persecution" seemed to have been lodged unshakably in me. I had the assurance that God was definitely going to bless and take care of us, but I also received the clear message that along with that, we should prepare to suffer persecution. It was not my imagination. I knew the Lord was highlighting that to me. Years later in ministry, that statement became a normal part of my life in ministry. God has blessed, but the enemy persecutes relentlessly. Both our bodies have gone through unimaginable afflictions, but God has been faithful. I will revisit our afflictions later. Angie was not the only one concerned about my responding to the call into ministry. A very good friend of mine bluntly said to me, "Be careful because you can lose your house and everything you have worked for." Another friend said, "Why are you leaving your wife behind to attend seminary out of town when you are trying to have children? How are the children going to come if you are away from her for three years?"

However, I was undaunted. Somehow, God graciously gave me enough faith to believe that He would work it all out. I said to Angie that I came to the United States with absolutely nothing and trusted God to take care of me. Was I now going to distrust Him because I had a few assets? The God who took care of my needs when I had nothing is the same God who will protect the blessings that He has so graciously given us. We sold all the stocks we had, we took out all my retirement savings, and I headed off to Missouri in the fall to attend seminary.

> Somehow, God graciously gave me enough faith to believe that He would work it all out.

CHAPTER 2

TRUSTING GOD IN SEMINARY

ANGIE AND I DROVE OFF in the fall to Springfield, Missouri. We drove so I could have a car there, and she flew back home. The journey was memorable in many ways. Angie was quiet, and she wept most of the nineteen-hour drive. On our way, somewhere in Ohio, my car broke down in the middle of the night at a traffic light, at about 2 a.m. I popped the hood open but had no clue about what was going on. We had absolutely no idea how we would get out of that. We prayed for the Lord to send us help.

Amazingly, a young white couple in a black pickup truck drove up a few minutes later and offered to help. They mentioned that there was a hotel less than a block away and that they could drive my wife there and come back for me. I trusted the Lord to take care of her. They called a tow truck and took off. They came back to wait with me for the tow truck to arrive. While waiting for the tow truck, the young lady said to me, "Would you be interested in coming with me home? I have never been with a person of your race. We have everything at home." I was so stunned that all I could say to her was "I am on my way to seminary!" I asked her if that was her husband who she was riding with, and she said no. I asked why they were out at that early hour of the day. Her response was that they just decided to get out of the house and ride around town a bit. I knew without a shadow of a doubt that the Lord had sent them out on an assignment to help us. They waited until the tow truck came and followed the tow truck to drop off my car at a repair place right next to the hotel. When they dropped me off, my wife had just come down into the hotel lobby to check on me. The young lady said to me, "Please do not tell your wife that I propositioned you."

I told my wife later, and we had a good laugh over it. But there was a lesson learned. The enemy was already at work to derail me from the call, right at the outset even before I set foot in seminary. It was a lesson I would not soon forget! The good thing is that I had covered myself with massive prayers before embarking on the journey. Continual prayer is critical to our lives every step of our Christian journey. We are to pray without ceasing because our adversary attacks without ceasing.

We got safely to Springfield, and I was graciously hosted by a lovely couple until I found a place to rent. Angie flew back to Maryland with a heavy heart. We had never been separated in our nine years of marriage, and now I was going away from her for three long years. She was going to be alone in that spacious house. For two weeks after she flew back to Maryland, Angie never took or returned my phone calls. It was a grieving time for her. I knew she needed some space to process all that was happening to us. Our lives were now on a totally different trajectory with a very unknown future in ministry.

The Lord had it all figured out though. Angie was not going to be alone at home. Remarkably, two of her sisters both won the United States Immigration Diversity program and relocated to America. They came to live with her in Maryland. They lived with her until I returned from seminary three years later. *Who could ever have imagined that?* I think that boosted her faith that God truly had it all figured out.

Life in seminary was ... a pure walk of
faith bathed in constant prayer.

Life in seminary was quite interesting. It was a pure walk of faith bathed in constant prayer. We used money from stocks and retirement savings to make mortgage payments for a while, but we both knew it would run out at some point. I tried to economize as much as possible. I was on a very strict budget and could afford absolutely nothing beyond the bare necessities. I got a part-time job as a retail associate and lived on a very sparing budget. I cooked every meal—usually rice, beans, and vegetables. I could not afford much beyond that. I learned to live by prayer and trust God to supply my needs. I vividly remember that the only time I could afford to buy an outside meal was when Burger King had a special. I was always excited because it afforded me the opportunity to eat something different. The Lord was gracious though, blessing me with many friends who would invite me to their homes for meals. Those were special moments for me. Those individuals have become lifelong friends, and we still keep in touch.

The Lord also touched the heart of a medical doctor friend of mine who religiously sent me $200 every month all through my stay in seminary. That helped to pay for my rent. That was nothing short of God graciously answering prayer for provision. I was used to having enough money, living in a nice house, and having the ability to travel wherever I felt like going, but things were different now. I was on a strict budget and trusted the Lord from day to day. I was living on the FROG (fully reliant on God) plan. I remember one day asking the Lord how I was going to make things work, given my tight financial situation. The answer I received was "The best place to eat is from the palm of My hand." I will never forget that response. I received that answer in a prayerful conversation while driving to work one afternoon. I knew God was assuring me that He had me totally covered. He never disappointed me.

Seminary was a great experience for me. I was focused on my academic work and spiritual growth. I was also active on campus and got elected as president of the Student Advisory Council. As the leader of the student body, that gave me a lot of interaction with my fellow students as well as great contacts with the administration. In particular, the academic dean (Dr. Edgar Lee) took an uncommon interest in me and became a friend and mentor. We stayed in touch even after school, and he came to preach in our church.

School was busy because I tried to take as many classes as possible so I could quickly graduate and join my wife back in Maryland. Most people could simply not understand the sacrifice of leaving my wife in Maryland for three years to pursue seminary studies. I stayed behind during summer for two reasons. First, I could not afford the airfare back home, and second, I wanted to take as many summer classes as I could to speed up my graduation. My academic load in the summer was quite heavy. I remember once taking what appeared to be too many classes, so I decided to see the professor and drop a class. I felt a bit overwhelmed. As I stood behind the professor's door ready to knock and enter, the Holy Spirit posed a question to me. "Have you asked Me whether you should drop this class?" I knew the Lord was speaking to me. I was rather stunned and decided that I had truly not prayed about it. The Spirit of God is so intimate and real. I quickly abandoned the idea and put in the extra work needed to take the class. I fervently prayed for grace and strength to carry the load and ended up with an A in the class. It was a big lesson to me: always ask the Lord for His direction. Pray about every little detail of your life, and never take anything for granted because God is interested in everything concerning you. He knows when you are overwhelmed, and He knows how to encourage, sustain, and pull you through every situation. His grace will always be sufficient for you.

Prayer definitely works. "Pray without ceasing." The Bible gives that admonition in 1 Thessalonians 5:17 (KJV) for a reason. We must bathe ourselves in continual prayer because God is interested in guiding every step of our walk with Him. Nothing in our lives is unimportant to God, including which courses to take in school and which courses to drop. It is especially important to pray for our children and teach and encourage them to pray about their school courses and future careers. The Bible makes it clear that every day of our lives has already been written in God's book. David reminds us of that in Psalm 139:16–17 (NLT).

> You saw me before I was born. Every day of my life was recorded in your book. Every moment was laid out before a single day had passed. How precious are your thoughts about me, Oh God. They cannot be numbered!

I believe that the God who created us for His own pleasure and purpose takes absolute delight in directing our steps to fulfill His purposes for us. We receive directions when we call upon Him in prayer. He loves when His children call upon Him. It shows our trust in Him and our desire to see His involvement in or lives, as any true father would.

God remained faithful to us and continually supplied our needs, sometimes in miraculous ways. I remember one summer when I missed Angie so badly and wanted to go home but could simply not afford it. Actually it was the only summer I went home during the three years I was away in seminary. I had a pastor friend who had given me the assurance that if I ever needed some help, I should let him know. So, I decided to take him up on his offer and went to speak to him after service one Sunday morning. I told him I needed some help to see my wife in Maryland. He was more than willing to help and asked me to come back for a check the next day. I felt grateful knowing that the Lord was going to use him to meet my needs.

As I got ready to open the door to my car and drive off, the Holy Spirit asked me a question. "Did you ask Me if this is how I intend to meet your needs? Go back and tell the pastor that this is not how the Lord intends to meet this need." I knew I was hearing from the Lord, but I was also pretty confused. Was this my imagination? Was it the devil trying to "steal" my blessing? I knew it was neither my imagination nor a trick of the devil, so I went right back to the pastor and told him not to bother writing a check to me because that was not how God intended to meet that particular need.

He was stunned and said, "Albert, are you sure?"

I said, "Yes, I am very certain."

He said, "OK, let me know if you change your mind."

I thanked him and left. I offered a prayer of apology to the Lord and asked that He would supply the money I needed to go east and see my wife for the summer. Time was running out, and I had to leave for Maryland as quickly as I could. My audacious prayer was for God to supply the need expeditiously. The money had to be enough to take me to Maryland and back and also pay two months of rent for the summer vacation because I was not going to be working.

The very next day, I picked up my mail after classes only to find that someone had mailed a gift of $1,000 to me. God does "exceedingly abundantly above all that we ask or think, according to the power that worketh in us" (Ephesians 3:20–21 KJV). He supplies "all our need according to his riches in glory by Christ Jesus" (Philippians 4:19 KJV).

At another point in time, close to the end of my seminary studies, we needed money to help with our mortgage, which was quite behind. We had depleted all our savings, our stocks, and my retirement account. There was nothing left to fall back on. I was very close to the end of my studies. My wife hates debt and gets stressed when finances get challenging. She asked how we were going to catch up with the mortgage. We needed about $7,000 to clear the arrears. That week, I asked my good friend and prayer partner to fast and pray with me about the issue. It was another audacious prayer. Where in the world was I going to find $7,000?

The truth is nothing is impossible with God (Luke 1:37 NKJV). Jesus tells us in Mark 11:24 (NLT), "I tell you, you can pray for anything, and if you believe that you've received it, it will be yours." I prayed audaciously for that huge amount because I believed that God was able. God answered our prayers, and all the money we needed came in to take care of the mortgage arrears. A thousand dollars of that amount came in all the way from Africa. God answers prayers, sometimes in rather astonishing ways.

All through these experiences, God was growing our faith and deepening our prayer lives. Angie had become a strong prayer warrior. She had to constantly be

> God answers prayers, sometimes in rather astonishing ways.

on her knees for divine provision and protection. We both grew in our faith and commitment to the Lord. A few months before finishing seminary to rejoin Angie in Maryland, I received this letter from her:

Dear ABK,

The past three years have been rather challenging, but God has been faithful to us.

I have learnt to trust God through all the challenging times we have been through.

I am glad you responded to the call to serve the Lord in full-time ministry.

You dragged me into this kicking and yelling, but you were right in saying that we would never be happy if we failed to do what the Lord was asking of us.

The past few months have been particularly challenging, but I take encouragement from the words of Habakkuk.

Though the fig tree does not bud and there are no grapes on the vines,

Though the olive crop fails and the fields produce no food,

Though there are no sheep in the pen and no cattle in the stalls,

Yet I will rejoice in the LORD, I will be joyful in God my Savior.

The Sovereign LORD is my strength; He makes my feet like the feet of a deer,

He enables me to tread on heights. (Habakkuk 3:17–19 NIV)

All my love,
Angie

CHAPTER 3

CALLED TO SERVE

DURING MY LAST SEMESTER IN seminary, my senior pastor from back home in Maryland called to ask if I would consider coming to serve as his associate pastor. This was the church in which I served as an elder and board member prior to leaving for seminary. I was a bit uncertain because I also felt a clear call within me to plant a new church in Upper Marlboro, Maryland. I asked my pastor to give me some time to seek the Lord about that. When I discussed it with Angie, she was all for it. While away in seminary, she had continued to serve actively in the church. I think my absence gave her even more time for the Lord's work. I had heard from Angie, but I needed to hear from God. I went into my prayer closet.

As I continued to seek the Lord about the ministry opportunity offered, I received an answer in the form of a question.

> What would you do if you stand before the Lord at the
> end of your days on earth and He asked you why you
> refused to help His servant when he needed you most?
> What response would you give? What would you say
> when the Lord tells you at the end of your days, "You
> did all I wanted you to do but at the beginning of your

18

ministry. I needed you to help in that church"? How would you respond?

I knew that question was God's way of answering my prayer.

That settled it for me. I called my senior pastor and said yes to the call to serve with him. He had been my pastor for thirteen years, and I had nothing but the highest love and respect for him. I had worked closely with him under very difficult circumstances, and I knew he was a genuine man of God who loved Jesus with all his heart. The only condition I gave him was that I felt called to plant a new church and would appreciate if he would give me his word to release me with his blessings when the time came for me to leave. I met with the church board—and later the entire congregation—and shared the same thing with them. Angie and I immediately settled into the church in our new role.

Brewing Crisis

Serving as the senior associate pastor was a growth experience for me. I had oversight of the church administration as well as the youth and men's ministries. My pastor assigned me numerous counseling assignments. I did a great deal of premarital counseling as well as regular marriage counseling. I helped to liaise between the various campuses of the church that had been established in different states. I was heavily involved in the preaching ministry as well.

I was suddenly a very busy pastor. It was not uncommon to see a long queue of people waiting to talk to me after service. The church loved us, and my senior pastor was very supportive of me. He called me "baby crab" because he said I reflected his work ethics. He said he was the "senior crab" and he had given birth to a baby crab (me). I was very close to him. I highly respected him, and he impacted my life with his genuine godliness.

I felt comfortable enough to point out to him things that I felt needed to be done differently. He took those suggestions well. Sometimes, he would smile at my suggestions and not say much in return. I remember a story he told me once after I asked why he had handled a particular issue a certain way. He said,

> Mama crab once took a walk with baby crab on the beach, and baby crab saw that mama crab was walking with a tilt. When baby crab asked mama crab for an explanation, mama crab simply answered, "You will understand when you grow up to be my age!"

This precious, experienced, godly, and very wise servant of God was telling me that there were things I would only understand after years of carrying the load of ministry. That was when he started calling me "baby crab." I will never forget the impact it had on me. It made me understand the need to respect the wisdom of those who have carried the load ahead of us. Sometimes, in our youthful exuberance, we tend to criticize the ways of our elders in spite of their wisdom and experience. No matter how gifted and anointed we might be, it is critical that, like Joshua, we learn to sit under Moses and receive every bit of teaching we can imbibe. It is definitely worth it. Having the privilege to serve as an understudy with a godly leader is a blessing to cherish.

Things did not take off smoothly when I first went on staff. There had been a brewing crisis for years, which finally came to a head. At the time of my employment, two other staff members—a music minister and a minister for outreach and evangelism—were added. Some of the leaders vigorously opposed the addition of all that staff. They were particularly opposed to the hiring of the music minister, who was also the pastor's son. There was a lot of tension in the church. Many of the top leaders left the church along with numerous members. Massive prayer is what got us through those turbulent times.

I remember one of the leaders who also happened to be one of my closest friends asking me why I had come to join "a sinking ship." I was stunned at his brazenness. It was right in a church service during greeting

> Massive prayer is what got us through those turbulent times.

time when he approached and said that to me. I simply responded that I had not joined a sinking ship because the hand of God was upon the church. He responded, "We will see." I also remember the animosity I faced from some of the leaders. There was a lot of anger and confusion. I was caught in the eye of the storm. I was totally ignorant of the angry undercurrents beneath the church when I responded to the call to serve.

I remember one particular individual asking if she could come and see me at home. She came with an angry complaint, which took me by surprise. She said she was angry with me because I had come to take a position that belonged to someone else. She was displeased with the staff changes the senior pastor had made. No one had been fired during the changes, but I had incurred her wrath because I had been appointed as the senior associate pastor. She was angry because she felt someone who was closely related to her should have been appointed to that position. I was simply stunned. Everything was now clear. I knew the only solution was to pray for myself and the church since my only desire was to serve God's people. Needless to say, Angie and I began praying fervently. Kneeling before God continually is a must in ministry because our struggle is not against flesh and blood, as the scripture reminds us in Ephesians 6:12 (NKJV).

I also recall another interesting experience. With the permission of my senior pastor, I decided to visit and talk privately with each of the dissenting leaders in the privacy of their homes. My goal was to listen to them and help address their concerns. When I visited one particular leader, he pointedly told me that the church was not going to survive. He was totally confident that the church was facing its demise. Again, I was shaken by how a mere mortal could so brazenly pronounce death on God's church because he disagreed with the decisions of the senior pastor. I simply responded that the church would not die. It would survive and thrive. He was so confident of his assertion of death that he asked me to give him a moment. He went into his bedroom and came back with his journal. He said, "I am writing down today's date and what you just said concerning the church not dying. I am confident the church will die, but if you are a true man of God, your words will come to pass."

A few months later, the leaders who were in disagreement with the pastor left along with many others. The attendance, along with the church's finances, plummeted. In fact, one minister preached a message titled "Ichabod" (1 Samuel 4:21 NIV) because he felt God's glory had departed and the church was in the throes of death. We must always remember that the enemy comes to steal, kill, and destroy, but Jesus came to give life in abundance (John 10:10 NKJV). God was about to give new life to His church, and He did. Mere mortals cannot write off God's church; not if God's children call upon Him in prayer!

I guess I can say, looking back this many years later, that I am a "true man of God" according to that particular leader's "prophetic" pronouncement because the church did not die. It thrived!

God Rebuilds His Church

Jesus made a promise that He will build His church and the gates of hell shall not prevail against it (Matthew 16:18 KJV). That is exactly what God did. He rebuilt His church. The stress and confusion being experienced were enormous, but we had grace behind us and energy and determination to forge ahead. We prayed, worked hard, and believed God to pull the church through.

He did it in a rather glorious fashion. Suddenly, there was an influx of people into the church! New immigrants from the war-torn countries of Liberia and Sierra Leone who had been graciously relocated into the country started coming into the church. They brought new energy to evangelize and expand. There was a surge in attendance. The plummeting finances were revived and greatly increased. My senior pastor, who up till then had not taken a proper vacation in several years, was able to travel outside the country for over a month, knowing that the church was in trusted hands. There was a new, refreshing spirit in the church. It was obvious that God had shown much grace. He had answered the bold prayers of His people to rebuild His church.

The hard work of building lives and serving God's kingdom continued. I helped my pastor cast a new vision for the church. He and I had a very close relationship. I was like a son to him. He had been my pastor and mentor for years. He had performed our marriage. I had served him as board secretary, helping him to navigate some of the treacherous waters of ministry all before coming to serve as his associate pastor.

The ministry was busy, and there was so much work to do with the new influx of people. I worked my heart out and barely had much time to myself. I was continually fasting and praying with people. There was actually a running joke behind the scenes that "if you take your needs to Pastor ABK, he will have you fast and pray." God graciously used us to impact many lives and renew many marriages.

The church was a praying church, and many prayer services were held to intercede for the needs of the people. I remember one particular instance when an altar call was made during a prayer service. All the pastors were at the altar praying with the people who had lined up. I noticed a particular gentleman who seemed to be moving wherever I went. It was obvious that he wanted me to be the specific person to pray for his needs. When I finally got to him, he told me about a type of addiction he had been battling. His voice was quivering as he spoke. He said he felt comfortable talking to me about his situation. I prayed with him and gave him an appointment to see me in the office the next day.

We met, and he described the pain and embarrassment of his addiction. As I listened to him, I felt the Holy Spirit directing me to ask him to fast and pray for a whole month. He was willing. He sincerely wanted to be set free, and it was imperative that the necessary spiritual help was brought to bear on the situation. This was not a battle to be taken lightly. I actually joined him for most of the fast. I continually met and prayed with him during that long fast. The Lord completely set him free. He was very grateful. He later became a valuable church leader and contributed greatly to God's kingdom. There were many instances of marriages that were healed due to fasting, prayer, and counseling.

There was a lot of fruit to our ministry. I attribute that to grace and prayer. Angie rebuilt the children's ministry based on a model I had developed during my master of divinity program in seminary. Many areas of the church were renewed, and lives were impacted. Most pastors would not entrust their pulpits to their associates, but my pastor dealt very differently with me. He had me preach on numerous occasions, and the church received my preaching and teaching ministry well. I was a bit concerned when one of the staff pastors called after I had preached one Sunday and said that our senior pastor should consider allowing me to preach more often because of my giftings. I knew it was a line that should never be crossed. I immediately told him I was very content with whatever opportunity I was given and that my senior pastor was the one to whom God had entrusted the church and the feeding of His children. That staff pastor never brought up the issue to my hearing again. I was not going to give the devil any entry point into my relationship with my senior pastor. Respecting and honoring the authority under which one has been placed by God is never to be taken lightly. Undermining authority can have devastating spiritual consequences. I was not about to be sucked in by the devil. Prayer undergirded us continually.

I also remember a particular Sunday service when my senior pastor was out of town and I preached. One of the elders came to me after service and said, "You have to be crowned king of preaching. Pastor should let you preach more often." I swiftly responded that my senior pastor reserved the right to do whatever he pleased with the pulpit and that I was no king of preaching. It was obvious that the enemy was trying to inject pride into my spirit. The Bible makes it clear that pride goes before a fall (Proverbs 16:18 NIV), and I was determined to have none of that. I also remember a leadership meeting in which we looked at how the different ministries were faring. The leader of the audiovisual ministry remarked that they had recently set a sales record about the number of tapes sold after I had preached one Sunday morning. It was not unusual to see people lining up to purchase tapes after I had preached. I prayerfully sought the Lord to uphold me and protect me from pride. Prayer was a vital part of our lives.

The Bible makes it clear that pride goes before a fall, and I was determined to have none of that.

Angie and I continued to respect, support, and serve our senior pastor. We had no children at the time, and we spent most of our time in ministry work. In fact, my senior pastor was so concerned that he called me one day and said, "ABK, you are working too hard. You need to take a vacation and rest. You need to pace yourself." That was when I realized that I was totally enmeshed in the work of ministry.

Through it all, however, my relationship with God grew stronger. I spent lots of time studying, reading, praying, meditating upon God's Word, and fasting.

During that hectic time of ministry, I also became a credentialed minister with the Potomac District of the Assemblies of God. While in seminary, my academic dean, Dr. Edgar Lee, encouraged me to pursue credentials with the Assemblies of God denomination even though I was a member of an independent church. Dr. Lee, highly respected in the denomination, was able to pave the way for me to be credentialed.

The church was very supportive, and many people, including my senior pastor, came to my ordination service. The Lord gave me a rather interesting gift on that day. As I chatted with well-wishers after the ordination service, I noticed there was a particular lady who had been waiting patiently to talk with me. She stood by and waited for the right opportunity, since she did not want to interrupt my other conversations. She mentioned to me as I walked across the stage to receive my credentials that the Lord asked her to tell me that He had His hand on my life and some great assignments for me in ministry. She said I needed to remain encouraged and focused. She said I needed to be strong, no matter what I experienced in the future. I had never met the lady and did not know who she was.

> In our walk with God, there are times when we simply have to quietly receive messages from the Lord and just ponder them in our hearts.

That message was rather interesting because a few months prior to that, I had received another message from another minister at our annual Pastors' Prayer Day at a retreat camp in Falling Waters, West Virginia. A lady came up to me and said,

"The Lord wants you to know that He has put you above the fray. Stay above the fray."

I had no idea what to make of it, but I kept it in my heart. In our walk with God, there are times when we simply have to quietly receive messages from the Lord and just ponder them in our hearts. Our minds are too limited to understand the vastness of God's plans for our lives. Some things just have to be received and not immediately pried into, until the Lord uncovers their meaning to us at His appointed time. As scripture says, the vision is for an appointed time (Habakkuk 2:3 KJV), and we must wait for it even if it seems to be delayed.

CHAPTER 4

TIME TO LEAVE AND PLANT

AFTER THREE YEARS OF FRUITFUL ministry, the Holy Spirit began to stir my heart about our next ministry assignment. It happened in a rather awkward way. At a staff pastor's meeting to consider the appointment of new elders to assist the pastors in their ministries, I had raised issues about a particular individual because I was concerned about that person's qualification for the position of church elder. I expressed my honest opinion, and the person's name was dropped from consideration.

At one church business meeting, the individual rather disrespectfully confronted me about the leadership appointments. Somehow, this person had gotten wind of my stance during the staff discussions about the appointment of the new elders. To my surprise, no one said a word to the person. Absolutely no one came to my defense! No pastor or any leader said a word. I felt as if the trust I had in my fellow pastors had been indelibly tainted! I looked at my wife and saw shock, hurt, and pain written all over her face. She left the meeting hall and made her way to my office. She was so confused by it all that she tripped on the carpet in the hallway and busted her lips. It was an evening of pain, shock, tears, and now bloody, busted lips. My wife, who was also my best friend, was in great emotional and physical pain, and I felt totally

27

helpless. I simply could not wrap my mind around the indignity of it all. We left after the meeting and drove back home without uttering a word to each other. I was simply in shock! There is something very difficult to regain once trust in a relationship is violated. When a person is abused and disrespected, the innocence and beauty of the relationship are tainted between the abused and the abuser. That was what I felt had taken place between us and those I trusted to have stood up for us. We both knew it without verbalizing it. We simply drove quietly home. The question was this: why did the Lord allow that to happen?

The next day, one of the most respected elders in the church called and said, "Congratulations, Pastor ABK. You just earned yourself a spiritual promotion. God is lifting you to the next level of your ministry." From that point on, I began to seek the Lord in fervent prayer about the future.

> I stayed at the altar of God in fasting, worship, and prayer. I needed to have clear divine direction for the future.

On July 4, 2000, I spent the entire day praying in the sanctuary. It was a day when everyone was out barbecuing and watching fireworks, but I stayed at the altar of God in fasting, worship, and prayer. I needed to have a clear divine direction for the future.

Was God trying to get my attention with that painful incident and experience? Was it time to move to the next assignment in His vineyard? Had I finished faithfully serving my purpose at our current church?

As I fasted and prayed, the Lord spoke to me through the scriptures, as He so often does. He brought Isaiah 62 to my attention, and I started meditating on it.

> For Zion's sake I will not keep silent, for Jerusalem's sake I will not remain quiet, till her vindication shines out like the dawn, her salvation like a blazing torch.

The nations will see your vindication, and all kings your glory; you will be called by a new name that the mouth of the LORD will bestow.

You will be a crown of splendor in the Lord's hand, a royal diadem in the hand of your God.

No longer will they call you Deserted, or your name Desolate.

But you will be called Hephzibah, and your land Beulah; for the LORD will take delight in you, and your land will be married.

As a young man marries a young woman, so will your Builder marry you.

I have posted watchmen on your walls, Jerusalem; they will never be silent day or night.

You who call on the LORD, give yourselves no rest and give Him no rest till He establishes Jerusalem and makes her the praise of the earth …

And you will be called Sought After,

The City No Longer Deserted.

(Isaiah 62:1–12 NIV)

This is a paraphrase of some specific things that caught my attention:

I will not remain quiet till her vindication shines out like the dawn; you will be called by a new name that the mouth of the LORD will bestow; you will be a crown of splendor in the LORD's hand; no longer will they call you deserted or your name desolate; the LORD will take delight in you; give yourself no rest and give Him no rest till He establishes Jerusalem and makes her the praise of the earth; never again will foreigners drink the new wine for which you have toiled; those who gather the grapes will drink it in the courts of my sanctuary; prepare the way for the people; raise a banner for the nations; they will be called a holy people; you will be called Sought After; the city no longer deserted!

I could not relate to the entire passage in my situation then. A lot of it seemed futuristic, but I knew without a shadow of doubt that the Lord was speaking to me both in the present and the future through this passage. The words leapt at me from the pages of scripture and became indelibly etched in my spirit. Over the years, the Holy Spirit has brought this passage to me time and again as the events of my life and ministry unfold. It was most poignant especially after about five years of planting the new church. That was when I gained greater insight into what God had said to me at the altar many years back. You and I can never fathom the complete unfolding of the actions of the divine counsel. Sometimes God may give us a glimpse of His inner workings to encourage us. Most times, He simply does not. The Bible makes it clear that the secret things belong to the Lord our God, but the things revealed belong to us and our children (Deuteronomy 29:29 NIV). All the Lord requires of us is simply to trust Him with all our hearts and not to lean to our own understanding. He wants us to acknowledge Him in all our ways, knowing that He will direct our paths (Proverbs 3:5–6 KJV).

You and I can never fathom the complete
unfolding of the actions of the divine counsel.

God does not want us to be anxious about the future. He wants us to rest in the complete assurance that His plans for us are for our good and never for evil. He has plans to prosper us and not to harm us. He has plans to give us hope and a future (Jeremiah 29:11 NIV). We must not be rattled by the unknowns of the future. We must not be doubtful whether God's word to us will ever materialize. When will my vindication shine out like the dawn? When will I become a crown of splendor in the Lord's hand? When will I no longer be deserted or desolate? When will the Lord take delight in me? When will the Lord use me to raise a banner to the nations? When will I be called "Sought After"? When? When? When?

The answer to our anxiety-laced questions is found in God's answers to the prophet Habakkuk when he found himself in the same dilemma. The prophet wanted answers from God.

> I will climb up to my watchtower and stand at my guard post. There I will see what the LORD says and how He will answer my complaint.

> Then the LORD said to me, "Write my answer plainly on tablets, so that a runner can carry the correct message to others. This vision is for a future time. It describes the end, and it will be fulfilled. If it seems slow in coming, wait patiently, for it will surely take place. It will not be delayed." (Habakkuk 2:1–3 NLT)

The Bible makes it clear that no matter how many promises God has made, they are yes in Christ (2 Corinthians 1:20 NIV). God's intention is not for us to anxiously wait for the fulfillment of His promises to us. His desire for us is to simply trust Him with our past, present, and future, knowing He will work all things out for our good (Romans 8:28 NIV). God is a promise keeper and a very good Father. He will always lead us beside still waters and restore our souls (Psalm 23:2–3 NKJV).

I spent several hours in the sanctuary fasting, praying, and meditating from early in the morning till after 6 p.m. when I left to go home. I felt confident that I had heard from the Lord and that it was time to plan toward leaving and planting the church the Lord had placed on my heart back in seminary and of which my senior pastor was well aware.

One thing was extremely important to me. I wanted to finish well. I wanted to leave my current church without any ill feelings whatsoever. I wanted to show my senior pastor the utmost respect as I transitioned. I did not want any schism to plague the church as a result of my departure. I committed myself to praying fervently for God to stay the hand of the enemy from the church.

I talked things over with my wife, and we both agreed that it was time to leave and plant the new church. We made an appointment to see our senior pastor and his wife at home. We thanked them and said we both felt it was time to plan and leave. However, we wanted to ensure that we left the church in a healthy way. We would put plans in place to train others for our responsibilities if my senior pastor so desired. We would give a year's notice to the senior pastor without breathing a word of it to another soul. During that one-year period, we would ensure that everything was put in place and that our departure would not have an adverse effect on the church. Our senior pastor's wife tried to convince us to change our minds, but we knew we had to leave, and we respectfully made that clear to them.

The plan was carried out exactly as we had talked about. No one knew except my wife and me—at least from our end. We trained others to become familiar with what we did. At the end of one year, pastor informed the board that we would be leaving in March of that year. The board seemed incredulous at the news. Some even expressed open hostility. These were people I had loved and worked with for years. I vividly remember the mocking laughter from one longtime member of the board. He asked what I would be doing, to which I replied that we would be planting a church in a different part of the county. He let out a very cynical ringing laughter, which I can hear to this day. The board asked that we stay for six months instead of the three-month notice we were giving.

Finishing well was important to both Angie and me.

I explained that the senior pastor had been aware of our departure for over a year and that we had been putting things in place all along with his total consent. Finally, we agreed to another three-month extension for a total of six months, ending in June.

We are grateful for the wisdom and grace God gave as we planned our departure. There was no disrespect toward our senior pastor during the private one-year notice we gave him. We did not slack in our responsibilities. We worked as hard as ever. During the next six months after our departure had become official, we continued to work hard at our responsibilities. Again, finishing well was important to both Angie and me. We continued to love and serve the church. It was the work of God, not the work of people. It was our Lord and Savior Jesus we served, not a mortal being. Jesus was our rewarder—not people. Many were sad and shocked to see us go. Some came and cried in my office. I remember one particular message someone left on my office voice mail. She simply said, "Pastor, the church you are going to will never love you as much as we do!" She was dead wrong. Our current church loves us very dearly. The leaders are especially supportive of the vision God has given us for the church. They are faithful and loyal.

A Wonderful Send-Off

The church held a send-off service for us. There was no dry eye in the auditorium. The elders and deacons outdid themselves with plaques, gifts, and compliments. One particular gift that touched me deeply was a "majesty plant." The entire church knew that one of my favorite songs was "Majesty" by Dr. Jack Hayford. I had sung it numerous times with the congregation. Typically, I would ask everyone to join in as the worship leader led us in that song. The Sunday school department got us a beautiful palm plant called "majesty," and I had tears in my eyes as I listened to the thought behind it. To crown it all, the church took a very generous offering for us, a total of $6,000. No such amount had ever been taken as a gift for any pastor. Even our annual Pastors' Appreciation Day offerings came nowhere close to that generous amount. The church truly expressed great love to us. We left on a very good note.

A couple of months after our departure, my senior pastor asked me to speak in the church, which I did. My relationship with my senior pastor was transparent and healthy.

I sincerely believe that it is important to finish well. It is important to honor the spiritual authority under which God has placed you. No matter how much we disagree with God's appointed authority over our lives, we must never be belligerent toward them. They have been divinely appointed to keep watch over our souls, and God holds them accountable. Scripture admonishes us,

> Obey your spiritual leaders, and do what they say. Their work is to watch over your souls, and they are accountable to God. Give them a reason to do this with joy and not with sorrow. That would certainly not be for your benefit." (Hebrews 13:17 NLT)

We must hold our spiritual leaders in high honor and give them utmost respect especially when God is transitioning us out of their ministries and oversight. Honoring leadership is a particularly important thing.

I still have a great relationship with our former senior pastor and his wife. We continued to visit them periodically. A few years after we had left, we visited them because he had suffered a stroke. It was a marvelous joy as they both laid hands on my wife and me and prayed heartfelt blessings and success over our lives and ministry. It is an important spiritual principle to honor those in authority and never to disrespect them.

We see a great example of this when David refused to kill or mistreat King Saul even when he had the opportunity to do so! Saul had become ungodly, and God had rendered judgment over his kingship. God had rejected him as king and anointed David to replace him. Saul had become so obsessed with

It is an important spiritual principle to honor those in authority and never to disrespect them.

killing David that he even hurled a javelin at his own son, Jonathan, for speaking favorably of David. Saul had thousands of soldiers tracking down David to put him to death. An account of Saul's insane obsession to harm David is captured in his slaughtering of God's priests. The biblical account is rather chilling.

> Then the king ordered the guards at his side: "Turn and kill the priests of the LORD, because they too have sided with David. They knew he was fleeing yet they did not tell me" …
>
> The king then ordered Doeg, "You turn and strike down the priests" … That day, he killed eighty-five men who wore the linen ephod. He also put to the sword Nob, the town of the priests, with its men and women, its children and infants, and its cattle, donkeys, and sheep. (1 Samuel 22:17–19 NIV)

Saul's heart had become darkened with wickedness. There was absolutely no fear of God in him. David could easily have justified attacking and killing Saul, but when David had the opportunity to kill Saul, he refrained. Saul had three thousand men solely dedicated to finding David to put him to death. I think the direct biblical account does more justice than any attempt to retell the story.

> He came to the sheep pens along the way, a cave was there, and Saul went in to relieve himself. David and his men were far back in the cave. The men said, "This is the day the LORD spoke of when He said to you, 'I will give your enemy into your hand for you to deal with them as you wish.'" Then David crept up unnoticed and cut off a corner of Saul's robe. Afterward, David was conscience-stricken for cutting off a corner of his robe …

Then David went out of the cave and called out to Saul, "My Lord the king!" When Saul looked behind him, David bowed down and prostrated himself with his face to the ground. He said to Saul, "Why do you listen when men say, 'David is burnt on harming you'? This day you have seen with your own eyes how the LORD delivered you into my hands in the cave. Some urged me to kill you but I spared you; I said, 'I will not lay my hand on my Lord because he is the LORD's anointed.'"
(1 Samuel 24:3–10 NIV)

Disrespecting, maligning, and dishonoring spiritual authority has consequences because those authorities were set in place by God. Spitting in the face of a pastor who has been used by God to shepherd you is spiritually damning. I have witnessed situations where individuals have undermined their pastors and polluted the church with untruths because they felt it was time to leave the church. In some instances, these are people who even claimed that God had called them into ministry! They forget the scriptural truth that we reap what we sow! David, the man after God's own heart, was called and anointed to succeed the very man who desperately tried to kill him. He set the godly example of not lifting a finger to harm Saul. It is an example worth following.

I used to give the microphone to everyone who was leaving the church, whether on a good or bad note, but I learned a valuable lesson along the way. A departing leader used the opportunity to unleash some rather negative feelings on the church. This was a person who had been nurtured and mentored in the ministry. The person pretty much said the church was following a man, not God. He left as soon as he had finished speaking. I felt blindsided and stunned, but I still did not learn from the experience. I was naive to the damage the enemy could do under those kinds of circumstances. I continued to give out the microphone until another bad experience. Another departing person used the opportunity after we had blessed her with gifts to say some subtly veiled castigating things about the church. That was the turning point. No more microphones for departing people unless I was absolutely sure of them.

Years later, another person came to tell me that he and his family were leaving the church. They came to my office as a couple during the week and said they were not returning for the impending Sunday service. They brought me a gift and thanked me, but I also knew that they had definite negative undercurrents. Every pastor knows those kinds of situations. I prayed for them and released them with my blessings in spite of some of the damaging things they had done behind the scenes. I had actually been quietly praying for the Lord to give them another place of worship if that was His will. I prayed and waited until God answered.

I prayed and waited until God answered.

A few weeks later, I returned a phone call the gentleman had placed to me. As we conversed, he mentioned that he was very disappointed and unhappy that I did not give him the microphone to say goodbye to the church after serving for several years. What I found puzzling was that there was no opportunity to do that. They informed me on a Tuesday that they were not returning to the church. So how in the world would I have given them that opportunity? Not that I would have done it anyway. I had already learned my lesson from previous experiences! I would have publicly blessed and released them but would not have handed the microphone for them to speak! The man's unhappy reaction on the phone convinced me that God spared His church from what could probably have been a rather awkward situation.

Leaving a church on a good note honors God. It is important to finish well. After all, Christians are not each other's enemies. We have all been redeemed by the same precious blood of Jesus. We serve the same God in different parts of one big vineyard. We are all valuable to God. There is no need for acrimony, hostility, or castigations.

The God we serve in one church is the same God we will meet in another church unless we really do not know Him! It is true that there are times when God would release a person from one church to another. It is also true that one should leave when it is evident that the Word of God is not being preached, that there is blatant immorality, or that Jesus is no longer the focus of the church. These are all real and legitimate reasons to leave a church, but the truth is some people leave churches because of personal issues that they justify with skewed theological reasoning. They leave because they disagree with leadership about one decision or the other. They leave because they were not elevated to some expected positions they wanted. They leave sometimes for rather trivial reasons that they carefully robe in spirituality! That, I believe, is displeasing to God.

I am of the opinion that, as much as possible, one must always leave a church in such a way as to be able to return to visit or worship in good conscience. I was determined to end my service at my former church with a good testimony. God helped Angie and me to conduct ourselves with utmost decency and to leave on a very good note.

We maintained a cordial relationship with the pastor who had watched over our souls for seventeen years and who had given us ministry opportunities to learn, serve, and grow. In fact, our senior pastor's wife and some leaders from our former church attended the opening service for the new church we planted, Renewal Christian Center. We were very grateful to the Lord.

CHAPTER 5

AUDACIOUS PRAYER OF FAITH: PLANTING RENEWAL CHRISTIAN CENTER

WE LEFT AT THE END of June, ready to plant the new church. We carefully avoided letting people know what we had been called to do because we did not want anyone to follow us as we left for our new assignment. Our senior pastor was of course well aware of our call to plant a new church. However, there was one sticky point. I was very good friends with the senior pastor's son, who had been serving as the music minister. He and I had been friends for years. In fact, on more than one occasion, I had to convince him to stay on staff with his father when he wanted to resign as a result of all the crisis in the ministry. He was a very principled and reliable person. He loved the Lord and had a heart of gold. At the time of our departure, he also resigned to attend seminary out of state. He was no longer employed by the church. His wife, who served as the church administrator for several years, had also resigned her position at the church a year earlier to take a job in the private sector. She was a gifted worship leader and excellent administrator who was very familiar with church administration. She was a trusted family friend.

A few weeks prior to our leaving, she came to my office and spoke these words to me:

> I know you will vehemently oppose what I am about to say to you, but please hear me out and think about it. I feel the Lord is asking me to come and help with the worship ministry in your new church. I know how you think, and I know you will definitely oppose my proposal, but I believe the Lord has put this on our hearts and we are prepared to help in every way we can.

My response was swift and immediate. "No, I don't think it's a good idea." She asked me to think over it and give her a response later. I felt rather awkward because everyone knew she and her husband were our close friends. We traveled and did many things together. We even vacationed together in London at one point. I was definitely in a quandary because I did not want the appearance of taking them away from their father's church even though the husband was relocating out of state and she herself was no longer actively involved in ministry at the church. I did not want to do anything to either raise eyebrows in the church or incur the displeasure of my senior pastor, but what if that was the Lord's way of helping us to get things started in the new church? I talked it over with my wife, and we decided to seek the Lord about it.

When she came a second time with the same request, I had an answer for her. I asked her to tell the senior pastor about it to get his blessing first. If he felt comfortable enough to release her, then I would be willing to have her come along to help with the new church. If he was uncomfortable with the proposal, then she could not come. I then asked her to let me know the outcome so I could personally follow up with the senior pastor.

A week or so later, she reported back that the senior pastor had agreed to let her help with the new church. I followed up by meeting with him to formally hear his thoughts. He was very gracious.

His exact words were "ABK, they are coming to help with God's work, so that is fine with me." They were a great asset as we labored together to lay the foundation for the new church.

Another couple who were friends of ours, who mostly lived outside the country because of their careers, had relocated to the US, and they became part of the core group as we worked to lay the foundation for the church.

A Jar of Pennies

How was the new church going to be funded? I had spent the first three years after school working in full-time ministry. My desire was to continue focusing on the new church in a full-time pastoral capacity. This, of course, required enough funds to do so. I had already resigned from my position as associate pastor at the end of June, which meant that from the beginning of July, I would receive no paycheck. However, I had faith that God would provide. We had seen Him supply our needs for three years in seminary. We had seen Him take care of our mortgage month after month. We knew we could trust Him to do the same, but *how* was God going to do it?

I went before the Lord with some rather audacious requests. I was trusting the Lord to meet every need in our personal lives and that of the church right from the beginning!

> I had faith God would provide. We had seen Him supply our needs ... but how was God going to do it?

After my resignation, I spent much time fasting and praying. I organized the initial core group of two families into a "praying machine." We met every day at our house to pray. I am a fervent believer in the fact that every divine vision comes with divine provision and that God's work done God's way will never lack God's resources.

When God called Moses to build the tabernacle, He gave him precise architectural plans from heaven and instructed him to set up the tabernacle according to the plan shown him on the mountain. God repeated this instruction in diverse ways. Moses was no builder though, so how was this going to be done, and where was the provision going to come from?

God knew exactly how to fund the tabernacle. First, He asked Moses to take an offering from everyone whose heart prompted them to give (Exodus 25:1–2 NIV). The generosity of the Israelites in giving toward the construction of the tabernacle was nothing short of astonishing. The Bible gives this account:

> They received from Moses all the offerings the people had brought to carry out the work of constructing the sanctuary. And all the people continued to bring freewill offerings morning after morning. So all the skilled workers who were doing all the work on the sanctuary left what they were doing and said to Moses, "The people are bringing more than enough for doing the work the LORD commanded to be done." Then Moses gave an order and they sent this word throughout the camp: "No man or woman is to make anything else as an offering for the sanctuary." And so the people were restrained from bringing more, because what they already had was more than enough to do all the work. (Exodus 36:3–7 NIV)

God also made further provision by endowing Bezalel and Oholiab with the requisite knowledge and skills to carry out all the construction needed. Again, the biblical account is heartwarming.

> Then Moses said to the Israelites, "See, the LORD has chosen Bezalel, son of Uri ... and has filled him with the Spirit of God, with wisdom, with understanding, with knowledge and with all kinds of skills—to make artistic designs for work in gold, silver, and bronze, to cut and set stones, to work in wood and to engage in all kinds of artistic crafts. And He has given both him

and Oholiab son of Ahisamak, of the tribe of Dan, the ability to teach others. He has filled them with skill to do all kinds of work as engravers, designers, embroiderers in blue, purple, and scarlet yarn and fine linen, and weavers – all of them skilled workers and designers." (Exodus 35:30–35 NIV)

God had commanded Moses to build a place of worship so He could dwell among the people and receive their sacrifices. God ensured that there was adequate provision for the vision. It is rather interesting to recall that before the Israelites left Egypt, God plundered the Egyptians and transferred their gold, silver, and other riches into the hands of the Israelites. God blessed them to be able to give generously toward His kingdom agenda, but God also instructed Moses that only those willing to give were to bring an offering. God knew that there were some whose hearts were not going to be moved to contribute to the building of the tabernacle in spite of the great blessings He had transferred into their hands from the Egyptians. It is sad to observe that many are blessed by God, but few are willing to give some of the blessings back to God to fund His kingdom. We are willing to take but unwilling to give to the very God who gives us the ability to acquire wealth. This is a sad way to live one's life.

God blesses us to bless and fund His kingdom agenda. God blessed all the Israelites as they left Egypt, but He asked Moses to receive the offering only from those whose hearts were willing. This is worth noting because God wants our giving to flow freely out of a genuine love for Him. He does not want us to give out of compulsion. Paul reminds us,

> It is sad to observe that many are blessed by God, but few are willing to give some of the blessings back to God to fund His kingdom. We are willing to take but unwilling to give to the very God who gives us the ability to acquire wealth.

43

> Remember this: Whoever sows sparingly will also reap sparingly, and whoever sows generously will also reap generously. Each of you should give what you have decided in your heart to give, not reluctantly or under compulsion, for God loves a cheerful giver. And God is able to bless abundantly, so that in all things at all times, having all that you need, you will abound in every good work. (2 Corinthians 9:6–7 NIV)

As I sought the Lord in fasting and prayer for provision to plant Renewal Christian Center, I was reminded of an interesting experience I had had in our former church. I had a habit of going very early to church and praying through the aisles well before anyone showed up, including the ushers. One day, as I was praying in the sanctuary, one of the ushers walked up to me with two grocery bags full of pennies. It was a rather interesting moment. She was a woman of very modest means and did not even possess a car. She rode the bus to church. The two bags were quite heavy, and she had walked quite a distance from the bus station to the church carrying them. She joyfully handed them over to me in the sanctuary and said, "Pastor ABK, I have been saving these pennies for a while, but yesterday, the Lord asked me to bring them as a gift to you." I was stunned beyond belief. She had brought her savings to me. It was a very sacred moment. I thanked her with a rather sheepish look on my face. I was quite overwhelmed and wondered what message the Lord was sending me.

As I stepped away to continue praying, the Holy Spirit immediately spoke to me concerning the pennies. "If you are faithful to Me, you will never lack the resources to do My work. I will always supply your needs. Even if it means bringing you pennies from all over town." So that was the message behind the pennies. I informed Angie about the precious pennies and decided to keep them in a big glass jar to serve as a memorial to God's faithfulness. Those were "sacred" pennies and could not be used for anything other than a testimony to glorify God. They were a memorial offering to Jehovah Jireh. In a sense, this situation reminded me of David's response when he was on the run from King

Saul and longed to drink water from a well in Bethlehem. His men risked their lives to get him the water he craved, but David poured it out on the ground as an offering to the Lord (2 Samuel 23:15–17 NIV).

As I prayed and sought God for divine provision for His new church, He reminded me of His promise with the pennies. I was greatly encouraged. I knew God was about to work a miracle, and He did. Our budget for the church was $78,000 for the first year. That was going to be enough to help pay my salary, rent a meeting place, and take care of other necessary expenses and supplies. We definitely needed God's provision. Our prayer was for God to touch the new congregation to be financially faithful when we began church services, but God was about to blow our minds. He surprised us with much more. He did exceedingly abundantly above all that we were asking or thinking (Ephesians 3:20 KJV). That is the God we serve!

One day, I received a call from a pastor in Virginia named Rev. Bill Frasnelli. I had never met him in my life. He asked me to come to his office. After a few questions and a lengthy conversation about what the Lord had called us to do, he mentioned that his church, Jubilee Christian Center in Fairfax, Virginia, had decided to come alongside us as a "mother church" to help us plant Renewal Christian Center in Maryland! God used another church in another state with a similar name to meet our needs! Pastor Bill's church decided to give us $5,000 a month to support us! This was nothing short of a miraculous answer to prayer. He explained to me that he and one of his board members had observed at our last denominational District Council that when new church-planting couples were introduced, everyone except Angie and I had a "mother church" standing behind them to help them plant the new church. They made it a prayerful concern, and the Lord had prompted their church to support us.

God answers prayers. We were waiting on Him in expectation. As David says in the psalms, "In the morning, LORD, you hear my voice; in the morning I lay my requests before you and wait expectantly" (Psalm 5:3 NIV). Our God had come through again. He had miraculously provided for His people. He had answered our audacious prayers! But wait. There was even more to come. God was about to put some icing on the cake. That icing was rather interesting.

> Our God had come through again. He had
> miraculously provided for His people. He
> had answered our audacious prayers!

About a year before we set out to plant, I ran into a seminary mate of mine, Steve Brimmer, at a church financial conference in Virginia. I casually said to Steve that we were in the process of planning to start a new church in Maryland and that I would be knocking on his door for some financial support when the time came. The truth is I had not met Steve since our seminary days and had absolutely no idea that he was pastoring in Virginia—our neighboring state! Steve said, "Sure, Albert," and we exchanged numbers.

Steve was very excited when I contacted him about a year later. He got back to me with the promise that his church, Centerpointe Church, would support us with $18,000 for our first year. So, guess what? The entire first year budget of $78,000 was met even before we had our first service. We truly serve an awesome and providing God! Audacious prayers attract audacious answers from heaven!

This wonderful divine provision meant that I was not going to lose a single paycheck. There would be no break. I was assured of a salary for the very next month and throughout the coming year! God's work done God's way will never lack God's provision. We were set to go!

Why the Name Renewal Christian Center?

Angie and I prayed quite a bit about the name for the new church. God had given us a vision, and we wanted a name that would tie into that vision. We finally settled on Renewal Christian Center. Our mission as a church is "Make Disciples for Jesus Christ" in line with the Great Commission given by Jesus in Matthew 28:19 (NIV). We want to see many souls saved and discipled into the kingdom of God. In line with that, the vision of Renewal Christian Center is to be a "spiritual hospital." A hospital is a place for healing the sick. As a spiritual hospital, Renewal is to be a place where lives are renewed for Jesus. The lost are to be saved, and the wounded, battered, and broken are all to be received with genuine Christian love and nourished with the Word of God and the power of the Holy Spirit.

> All who come must encounter the renewing power of God's Spirit.

The sick are to be healed physically, mentally, and emotionally. All who come must encounter the renewing power of God's Spirit. The name Renewal Christian Center denotes the fact that lives must be renewed for Jesus Christ. Christ is to be the foundation for the renewal of lives. It is to be a "center" because we believe that the church must be a center where Christians are trained, nourished, equipped, and empowered to reach out into society and touch people with the love of Jesus. We also settled on the name Renewal because we fervently believe that the church must be a catalyst for spiritual renewal and revival in society. For several years, we have been praying for God to give us the privilege of experiencing His presence in a mighty renewal that will engulf the entire Washington, DC, metropolitan area and beyond. That is the church that God called us to plant. We have diligently prayed this at 5:30 in the morning every week for several years now. We anticipate a move of God, and we want Renewal Christian Center to be a part of this move of God.

In the early summer of 2000, the Lord opened the door, and my wife and I stepped out by faith in obedience, not knowing where resources would come from to support the church or where my next paycheck would come from. Yet our faithful God had it all figured out and used two churches to meet our budget to the penny. The faithfulness of God is simply astonishing.

Two families stood with us as the initial core, and the Lord used them in diverse ways to help establish the new church. One of the families made a donation of $2,000 to buy our first keyboard. We met constantly to pray and plan. It was a lot of hard work bathed in audacious prayers.

By August of our starting year, the initial core had grown to eleven people with one child in the womb. The church had no meeting place to get things going as we prepared for our first service during the fall, but the Lord worked it all out. Our house was quite spacious, but the basement was unfinished. It seemed the ideal place to start things off. An architect friend graciously designed the basement to accommodate an office and a meeting place, charging us absolutely nothing. The Lord was on the move again.

There was another interesting development. Our neighbor across from us was a builder. He built our basement for us at a very reasonable cost. Again, we withdrew money from my retirement account to fund the construction so the church could have offices and an initial meeting place. It was another pure act of faith. Over the years, God has replenished all that we took out both at our initial call to ministry and in funding the basement construction. We wanted the church to save as much money as possible, so we allowed the church to use our house for various things for seven years at no cost to the church.

The Lord was on the move again.

The church administrator had a key to our home, and she could come and go as she needed to. The church treasurer also had a key and could come and go as she needed to. Later, the music minister, who also served as my associate, had a key and an office in our house. We had converted the guest room and another bedroom into administrative offices. Monday intercessory prayer meetings and all church meetings were held in our home. Our fridge was regularly ransacked for whatever was available. This went on for seven years, but we did it with much love and joy. I still recall a comment made by a member when we found a place that we briefly used for offices. It had originally been rented by a lawyer, and he wanted to share it with a tenant. It was rather costly and crammed, and it did not work out too well, so we did not renew the lease. We moved things back to our home. The member's comment was a lament. "I will surely miss going into pastor's fridge to find a drink!"

Having the church offices in our house was not without its challenges. One interesting challenge was that the Lord blessed us with twins in 2001, so we had a full house unlike before. We had absolutely no privacy since we hosted all kinds of church activities at our house. I clearly remember one instance when someone with a key to our house opened the door without even bothering to ring the doorbell! I had to instruct every keyholder from that point on to give us a little privacy by ringing the doorbell! The Lord gave us sufficient grace to do that for seven years. We trusted God for strength all the way, and He never let us down.

CHAPTER 6

PRAYER IS A SINE QUA NON

TRUSTING GOD ALL THE WAY in any assignment requires lots of prayer—sometimes very audacious prayers. Prayer is a definite sine qua non (literally in Latin, "without which, not" (i.e., an essential condition, something absolutely necessary)) if one is to handle life and destiny as God intends. Prayer helps us to know the will of God for our situations and gives us confidence to courageously navigate the uncertain currents we encounter along the journey of life.

> We knew we did not stand a chance
> if the church was not founded on prayer.

We knew we did not stand a chance if the church was not founded on prayer. I am an intercessor, and I know the power of prayer, so we started things off by training a group of intercessors for the church. For two years, I met with a group in our basement from 7:00 to 8:30 p.m. every Monday night. In those years, I led most of the prayers, periodically allowing my wife and another seasoned member from the initial core group to lead. The Lord was extremely gracious, and all the hard work paid off. I used that time to train the core intercessory group for the church.

I noticed that one particular person had the drive, interest, and humility needed for intercession. I knew she had the potential to be trained to lead the prayer ministry. The problem was that I saw the potential, but she did not see that in herself. She simply said, "Pastor, how can I ever pray like you? I don't feel qualified for that responsibility." However, I did not give up on her. I convinced her to take the opportunity to give the Holy Spirit the chance to perfect her as an intercessor. Fortunately, she agreed, and she has ably served for years as the leader of the prayer ministry. She has done an outstanding job with the ministry. For two years without fail, she would come to our house from 7:00 to 8:30 every Saturday morning for us to intercede for God's work. This was after we had already been on the church prayer line from 5:30 to 6:00 that morning. She has become a passionate intercessor. Her giftings and passion are a great blessing to God's kingdom.

We believe in prayer as a church because Jesus said, "It is written: 'my house shall be called a house of prayer'" (Matthew 21:13 NKJV). I believe in prayer, and Renewal is a praying church. In fact, members have all kinds of jokes about my prayer life. On several occasions, funny skits have been presented during Pastor's Appreciation services about how I would end every conversation with a prayer. Some have quipped, "When the pastor calls you, his first question is 'How are you doing?' Before you even get the chance to answer, he would say, 'Let's pray a little!'" I have been made fun of for praying with people after saying hi to them in the parking lot! Well, all jokes aside, we believe in prayer as a church, and we have gone to great lengths to get the entire church involved in prayer.

The Prayer Life of Renewal Christian Center

Daily 5:30 Prayer Line

We have created different opportunities for people to be involved in prayer. First, we have a daily 5:30 a.m. prayer time over the telephone. This is a time of intercession open to the entire church.

Teams have been created for each day of the week, and specific prayer points are prayed through on a daily basis. Each day of the week has an assigned team leader. The team leader, along with three to five other intercessors, take turns to lead prayers over a dedicated phone line from 5:30 to 6:00 a.m. once a week. Members of the church are encouraged to call in to the prayer line on whatever day suits their individual schedules. The teams pray through their assigned prayer focus for three months at a time. We rotate the teams on a quarterly basis through the year. Leaders are moved around to head other teams as the need arises.

Here is the breakdown of the daily prayer points, rotated so that every month, each team gets to focus on a different set of prayers:

Sundays
Renewal Christian Center's leadership: pastors, ministers, deacons, and the leaders of the various ministries, including worship, prayer, outreach, men, women, youth, transportation, care call, hospitality, media, and all other ministries. We pray

- that each leader will walk in holiness, integrity, and righteousness;
- that each leader will walk in divine health and strength;
- for divine protection for each leader;
- that each leader will be strong, active, and passionate in their ministries.

Mondays
A strong spirit of evangelism at the church. We pray

- for everyone to have a strong spirit of outreach and evangelism;

- that each person will have a passionate desire to proclaim the gospel and lead others to Jesus and discipleship at Renewal Christian Center;
- for God to grow His church through Spirit-empowered evangelism and the preaching of the gospel accompanied by signs and wonders;
- that God will be glorified through the salvation of many souls and that our community will be transformed by the gospel of Jesus Christ;
- that the Holy Spirit will fortify and protect the church from any demonic activities.

Tuesday

Prosperity of our church members. We pray

- for faithfulness in tithes and offerings and for the church to be a 100 percent tithing church because financial faithfulness to God opens the windows of heaven upon our lives;
- that our jobs, businesses, and finances will be blessed;
- that God will meet the needs of everyone at Renewal: healings, family and marital challenges, legal issues, etc.;
- that our children will be safe and excel at school;
- for the protection and prosperity of our members and God's favor over our lives so we can do exploits in His kingdom;
- that our members will walk in obedience to God's Word.

Wednesday

Pastor and his family. We pray

- for the well-being of the pastor and his family—that they will walk in divine health and strength;
- for God's protection to be upon him and his family;
- for the direction of the Holy Spirit to be clear to the pastor and that he will listen to God's voice and follow God's direction;

- that the pastor will walk in holiness, integrity, and righteousness and that he will always be a servant leader who walks in humility;
- that the pastor will operate under a mighty anointing and the gifts of the Holy Spirit;
- for God's favor so the pastor can lead the church to fulfill its God-assigned vision.

Thursday

The gifts of the Spirit and signs and wonders. We pray

- that the gifts of the Holy Spirit will be mightily manifested and that signs, wonders, and miraculous healings will characterize the services at Renewal;
- that Renewal will fulfill its calling to be a spiritual hospital so that the lost will come to Christ, the blind will see, the lame will walk, the deaf will hear, the barren will be fruitful, demonic bondages will be broken in the lives of people, captives will be set free, and all kinds of physical, mental, and emotional healings will take place;
- that God will make Renewal Christian Center a lighthouse in the Washington, DC, metropolitan area;
- for the success of our cell groups.

Friday

Revival. We pray

- that God will be merciful to His church and pour out His Spirit upon us in a mighty way;
- that the presence of the Holy Spirit will be felt in every service;
- that God will revive Renewal and give us the privilege of experiencing His presence in a mighty revival that will engulf the entire Washington, DC, area and beyond;
- that each of us at Renewal will be deeply convicted and repent from every sin;

- that each of us will have a zeal for God and His kingdom agenda;
- that each of us will live holy lives based upon the scriptures;
- for a spirit of joy, worship, and liberty in the Spirit to engulf the services at Renewal;
- that God will protect the genuine and warm Christian love and care that has always characterized Renewal Christian Center.

Saturday

Breaking demonic resistance as well as cleansing and protection. We pray

- that God will destroy every demonic resistance against the church that will seek to derail us from fulfilling our divine vision;
- that the Holy Spirit will drive out any spirit of offense, negativity, and murmuring in the church;
- for God to place a hedge of protection around the church so the enemy will not be able to steal, kill, and destroy;
- against flattering and corrupting tongues that may seek to influence members negatively and dampen their enthusiasm and love for the Lord.

Daily Prayer Points

In addition to these weekly prayers, each team prays the following daily prayer points:

- We pray for God to protect missionaries around the world, provide for their needs, anoint them, and make their work fruitful.
- We pray for the protection of God's church around the globe and for God's shepherds to fearlessly and truthfully proclaim the anointed Word of God, yield to the Holy Spirit, and be a mighty army that bears much fruit to glorify God.

- We pray for the protection and blessing of all our members so we can do exploits for the kingdom of God.
- We also pray for pastor and his family for divine protection, health, and favor to lead Renewal to fulfill its vision and destiny.
- We pray for the country, the president, and the leadership of the United States as well as the other nations of the world.

These might seem rather numerous, but we have trained ourselves to do this within the allotted thirty minutes so the intercessors can be released to go about their day. In addition to the prayer points, we have available various passages of scripture to back up the weekly prayer points.

Monday Night Prayers

On Mondays, the intercessors meet for prayers from 7:00 to 8:30 p.m. Two separate teams rotate on Mondays. Each team has an assistant, and the leader of the prayer ministry oversees the teams and works closely with me.

Each team has about five or six intercessors who lead the weekly prayers. Every intercessor has the freedom to wait on the Lord and come up with their own prayer points as the Holy Spirit leads them.

In addition to that, there are specific prayer points prayed every Monday night.

- We pray over the requests submitted by members and various requests from the church's web site.
- We pray for all missionaries and God's church around the world.
- We pray for the outreach ministries of the church.
- We pray for the pastor and his family.
- We pray for the president of the United States and other world leaders.

Prayer Rallies

We also meet every last Friday of the month to pray from 7:00 to 10:00 p.m. Typically, we fast on the Friday of the prayer rally. We have trained leaders who lead the prayer rallies.

Monthly Men's Prayer Breakfast

On the second Saturday of every month, the men gather to fellowship and pray.

Daughters of the King

The ladies also meet on the second Friday of each month to fellowship and pray.

Outreach Ministries' Monthly Prayers

The outreach ministries also meet one Friday a month to pray for their ministries and the salvation of souls.

Sunday Morning Intercessors

Each Sunday morning, a group of intercessors meets to pray prior to the service. They focus on covering every aspect of the service.

Intercessors' Quarterly Prayers

Once every three months, I meet to pray with all the intercessors in the church. This involves those who lead the morning telephone prayers, those who lead the Monday night prayers, and those who lead the Sunday morning prayers. Everyone who functions as an intercessor is encouraged to attend the quarterly prayers. I focus on lifting the intercessors before the Lord and praying for their own needs.

Pastor's Sunday Prayer Team

Sometime ago, I felt prompted to pray with a group every Sunday. I chose intercessors who had a passion for the vision God had given us and who lived close enough to our home to reduce the burden of driving long distances. This was a quiet, unannounced group who focused on praying behind the scenes. In our first year of engaging in this, we met after church every Sunday to pray from 2:00 to 3:00 p.m. The following year, we began meeting on the first Sunday of each month.

Annual Twenty-One-Day Fast

Every year, the church undertakes a twenty-one-day fast in January. We normally have a theme for each year. We have scriptures and prayer points for each week of the fast.

- Typically, the first week is used for personal cleansing and repentance.
- The second week focuses on praying for our church as well as the global church and the leaders of various nations.
- The third week is used to focus on our personal needs and to ask God to protect and favor us through the new year.

Prior to starting the yearly fast, we give out prayer cards for everyone to write down their prayer requests for the year. We typically collect the cards on December 31 and pray over them throughout the fast.

No doubt all these volumes of constant prayers have placed a covering of divine favor over the church.

We believe that putting God first causes Him to add all other things unto us. It is always a thrill to see people line up at the end of the year, during our December 31 end-of-year service, to testify and praise God for answered prayers.

No doubt all these volumes of constant prayers have placed a covering of divine favor over the church. For the eighteen years we have pastored the church, hospital visitations have been minimal, accidents have been virtually nonexistent, our children have been graduating from high school, and almost 100 percent of them go to college year after year. There have virtually been no issues of drug addiction or any disturbing moral issues among our youth. God has been extremely gracious to us as a church.

Prayer Promptings from the Spirit

Numerous times I have felt the prompting of the Holy Spirit to pray over certain specific prayer points.

A good example is what I received one December morning when I was at the Mayo Clinic in Minnesota for my wife's heart surgery. The Holy Spirit gave me some points for prayer. One of them was to pray that no leader in the church would be taken captive by Satan to do his will and that my reputation and relationships would be protected by God. All through the year, I focused on those prayers along with scripture passages I had received.

One interesting thing that came directly out of that season of prayer was in connection to the relationships around me. Over the years, I have seen people leave the church for various reasons. Some of those situations have been revealed to me by the Holy Spirit in advance, but two particular leaders left in a rather dramatic and unexpected fashion, which could have been despairing had the Lord not directly prepared my spirit through prayer to anticipate and handle those situations. One of those who left was a member of my inner prayer circle and a very valuable leader. This person was financially faithful, a top giver, a great intercessor, a lover of Jesus, and a remarkable supporter of my family and the vision God had given to Renewal Christian Center. She decided to take a break from the church after disagreeing with a decision at a leadership meeting. But I never gave up on her. I will tell her story later.

The other person was a trusted individual who had been a member of the church for several years. This individual would do anything for my family. He would drive me to the airport and pick me up from the airport from my travels around the world no matter what time of day it was. He did this for many years. He was extremely protective of our family and even testified both in private and publicly in church that God had assigned him to my family! He was a dedicated and trusted individual. He mentioned to me privately that God had always watched over me "because of the genuineness of [my] heart and character."

Those were his exact words. At one point, he went into a crisis of faith and experienced some depression. I relentlessly prayed and counseled him until God graciously healed him and brought him out of it. His words to me after his recovery were that God had assigned him to be behind us in ministry.

Surprisingly, however, he and his family left about a year later without even bothering to inform us. The sad thing was that I tried unsuccessfully to meet with them several times. It all seemed rather puzzling and inexplicable.

> This experience could have shaken our faith ...

This experience could have shaken our faith, even in our most trusted leaders, and made it difficult to trust and work with people at a time when it was obvious that God was moving the church to a new level of spirituality. We needed to trust others with sensitive responsibilities, but who could you count on after such an experience with a close and trusted leader of many years? People can be valuable, but our greatest confidant should be God. He is the only friend who sticks closer than a brother (Proverbs 18:24 NIV). He has also promised to be with us through the fire and the raging rivers of life (Isaiah 43:2 NLT). He is the only one who loved us enough to die for us willingly on the cross in spite of our sins. He is the one who truly takes the bullet for us every day.

We are human, and trusted friends are extremely helpful; however, we must learn never to place our full trust in any human being because scripture makes it clear that it is a curse to put our trust in mere humans (Jeremiah 17:5 NLT). We must certainly be grateful for the people God blesses our lives with, but our trust in them should never replace our trust in God. We should always remember that even the most trusted people and leaders can disappoint us. Humans have feet of clay and can crumble at some point.

We must certainly be grateful for the people
God blesses our lives with, but our trust in
them should never replace our trust in God.

In the same way that people sing your praises, they can rise up against you to "eat up" your flesh (Psalm 27:2 NKJV). Husbands and wives who joyfully say, "I do," at the altar of marriage can also say, "I don't," at the court of divorce. We should trust and enjoy every relationship without the stress of suspicion. However, when circumstances change and trust is broken, our faith in God is what will see us through. Because we live in a sin-infested world, husbands turn against wives and wives against husbands even to the point of murdering them for things like money or love affairs. Children murder their parents for money. Business partners can turn against their colleagues. People betray the trust of long-standing friends. Even churches can turn against their pastors at the instigation of a few dissatisfied leaders! This is the reality of life and particularly of leadership. It involves pain—sometimes unexpected pain and lots of it. It is valuable pain designed by God to make you though, not break you. In the words of Samuel Chand, "You will only grow to the threshold of your pain."[3]

The good news is that the painful experience I had had very positive fruit. As scripture says, in all things, God works for our good (Romans 8:28 NIV). This painful experience helped me reevaluate who I could really trust around me. I once heard someone say we must learn to distinguish between "confidants," "comrades," and "constituents."

- *Confidants* are those we can trust through thick and thin. We have the assurance that they have our backs no matter what happens.
- *Comrades* are those who would work hard alongside us to contend for the vision that God has given us. However, they

cannot be trusted as confidants. There is a limit to the depth
of the relationship.

- *Constituents* are part of the larger congregation. They can come
and go as they please. They can't be depended upon at any
personal and deep level. They will stay with us as long as their
needs are being met. Any slight form of dissatisfaction can
cause them not to show up any longer. They can walk away in
a heartbeat without bothering to say goodbye.

This distinction was a much-needed insight and body of knowledge
that helped transform my leadership skills. I had always practiced it but
had never had it articulated in such a clear and meaningful fashion. It
helped me to really know and value those who could truly be trusted
as confidants and others who only had to be understood as comrades
or constituents. Let me expand on this from my personal observations
and understanding and share some lessons.

- *Sometimes comrades push hard in an effort to be treated as confidants,
but that is a tragic mistake.* Confidants grow naturally into their
role with time without any overt push on their part to earn a
special place in one's life. It is a natural development. Comrades
must remain comrades, and confidants must remain confidants.
That distinction is extremely pertinent to the health and well-
being of any leader and any organization. Constituents are easy
to spot and work with, but the distinction between confidants
and comrades is not that easy to see. It takes time and focus to
distinguish between the two. If not appropriately distinguished
though, the oversight or mixture can prove costly for the leader
because when the wrong person is allowed into one's circle of
influence as a confidant, the damage can be incalculable. There
must be a constant test and evaluation of a leader's inner circle
in an intentional, prayerful, yet unobvious manner. No red flag
should ever be ignored, as this could prove rather damaging.
Simple things, such as a sudden consistent failure to return calls
or messages or failing to attend meetings without proper notice,

show an erosion of passion and possible loss of interest in the vision and support for the leader and the organization. These are valuable red flags that should not be ignored. They should be regarded as cautions. It could well be that a confidant or even comrade may be losing his or her passion or even nursing some form of grudge or dissatisfaction.

- *The only sure protection a leader has is to live a life of integrity and uprightness.* One's character must always be transparent and defensible even though we can never claim a flawless existence. As one saying goes, "If we take care of our character, God will take care of our reputation." We must live a life of constant introspection, prayer, and repentance. We must pour out our hearts first to God and then to our most trusted confidants as we feel directed by the Spirit within us. Even if people were to leave and say the most terrible things about us, our character will take care of our reputation. People will mostly trust what they know to be foundationally true about you and not necessarily what someone else says to the contrary. When people personally know you as a person of integrity, they will not be easily swayed by what your detractors might say in a bid to justify themselves and damage you. We must always remember the words of Paul in his vintage years to the young pastor Timothy.

Flee the evil desires of youth and pursue righteousness, faith, love and peace, along with those who call on the Lord out of a pure heart. Don't have anything to do with foolish and stupid arguments because you know they produce quarrels. And the Lord's servant must not be quarrelsome but must be kind to everyone, able to teach, not resentful. Opponents must be gently instructed, in the hope that God will grant them repentance leading them to a knowledge of the truth, and that they will come to their senses and escape from the trap of the devil, who has taken them captive to do his will. (2 Timothy 2:22–26 NIV)

- *Learn to love in spite of your pain.* I came to the conclusion that God will never move you to the next level of greatness in service if He has not tested you with trials. Trials produce inner pain, which leads to refinement of our character. The pain caused in us is used by God for our own refinement and strengthening so we can develop what it takes to handle the bigger challenges that inevitably come with expanded territories, responsibilities, and influence. When people see us handling pain with a transparent dependence on God, we earn their trust, respect, and support. They are more prone to follow us into unchartered waters. They become more willing to fight alongside us to accomplish the vision. God is able to trust us with greater responsibilities and blessings after we have been tested by Him and not found wanting. He elevates us after we have been tried and come forth as gold (Job 23:10 NIV). Testing is painful but good for our lives because of what it accomplishes in us.

One of the biggest tests is how we think of people who leave us, sometimes with great hurt and disappointment. Always remember that the people who part ways with you were once God's instruments of blessings for your life. It is wonderful when people leave on a good note, but that is not always the case. When they leave, whether on a good or bad note, never harbor animosity in your heart against them. Don't hold grudges. Release them with a pure heart. Their work is done. God will take care of you and them as well. You are God's child, and so are they. Leave it all to God. He will heal you and restore whatever He has allowed the locusts to eat (Joel 2:25 NKJV). That is His specialty. He never fails. You cannot jeopardize God's anointing on your life by harboring anger, bitterness, or discontent. That grieves the Holy Spirit and makes it difficult for Him to use you in an unhindered way.

Our Lord Jesus is the supreme example of how to handle disappointments and even betrayals from trusted people. Peter was not just among the twelve disciples; he was also a member of Jesus's inner circle of three. He was a confidant. Peter was the one used by God to reveal the true identity of Jesus as "the Christ, the Son of the Living God" (Matthew 16:16 NIV). Peter was one of the three out of the twelve who were allowed to experience the transfiguration of Jesus on the mountain. Peter had the privilege of seeing Moses and Elijah appear with Jesus and the countenance of Jesus completely changed so much so that His face "shone like the Sun, and His face became as white as the light" (Matthew 17:2 NIV). Peter heard the voice of God the Father booming from heaven, "This is my Son whom I love; with Him I am well pleased. Listen to Him" (Matthew 17:5 NIV). This was such a deep spiritual insight that Jesus told Peter and the other two disciples not to tell anyone about it until after His resurrection. Jesus was trusting them with a deep spiritual revelation. Peter was the one to whom Jesus said, "You are Peter, and on this rock, I will build my church, and the gates of Hades will not overcome it" (Matthew 16:18 NIV).

> Our Lord Jesus is the supreme example of how to handle disappointments and even betrayals from trusted people.

In fact, Peter was so sure of his love and loyalty to Jesus that he said to Jesus, "Even if I have to die with you, I will never disown you" (Mark 14:31 NIV). The truth is though that Peter denied Jesus three times. Yet the most fascinating thing is that Jesus restored Peter after he had betrayed Him. The one who turned his back on Jesus was restored and asked by Jesus to take care of His flock. So what if Jesus had written Peter off in anger and never given him a second chance? Obviously, the kingdom of God would have lost a most valuable contributor.

So no matter how terrible people may behave, we must leave them in God's hands and never angrily or bitterly write them off. This is not to deny the fact that there are times when God will allow people to walk out of your life or ministry for your own good. You must acknowledge those situations and not try to prevent such departures. Our omniscient God knows exactly which chess pieces to move at the right time. Simply trust Him because He knows exactly what to do and is working everything out for your good. Even in those situations, don't allow any form of bitterness to infest your heart. Never write people off. Let God do the writing off!

Another wonderful illustration of not writing people off is exemplified in the relationship between the apostle Paul and John Mark. Paul and Barnabas had a wonderful working relationship. Barnabas was the one who stood with Paul and introduced him to the rest of the disciples when everyone was afraid and skeptical of Paul (then called Saul) because of his previous persecution of Christians (Acts 9:27 NIV). Paul and Barnabas went on a missionary journey together after the Holy Spirit called them out of the church at Antioch (Acts 13:2). They took with them John Mark, a cousin of Barnabas, but Paul became displeased with John Mark because he deserted them on the trip. The biblical account speaks eloquently about this.

> Sometime later Paul said to Barnabas, "Let us go back and visit the believers in all the towns where we preached the Word of the Lord and see how they are doing." Barnabas wanted to take John, also called Mark, with them, but Paul did not think it wise to take him, because he had deserted them in Pamphylia and had not continued with them in the work. They had such a sharp disagreement that they parted company. Barnabas took Mark and sailed for Cyprus, but Paul chose Silas, and left, commended by the believers to the grace of God. (Acts 15:36–40 NIV)

Even though John Mark was the cause of a hot dispute and a ruptured relationship between Paul and Barnabas, it appears that Paul never completely wrote John Mark off. This is attested to by the fact that years later, Paul wrote to Timothy concerning John Mark, "Get Mark and bring him with you, because he is helpful to me in my ministry" (2 Timothy 4:11 NIV). I believe the apostle Paul requested that Mark rejoin him in ministry because he did not write him off—even though Mark had painfully deserted him earlier on.

No matter what desertions you face in life, do not write people off because they could repent and become even more valuable to you than before. Of course, you have to use discernment and wisdom to ensure that there is genuine repentance and that the person is not seeking to come back for ulterior motives. I had the experience of one leader who left after a sharp disagreement in a meeting over the direction of the church. She did not agree with a decision I wanted to take. It happened at a meeting of the leadership. (This is the story I promised to tell earlier.) This valued leader expressed her frustration and requested to step down immediately from every leadership role she had in the ministry. This person was very loyal and valuable to the ministry. She was a generous giver and a wonderful intercessor. I could attest to her character as being impeccable! She had been in the ministry for several years and had also headed a very important ministry in the church for many years!

I was stunned by her decision to resign with immediate effect. She asked to be given time off from the ministry, and she left the church for a while to seek the Lord. Incidentally, I dropped her off at her house after the meeting. You can imagine how interesting the ride was! She stopped attending the church for over a year! She virtually cut off communication

> No matter what desertions you face in life, do not write people off because they could repent and become even more valuable to you than before.

with most people and would not return any calls, but somehow, my love for her never waned. I kept in touch with her. I would constantly call and check up on her. Several months after she had left, she had a very challenging family situation. I went alongside the family and stood with them through that difficult trial. I rallied the church to stand with her and the family.

This precious lady ended up coming back to the church. I never wrote her off, and I am convinced that her future contribution to God's kingdom is going to be even more remarkable than before. In a conversation with one of our leaders, that leader remarked to me, "Pastor, the way you handled the situation is astonishing to me. You have truly challenged me to learn to continually express God's love no matter what the situation might be."

It is also interesting that just before the former close leader who helped with all my travels left, God raised up a replacement who lived quite close to our house. This individual retired just at the right time and was available to help with all kinds of situations. His wife, also an amazing gift to the church, constantly jokes that God retired her husband from secular employment to use him in His kingdom. We need to pray proactively and listen to what the Lord reveals or intimates into our spirit. Because I had prayed vigorously in advance, the changes I was seeing in the leadership around me were much easier to handle. When God allows a person to leave, it is always for a reason. We can either look back in nostalgia, constantly cling to the memories of the past, and refuse to let go, or we can trust God and look ahead with confidence to the new things God has in store for us!

We need to pray proactively and listen to what the Lord reveals or intimates into our spirit. Because I had prayed vigorously in advance, the changes I was seeing in the leadership around me were much easier to handle.

When God was about to commission Joshua to lead the children of Israel into the Promised Land, God's first words to him were that Moses was dead. God said to Joshua, "Moses my servant is dead. Therefore, the time has come for you to lead these people, the Israelites, across the Jordan River into the land I am giving them" (Joshua 1:2 NLT).

This was not simply a factual reminder but a spiritual repositioning of Joshua's entire orientation into the new things God had in store for him. God wanted Joshua to understand that the days of Moses were over. Moses had done his part. It was now time to move into the future. God wanted Joshua to understand that in spite of the amazing miracles Moses had been used by God to perform, it was time for Joshua to forget the past and press on into the future. God said to Joshua, "Today, I will begin to exalt you in the eyes of all Israel, so they may know I am with you as I was with Moses" (Joshua 3:7 NIV). God could not have exalted Joshua if he had clung to the accomplishments of his mentor and much revered leader, Moses, and refused to look ahead to the new things God had in store for him! Joshua had to forget the past and look ahead to the new things God had for him.

In our own spiritual journeys, it is important to recognize when "Moses" is "dead." We must be grateful for the "Moses" in our past journeys, but we must focus on the new people God wants to use in our lives to accomplish His purposes. The people God used in our past might not necessarily be the same people God would use in our current or future situations. Never be bitter when God allows a "Moses" to "die" out of your life because He may have somebody new to fit your current needs.

A Prompting in the Parking Lot at Sam's Club

I had pulled into the parking lot at a Sam's Club one day and immediately felt the prompting of the Holy Spirit about some specific things to pray about. So I picked up a piece of paper and started jotting them down.

These were the prayer points:

- Pray and believe God for the church to be blessed enough to support one hundred missionaries in one hundred countries.
- Pray for a fervent spirit of evangelism to engulf the church.
- Pray that revival will break out in the church and that it will engulf the entire Washington metropolitan area.

- Pray that Renewal will be a rallying point of prayer for the entire Washington metropolitan area.
- Pray that God will use each member of our family to our full potential.
- Pray for the worship team of the church.
- Pray for a deep insight into God's Word.
- Pray to proclaim the Word with great anointing and an attestation of signs and wonders.
- Pray for the church to be faithful in tithes and offerings and to give generously.
- Pray that the church will walk authentically with Jesus and pursue holiness and righteousness.
- Pray that the Wednesday Bible studies at the church will become a powerful discipling time for many people in the community and not just in our church.

These prayers have become part of my regular prayer points.

Whatever the Holy Spirit prompts must be an important focus of prayer because we flow with the move of God when we remain prayerful. God does everything according to His sovereign calendar. A prompting from the Holy Spirit to pray simply means God wants us to be ready for what He is about to do. We may not necessarily understand why, but it is always important to submit to the promptings of God's Spirit in our prayer lives. That is how the Spirit will entrust us with deeper revelations concerning the things of God and how to prepare ourselves spiritually to be used by God in specific assignments. The truth is you never know what God might be up to!

It is quite interesting to note that some of those prayer points are already becoming a reality. The fruit is already beginning to spring forth.

Prayer of Commitment and Renewal

Some time ago, I began praying a prayer of renewal and commitment on a daily basis. This is the prayer:

I am crucified with Christ; nevertheless, I live. Yet not I but Christ lives in me. And the life I now live in the flesh, I live by the faith of the son of God who loved me and gave Himself for me. (Galatians 2:20 KJV)

Lord, today I renew my covenant of love and servanthood to You. With the help of the Holy Spirit, I purpose to live a crucified life for You by the faith of the Son of God who loved me and gave Himself for me.

Please Father, all I ask is that the Holy Spirit will use me mightily to bring honor to Jesus. Pour out Your Spirit upon me in an extraordinary way to proclaim the gospel of Jesus Christ. Attest to my preaching of the gospel and vindicate my call by saving countless numbers of souls and healing lives, sicknesses, and diseases to let the world know that Jesus Christ is the same yesterday, today, and forever and that Jesus still saves and heals.

Let me live in absolute awe of You, and let my life praise You in every way. I present myself as a living sacrifice to You today.

Several months after praying that, I heard within me what I felt was a response from God.

I have heard your cry. I will show you My glory. I am pleased with you not because of yourself but because you live in My Son, you move in My Son, and you have your being in Him.

You are crucified with Him, and the life you live is by the faith of My Son who loved you and gave himself for you.

Because I am pleased with My Son, I am pleased with you; for you are in My Son. I showed My Son My glory and continue to show My glory through Him. I will show you My glory because you are in My Son. Abide in Me, and let My words abide in you. That will ensure that all your requests will be granted.

That was an exciting assurance. I believe with all my heart that I will see the glory of God as I continue to pray and minister faithfully before Him. For years, I have been praying the prayer of the prophet Habakkuk. "LORD, I have heard of your fame; I stand in awe of your deeds, LORD. Repeat them in our day, in our time make them known; in wrath remember mercy" (Habakkuk 3:2 NIV).

- I look forward to God renewing His works in signs, wonders, and salvations.
- I look forward to discipling many people to live authentically for Jesus.
- I look forward to a massive renewal from the Holy Spirit and people flocking to the house of God, hungry for the truth of God's Word.
- I look forward to God-centered preaching that drives people to their knees and causes their souls to hunger after the presence of God.
- I look forward to people living in joy regardless of their circumstances because the joy of the Lord is their strength.
- I look forward to people confidently declaring that

> whatever were gains to me I now consider loss for the sake of Christ … I consider everything a loss because of the surpassing worth of knowing Christ Jesus my Lord … I want to know Christ— yes, to know the power of His resurrection and

participation in His sufferings, becoming like him in His death. (Philippians 3:7–10 NIV)

- I look forward to people joyfully declaring,

  I know what it is to be in need, and I know what it is to have plenty. I have learned the secret of being content in any and every situation, whether well fed or hungry, whether living in plenty or in want. I can do all things through Him who strengthens me. (Philippians 4:12–13 NIV)

- I look forward to people saying, "to live is Christ and to die is gain" (Philippians 1:21 NIV).

I believe our heavenly Father is purifying His church and preparing churches around the world through which He can manifest His glory. We live in a time when God is marginalized and Christianity seems to be having no visible impact on society because God's children are not authentically living for Jesus. We are not praying audaciously for God to move in our lives, in His church, and in society. There must be a renewal, and there will be a renewal. The glory of God must be seen even amid the darkness and malaise that has engulfed society.

The words of the apostle Paul to Timothy are instructive.

But mark this: There will be terrible times in the last days. People will be lovers of themselves, lovers of money, boastful, proud, abusive, disobedient to their parents, ungrateful, unholy, without love, unforgiving, slanderous, without self-control, brutal, not lovers of the good, treacherous, rash, conceited, lovers of pleasure rather than lovers of God—having a form of godliness but denying its power. (2 Timothy 3:1–5 NIV)

Preach the word; be prepared in season and out of season; correct, rebuke and encourage—with great patience and careful instruction. For the time will come when people will not put up with sound doctrine. Instead, to suit their own desires they will gather around them a great number of teachers to say what their itching ears want to hear. They will turn their ears away from the truth and turn aside to myths. (2 Timothy 4:2–4 NIV)

These words of Paul are aptly descriptive of the times in which we live, but I am also confident that it is a unique opportunity for God's church to arise and shine. I believe the light of Christ must penetrate the darkness around us because Christ is the only hope of humanity. The church must actively believe this and practically live it out.

I am encouraged by the words of Isaiah.

We must not shirk our responsibilities. Heaven is counting on us to clothe ourselves in the power that God has already made available to us and to effect changes in this dark world through righteousness, obedience to God's Word, and faith in the promises of God.

Arise, shine, for your light has come, and the glory of the LORD rises upon you. See, darkness covers the earth and thick darkness is over the peoples, but the LORD rises upon you and His glory appears over you. (Isaiah 60:1–2 NIV)

God's church must rise and shine amid the engulfing darkness we see. God's people must pray, live righteously, and step out in the power of the Spirit to confront the darkness engulfing the world. That is our divinely assigned duty and destiny. We must believe and act on it. The power of God is available for us, and the authority of heaven is behind us.

We must not shirk our responsibilities. Heaven is counting on us to clothe ourselves in the power that God has already made available to us and to effect changes in this dark world through righteousness, obedience to God's Word, and faith in the promises of God. We must pray that God will manifest His power through us as we press on to accomplish His kingdom agenda.

CHAPTER 7

AUDACIOUS PRAYERS TO BE BLESSED WITH CHILDREN

MY WIFE AND I HAVE been married for over thirty years now. For the first seventeen years, we were childless. For three of those seventeen years, I left my wife by herself in Maryland to attend seminary in the Midwest. I saw her briefly only a couple of times during those three years, except for one summer that I spent fully with her.

We had been praying and trusting God for years to bless us with children. It is rather interesting that soon after our marriage, my wife said she would definitely want us to adopt children along with our biological children. So adoption has always been part of our thinking. The plan was to have our biological children first, followed by adoption. After several years of waiting, we decided to adopt.

The Spirit of God was simply about
to reveal the blessings ahead of us.
The prophetic word was soon to unfold.

The ways of the Lord are very interesting. One day, we had a guest minister in our former church. She had a prophetic gift, and as she was ministering, she called Angie and me. She said, "I see two children beside you." She had absolutely no idea that we had no children. The Spirit of God was simply about to reveal the blessings ahead of us. The prophetic word was soon to unfold.

Another interesting thing was that in my last class in seminary, which was on worship, the professor asked us to draw out our vision for the next five years on a piece of paper. I drew a man wearing a graduation gown with two kids beside him and a plant shooting out of the ground. The graduation gown represented the fact that I wanted to earn my doctorate within the next five years. The two children represented the fact that I was believing God to bless us with two children within the next five years. The plant shooting out of the ground represented the fact that I wanted to plant a church within the next five years.

The Bible says, "Write the vision and make it plain on tablets" (Habakkuk 2:2 NKJV). The Bible also makes it clear that to him who believes, all things are possible (Mark 9:23 NKJV). So to me, that piece of paper was not a wish list. It represented something that I was going to believe God for. I was simply writing down the vision and making it plain on paper. I believed that God was going to bless us with children, help us plant a church, and enable me to earn a doctoral degree. By the grace of God, all three things happened within five years.

I prayed audaciously and specifically for those three things to happen. About a year before we were blessed with children, I had a dream just prior to my birthday. In the dream, I saw a little boy with what appeared to be straight hair and a very fair complexion. I was a bit puzzled by the features, but I said to my wife that God had given me a birthday present. I was puzzled because neither of us is fair in complexion. The interesting thing was that the following year, God blessed us with our twins—a boy and a girl—and my son's complexion and features were exactly as I saw in the dream.

The twins were born on September 25, and my birthday is September 30. What a wonderful birthday present from the Lord. I have a picture in my office of my son taken when he was about a month old. It is a vivid representation of what the Lord had revealed to me in the dream.

How It All Happened

After seventeen years of marriage, we decided to adopt children. This had always been a desire of my wife. We worked with an adoption agency that proved to be excellent. After everything had been done, we were told that there were twins who were up for adoption, so we should put together a compelling case to the natural parents as to why we would be the best couple to adopt the children. I was actually away in Springfield, Missouri, taking some doctoral classes, when Angie called to inform me about the twins. She was wondering if I would be prepared for the responsibilities of raising twins. I excitedly told her yes! There were two other couples who were interested in the children as well. We were very excited and very interested. We created an album of our story and presented it to the adoption agency to be given to the birth parents. We never met the parents because they expressed a desire not to meet the prospective adoptive parents. I believe parting with the twins was a painful experience for them, but they knew that was the best thing to do if the children were to have a bright future.

Along with the album we created, we wrote our story as a couple. Below is the letter we sent to the birth parents to make our case.

Dear Birth Parents,

Angie and I wish to express our appreciation for the difficult but wonderful step in considering an adoption plan for your children. We know you have not made this decision in haste. It has involved deep emotions and pain. We can never pretend to understand the emotions you are experiencing now. We can understand, however, that your decision is motivated by a deep and unselfish desire to find a loving and caring home for your children. Our prayers are with you as you make this very important decision.

It is only natural that you would want to know as much as you can about us. The pictures we have assembled are an attempt to tell our story. We were both born in Ghana, West Africa, into large, nurturing families. I come from a family of ten. I am the third of nine surviving children. My father passed away at the age of eighty-eight almost two years ago. My mother currently resides in Ghana and has been able to visit with us. Angie also comes from a family of ten and is the third of eight surviving children. Her mother passed away in 1986.

Our siblings are spread over different parts of the world—Ghana, Canada, Italy, England, and here in the United States. This provides us with the unique opportunity to travel and visit with them and see other countries. We enjoy time spent with our families when we travel to see them and the many occasions when they come to see us here.

Angie and I met in England through a mutual friend while she was in college. We instantly liked each other and became very good friends. I particularly took to her because of her intelligence and very sociable nature. She brought life wherever she went. She says she liked me because I am gentle and kind. We were very good friends for five years before we got married. Destiny meant for us to be together because we both journeyed separately to the United States and lived our lives, but our friendship continued until we got married. We have been happily married for fifteen years now. Together, we share a loving relationship that we thank God for. Now we are excited about this opportunity to become loving parents and look forward with much joy to the children the Lord blesses us with.

Angie is a biologist and works as a senior research associate with a biomedical company. She studied pharmacology in college and enjoys what she does. I am a minister. I studied economics and political science in college, but when I felt the call into ministry, I went back to get a graduate degree in theology. I feel very fulfilled as a pastor. Angie and I both thoroughly enjoy helping to meet the spiritual, emotional, and social needs of people. We feel very blessed and fortunate.

We believe in God and family. We believe that a home should be a haven of love, care, and joy and that a child will be truly nurtured by the love we give. Integrity and hard work are both important principles in our lives. Our strong relationship comes from the mutual respect and trust we have for each other, which has nourished our home and marriage.

Choosing to adopt is an act of love and sacrifice. If you choose us, we promise to love and nurture your children with a lot of tenderness. We will provide a safe environment and give them the best opportunities in a loving Christian home.

Thank you for taking the time to read this letter, and may God bless and help you as you make this important, difficult, and selfless decision.

Sincerely,
Albert and Angela

Decision Time

With our letter and photo album making our case, we waited for the biological parents to make their decision as to which of the three prospective adoptive families they would choose for their twins.

We spent time fasting and praying and believing God to bless us with the twins. The Lord was gracious. The biological parents chose us to become the adoptive parents! We were overjoyed.

> The Lord was gracious. The biological parents chose us to become the adoptive parents! We were overjoyed.

The twins were born in Baltimore, Maryland, only an hour's drive from us. They were in the care of some wonderful foster parents in a place called Poolesville in Maryland. We arranged to see them quickly. A bunch of our close friends and family members went with us to see them one evening. They were simply adorable. A boy and a girl! The boy looked just like the face I had seen in my dream. I could not believe my eyes! What a blessing we were about to receive! The necessary paperwork was done, and we brought the twins home when they were barely a month old.

But there was one more hurdle to be cleared. Legally, we were to keep the twins for a month while the biological parents made the final decision about whether or not they still wanted to give the children away for adoption. The wait seemed like eternity. We would only know the final decision by 6:00 p.m. on day thirty!

I went away to a place off the Chesapeake Bay during the last three days prior to the final decision to fast and pray. This is one of my favorite getaways by the water. I would go there periodically to meditate and seek the Lord for a few days. I spent those days in fervent prayer asking for God to favor us by touching the hearts of the birth parents not to change their minds. I returned home in the afternoon to wait with Angie for the call. Was it going to be a yes or a no? It was a tense last hour prior to 6:00 p.m. Angie was by the telephone in my basement office, and I was working on some musical equipment with a friend who had stopped by. The friend had no idea about what was going on in our lives concerning the twins. Shortly after 6:00 p.m., the phone rang, and Angie let out a loud joyous scream. My friend almost panicked. Angie came out screaming excitedly, "We have the twins!

We have the twins! We have the twins." The evidence was clear. God had answered another audacious prayer!

Life was going to change radically for us! We were now going to parent our twins, continue planting the church, and plan for me to finish my doctoral studies! We needed a lot of grace and help. Overnight, we had become the parents of newly born twins! God provided abundant help to handle our radically changed household. Our first decision was for my wife to stop working outside the home in order to take care of our children. After six months of having nannies, she became a full-time mom. We had to completely rework our budget. The Lord graciously provided all the help we needed to take care of the twins.

Our church family rose to the occasion, and several of the ladies would come to our home to help babysit, bathe the children, wash clothes, clean feeding bottles, and clean the house or cook for us. The twins were simply adorable, and people were constantly showering them with gifts.

God has been extremely gracious, and they are growing up wonderfully. They both love and serve the Lord. They are very gifted musically. Sam, my son, became the church drummer at age nine and has been playing the keyboard in the services since he was about fourteen years of age. Sara, my daughter, is a very gifted singer. She is one of our valued worship leaders and helps in the media department. They both serve on the dance and the drama teams as well. They are both excellent with their academic work. We could not have asked God for more! We feel very blessed for the gracious hand of God upon our lives. God simply loves to bless His children. His promise is that if we abide in Him and His words abide in us, we should ask for what we wish, and it will be done for us (John 15:7 NIV). God continues to watch over His word to perform it. He does answer prayer, no matter how audacious it might seem! Nothing is too big to believe God for. I heard someone once say that what God cannot do, does not exist!

At the time of concluding this book, the twins are away to begin their college education at the same university. It is interesting that they found a church to fellowship at that is a walking distance from campus. One week after stepping into the church, my son became the keyboardist, and my daughter was leading the worship. Prior to that, the church had been worshipping by using music videos. When I spoke with the pastor by phone after one service, he simply said, "They are an answer to prayer." God took care of the void created by the departure of our children to college by blessing us with another gifted musician and worship leader. He then transferred our children into another portion of His vineyard in answer to another pastor's prayer.

God continues to watch over His word to perform it. He does answer prayer, no matter how audacious it might seem!

God does answer prayer! Prayer works!

CHAPTER 8

AUDACIOUS PRAYER: WE NEED TO BUILD

WE STARTED RENEWAL CHRISTIAN CENTER in the basement of our home. For seven years, we had the church office there. We first started holding services in a hotel and then moved to a school facility. Part of our vision was for the church to buy a piece of property and build a campus. Meeting in a school for services has numerous challenges, but the Lord has been extremely gracious. We have been blessed with very faithful and dependable workers. Many of them have been setting up and packing up after services for several years. For years, there was even a time when we kept all the church equipment in our garage to be hauled for services and brought back after each service. Through the heat, rain, and snow, the workers assigned to this difficult task have never complained! All our efforts to rent a commercial space to give us greater stability as a church never materialized. There was even a time when we signed a contract for a very spacious commercial space, but the owners suddenly pulled out.

We decided to put our efforts into acquiring a piece of land on which to build. The Lord blessed us with a good Realtor who led our efforts. We found a twenty-three-acre piece of property strategically located off the highway and started negotiations for purchase. Initially, the property was priced at $2 million at the height of the real estate boom. It was relisted at $1.5 million, and we negotiated and signed a purchase contract for $1.3 million. We secured a bank loan to buy. Strangely, however, the buyer suddenly seemed uninterested in selling the land. For six whole months, he would not sign the contract. It appeared he wanted more money.

We had only one recourse: prayer! I asked the church to pray fervently for the release of the property for our purchase. I vividly remember taking the contract, spreading it out, and calling for an answer from heaven. I would call the owner of the property by name and ask God to touch his heart to sign the contract. I would always have the contract before me as I cried out to the Lord. This type of prayer reminded me of when King Hezekiah received a letter from Sennacherib, the king of Assyria, defying Jehovah and threatening to invade and destroy Jerusalem. The biblical account declares,

> Hezekiah received the letters from the messengers and read it. Then he went up to the temple of the LORD and spread it out before the LORD. And Hezekiah prayed to the LORD: "LORD, the God of Israel, enthroned between the cherubim, you alone are God over all the kingdoms of the earth. Give ear, LORD, and hear, open your eyes, LORD, and see; listen to the words Sennacherib has sent to ridicule the Living God. It is true, LORD ... Now, LORD our God, deliver us from his hand, so that all the kingdoms of the earth may know that you alone, LORD, are God." (2 Kings 19:14–19 NIV)

For six months, I spread out the contract before the Lord in the basement of our home, believing for a divine intervention. God answered our cry in a marvelous way.

One day, during the Sunday

We knew that God had answered our prayers in a superb fashion!

morning service, I heard a word in my heart that I felt I needed to share with the church. "There are some here who have made large pledges but who will not stay to honor those pledges. Don't worry when that happens because the Lord will build His church." I shared that message right after the worship time, and I could see the shock on some faces. The truth was that people were content with the church and were simply surprised that anyone would think of leaving after we had so joyfully made those financial pledges! There was unity and absolutely no reason for people to complain! We had simply become too comfortable in our blessings. On our drive home, my wife said to me, "Honey, did you really have to share that with the church? People are going to be confused because everything seems to be going well." I simply responded that I believe the Lord wanted me to share that. I am certainly glad I did because things were about to change. And they did.

One day, my wife and I were driving on the highway past the property when I noticed a new sign advertising the property for sale. I immediately called our Realtor to find out what was happening. He called the owner for an explanation because we already had a contract to buy the land. All we needed was his signature! The truth is the Lord was up to something interesting. The real estate market had taken a downward turn because of the looming depression. We ended up renegotiating the price of the property and bought it for $812,000, which was $500,000 less than the originally contracted price! The seller had encountered bad financial times because of a divorce situation and was highly motivated to sell. In fact, things were so desperate for him that we had to advance to him $10,000 ahead of the closing date. I still remember signing the modified contract between us, the Realtor, and the seller on the open tailgate of the owner's red pickup truck! I can't shake off the vivid recollection of the expression on the face of the seller when we finally signed the closing documents for the property. He looked at me and said, "Reverend, you know you should have paid $2 million for this property." He was not happy at the turn of events, but we knew that God had answered our prayers in a superb fashion!

One morning, in my quiet time, the Lord highlighted a passage in

Ephesians that has deepened my faith greatly and increased my audacity in prayer. The passage reads,

> I also pray that you will understand the incredible greatness of God's power for us who believe in Him. This is the same mighty power that raised Christ from the dead and seated Him in the place of honor at God's right hand in the heavenly realms. Now He is far above any ruler or authority or power or leader or anything else—not only in this world but also in the world to come. God has put all things under the authority of Christ and has made Him head over all things for the benefit of the church. And the Church is His body; it is made full and complete by Christ, who fills all things everywhere with Himself. (Ephesians 1:19–23 NLT)

As many times as I had read that passage in the past, that morning was a eureka moment for me. I came into a completely different and deeper understanding of the power behind our prayers and why we must pray audaciously. Our faith must be without borders when we come before the throne of God to petition Him in prayer.

The power that God has put in us to accomplish His kingdom agenda is described by Paul in the above passage as being of "incredible greatness." It is that same power that raised up Jesus Christ from the dead. This simply means that we can depend upon God's mighty power to raise every dead situation back to life if we discern it to be the will of God. This is mind-boggling authority. It tells me that as God's children, we are not destitute people. If we are truly anchored in Christ, then no situation or condition should ever render us powerless. In fact, this assertion is buttressed by the assurance that Jesus gives us in Matthew 28:18–19 (NLT). "I have been given all authority in heaven and on earth. Therefore go ..." Wherever we go, we must function at the highest level of authority. God has granted us the power to live and function with authority in whatever calling and responsibility He has assigned to us on earth. This should give us unparalleled confidence every day of our lives.

We are also reminded in the Ephesians passage that no authority, leader, or power in the seen and unseen world, present or future, known or unknown, even comes close to the authority that Christ has. Our Lord Jesus is simply supreme. Everything is completely under His dominion and control! But what is even more astonishing and exciting is that "God has placed all things under his feet and appointed him to be head over everything for the church" (Ephesians 1:22 NIV).

This passage has remarkable implications for the church and how we view and relate to the powers, authorities, and institutions around us. So by practical extension and application, this means that every earthly authority, institution, power, person, and resource must work to further the advancement of God's kingdom agenda through His church. It means that the federal, state, county, and local governments—as well as all financial institutions and every conceivable institution and power structure—must all work to favor God's church to advance God's kingdom agenda.

Nothing should be impossible for us to accomplish
if we truly function according to God's will!
This is a strong basis for audacious prayers.

Every existing authority must function to favor God's church because Christ "fills all things everywhere with himself." Nothing is outside the control of Jesus, and nothing should be outside our control if we truly live in His will because scripture makes it clear that we live in Him, move in Him, and have our very existence in Him (Acts 17:28 NIV). Nothing should be impossible for us to accomplish if we truly function according to God's will! This is a strong basis for audacious prayers. In fact, I believe that is precisely why the writer of Hebrews enjoins us to come boldly before the throne of our gracious God because we will find mercy and grace to help us in our time of need (Hebrews 4:16 NIV). Our heavenly Father expects us to pray to Him in reverence yet with audacity. We have a basis to pray audaciously! We prayed with audacity for God to cause the seller to release the land to us, and He answered in a spectacular way by causing the land to be sold to us at a $500,000 reduction in price! Audacious prayers based upon the will of God will never fall on deaf ears. Heaven will always answer.

CHAPTER 9

AUDACIOUS PRAYER: OH LORD, PURGE YOUR CHURCH

THE CHURCH WAS VERY EXCITED after we purchased the land. The Lord had helped us greatly, and we were able to raise an amount of $306,000 within a year toward the purchase. This was in addition to the regular giving for the church. It was an exciting feat for a church of our size. Some gave as much as an extra $50,000 toward the land in addition to their regular giving to the church. There was great unity to accomplish the vision of the church. God was blessing His people in many ways. Couples who had been barren for years were being blessed with children as we fasted and prayed. Some were even blessed with twins. I remember a particular couple who had tried for years to conceive without success. They called to ask if they could see me at the office. They came that afternoon, broken. The doctor had given them the bad news that the woman was barren and would not conceive. As I saw her tears of pain and anguish, I simply asked them to join me in fasting and praying for an extended period to believe God to bless them with children. After a time of fasting and prayer, God answered, and today, they have two children: a boy and a girl. People who had a dream of owning their own businesses were able to do so.

Many people with all kinds of very difficult life issues received amazing answers to their prayers.

I have been especially blessed by the stories of our single mothers. I remember a phone call I received from one particular lady who was raising her son by herself. I was on my way to a meeting out of state when I received that phone call. I pulled off the road to talk with her. The lady was in tears. She mentioned that she and her son had just returned from a trip out of the country. She said that within an hour or so after getting back home, her son lost his ability to walk. She had rushed him to the hospital, but nothing seemed to be working so they were back at the house. I assured her that I would come and pray with her on my return. I asked her to join me in fasting and prayer and to believe God to heal the son. God was gracious, and the boy was completely restored. The lady became a very productive member of the church. Numerous single mothers joined the church. We pastored, nurtured, counseled, and stood with them. Years later, they were successfully raising their children, and many of the children are in college. Some of those single mothers went on to acquire college and even postgraduate degrees. One very wonderful blessing is that all our high school students were graduating and going on to college. God was shining His face on the church! The members were grateful for God's divine presence.

God was gracious, and the boy
was completely restored.

People were so blessed that five families came together and bought us a vehicle costing $40,000. One individual had approached me with the offer that a few of them wanted to bless me with a new vehicle. Even though I was driving an old vehicle, it was a very reliable one and served me well, so I declined the offer. Somehow, I enjoy driving old, well-maintained cars! I said, "Let those gifts be channeled into the building fund we are about to establish." He came persistently with the offer for a whole year. Finally, he convinced me by saying, "Pastor, you are blocking our own blessings by your refusal to accept the gift of a car from us."

When we received the new vehicle, I said to my wife that she should drive it. I wanted to continue driving my old car and give my wife's van to a lady in the church. The lady had started coming to the church as a result of our homeless ministry She attended church faithfully. She was getting back on her feet and needed a car. I called her to the front of the church one Sunday and gave her the keys to our family car! There was so much jubilation in the church! Some were weeping at the gesture! Only a little while back, the lady was in a homeless shelter with her three children. Through the outreach ministry of the church, she came out of the shelter. A member found her a job in her place of employment, and her life was radically transformed! Today, she has advanced on her job, and her children are serving with her as valuable members of the worship team. The power of God was at work in our midst. The wounded, broken, and destitute were being received with love and nurtured in God's kingdom.

We also embarked on a campaign to raise funds to build a campus. The pledges that came in were over $1 million to be redeemed within three years. Some of the pledge amounts were very sizable, but I knew it was possible to raise that amount. The dream was becoming a reality!

Amid all the blessings, however, spiritual coldness was beginning to seep in. The Lord brought the gradual spiritual coldness to my attention. It is a day I will not forget. I vividly remember getting the sermon ready to preach at the church's tenth anniversary when the Lord arrested my attention. A statement flooded my spirit. "This is not the church I called you to plant." I was a bit stunned, so I started listening to what was flooding my heart. "The church is blessed. Answers are being received to all kinds of prayers, but the hearts of the people are getting cold. The blessings have become more important than the giver of the blessings."

I knew I was hearing from the Lord. It was all true and very convicting. My response was "Oh Lord, please purge your church." That is one of the scariest and most audacious prayers I have ever prayed! But I knew it was better for God to have His way than for me to chart a course for God! I reflected over the message and changed my sermon completely. I preached to the church that Sunday and mentioned what I believed I had heard from the Lord.

I confessed that many had become cold spiritually after we had received so much blessing from the Lord. Many were no longer attending the midweek Bible studies and prayer meetings that they had so faithfully attended over the years. I mentioned that I had asked the Lord to purge His church so that those who truly loved the Lord would remain to serve Him.

> "Lord, afflict the comfortable and comfort the afflicted."

Sometime later, certain leaders began questioning the need for us to spend so much money to put up a church building when there were many hungry people in Africa who could benefit from the money! The interesting thing was that some of the same people who were complaining were busy putting up mansions in Africa even though they did not live there!

Each Sunday when I got up to preach, part of my prayer was "Lord, afflict the comfortable and comfort the afflicted." I did not realize that some in the congregation were disturbed by that prayer. A few people actually spoke to me about that. So I took the time to explain one Sunday morning that there are times when God would afflict us when we get too fat and comfortable and stray from Him. In those situations, affliction would help put us back on track. I reminded the church of the words of the psalmist.

> Before I was afflicted, I went astray, but now I obey your word. You are good and what you do is good; teach me your decrees ... It was good for me to be afflicted so that I might learn your decrees ... I know, LORD, that your laws are righteous, and that in faithfulness you have afflicted me. (Psalm 119:67, 71, 75 NIV)

The truth is we hate to hear admonitions and corrections when we are straying from the Lord.

Even when we are sitting on the deck of a sinking *Titanic*, we want to comfortably sit and sip a cold drink and be assured that it is all a dream, a huge hoax, and that all will soon be well. The Scripture clearly teaches, however, that effective shepherding of God's flock involves encouragement as well as admonition and even correction and rebuke. That is not easy to do!

The words of Paul to Timothy are quite succinct. "Preach the word; be prepared in season and out of season; correct, rebuke and encourage—with great patience and careful instruction" (2 Timothy 4:2 NIV).

We should not forget the words in Hebrews 12 about the value of divine correction.

> For the LORD disciplines those He loves, and He punishes each one He accepts as His child. As you endure this divine discipline remember that God is treating you as His own children. Who ever heard of a child who is never disciplined by its father? ... No discipline is enjoyable while it is happening—it's painful. But afterward, there will be a peaceful harvest of right living for those who are trained this way. So take a new grip with your tired hands and strengthen your weak knees. Mark out a straight path for your feet so that those who are weak and lame will not fall but become strong. (Hebrews 12:6–12 NLT)

I was convinced about the necessity to submit ourselves to a divine purge in our hearts and lives and even numerically in the church, if God so chose. It was evident that God was going to purge us. I said one Sunday that even if there were only ten people left as a result of a divine purge, I would not be worried because God can always rebuild His church. I also remember one particular leadership meeting when I said, "There are some here who will not be with us by the end of the year!" Again, I saw the discomfort on numerous faces, but I was convinced that the purge was afoot. Not surprisingly, we had numerous people who came to me and said, "The Lord has asked me to leave the church." I would always bless them and release them. One particular situation I will not forget is an individual who came to me and said, "The Lord has been asking me to leave the church for the past two years." I released her, wondering why she had been hanging around for two whole years if the Lord had asked her to leave!

I preached a series of messages on "the remnant" to prepare the church for what was ahead. It was such an important thing to do because it fortified the church against any form of discouragement. I assured the church that God is always able to build with a remnant. One very comforting passage I used was from Zechariah.

> "Two thirds of the people in the land will be cut off and die," says the LORD. "But one-third will be left in the land. I will bring that group through the fire and make them pure. I will refine them like silver and purify them like gold. They will call on my name, and I will answer them. I will say, 'these are my people,' and they will say, 'The LORD is our God.'" (Zechariah 13:8–9 NLT)

Slowly but surely, the purge was on. The landscape changed drastically. We appointed new board members for the church. All the former board members left, except one. The one left standing was a part of my inner prayer group. We lost about $100,000 in income during the purge. We had to be strong, trust the Lord, and pray our way through. Times were very challenging, but God remained unquestionably faithful. We never missed fulfilling any of our financial obligations as a church! I had decided prior to the purge not to take a raise. For several years I declined the raise the board granted me. It was a rather frustrating experience for the board to see me decline a raise year after year after they had spent hours discussing things. This went on for seven years! There were numerous Pastor Appreciation Day gifts that we declined to receive from the church, but God was exceedingly faithful and wonderfully supplied all our needs. We also appointed deacons and ministers for the first time right after the purge. Prior to that, we had never appointed any deacons or ministers. I just did not feel that the time was right! The spiritual atmosphere in the church was becoming cleaner, and the presence of God began to intensify in our midst. I kept telling the church that those who did not buckle up will become bystanders watching a whole new group of people coming in to work for God!

God surprised us by bringing in a whole new crop of seasoned, mature Christians hungry to work for the Lord. Some started off reworking the social media department and the church's web site. Some developed a new app for the church. Some started new things in the outreach ministry. Some were seasoned intercessors. Some began revitalizing the missions department. The Lord blessed us with a very gifted and anointed worship pastor who would not take a penny from the church. He and his wife had come to visit the church because they were in transition and had been visiting different churches for two months. The day they visited our church, I had decided to use the service for testimonies to highlight some of the wonderful things God had accomplished in the lives of His people at Renewal to kick off a Building Fund Pledge Drive. Some single mothers testified about the support they had received from the church in raising up their children. Others talked about how their lives had been changed and impacted since they joined the church. My goal in the service was to encourage the church to understand that our campus was not just going to offer us our own place of worship but would also give us the opportunity to touch and change lives. The various testimonies given were simply to buttress that fact.

> God surprised us by bringing in a whole new crop of seasoned, mature Christians hungry to work for the Lord.

The visiting worship leader came up as I was about to wrap up the testimony session and asked if he could say a word. He mentioned that they felt the presence of the Lord as soon as they entered the sanctuary and that the

Lord had confirmed to them during the service that Renewal was to be their new place of worship. He had a check in hand and mentioned that they had been waiting to give their tithe to the church the Lord would direct them to. They were giving that check to Renewal because it was going to be their new church home. Their presence has been a great blessing to the church. They both love the Lord sincerely, and as our new worship pastor, he has brought a new dimension to the worship ministry of the church. He is definitely an answer to many years of prayer! God continues to build His church.

A Pleasant Surprise

The building fund offering we received that day was an answer to a very audacious prayer. I belong to a network of churches in the Washington, Maryland, and Virginia area called the Potomac Ministry Network. We have an annual pastors' conference in May each year and an annual pastors' retreat in October. Almost without fail, I would return from those conferences, especially the one in May, with a distinct word from the Lord. During one particular conference, I heard no clear word from the Lord. However, on the last day of the conference, I responded to an altar call during a communion service. The altar call encouraged us to come and lay our burdens at the altar.

> Certain audacious prayers can be quite scary because we have no idea what the Lord might do, how long it might take, or even how messy the process might be before the prayer is fully answered.

I decided to lay two things at the feet of Jesus: the burden of raising enough money to build our campus and place of worship and the burden of healing for my body. I prayed fervently, thanked God, and left the altar. Sometime later, I wrote down an audacious request asking the Lord to bless us with $100,000 in a single offering toward our building fund. That was a very bold request considering the size of our congregation at the time, but the Lord answered, and we received $116,000 in that single offering. In fact, the total amount that came in for the building fund in two months was $250,000. That was nothing short of amazing! I had the audacity to believe God for $100,000, but He did immeasurably more than that!

The purge was definitely worth it. God cleansed the atmosphere in the church and began to touch the hearts of His people. I must confess that certain audacious prayers can be quite scary because we have no idea what the Lord might do, how long it might take, or even how messy the process might be before the prayer is fully answered. When you feel a prompting to undertake an audacious task for God though, exercise courage and back up the desire with audacious prayers, and God will certainly come through. The road may be long and hard. Some may desert you on the journey, but the One who put the vision in your heart will never leave or forsake you. He will strengthen and uphold you to the very end.

CHAPTER 10

AUDACIOUS PRAYER: "LORD, HEAL MY WIFE!"

ANOTHER AUDACIOUS PRAYER THE LORD graciously answered was for my wife, Angie, to be healed from a disease that had already taken the life of two of her sisters. One time she gave a talk on her journey to healing. This chapter will tell her story from an excerpt of the talk she gave, and I will pick up my narrative in the following chapter.

Angie's Story

First of all, we all need to be on the same page—that sicknesses and diseases do not come from God. If sickness comes from God, then Jesus would be acting against the will of God in healing the sick. Second, in Acts 10:38, we read that Jesus is a healer. Third, the Word of God is the basis for every healing. The key to divine healing for today is in the Word of God, and the healing power in the name of Jesus. Because Jesus Christ is the same yesterday, today, and forever, we should believe to be healed by the power of His name just as when He walked on earth.

I had a disabling autoimmune connective tissue disorder that is typically chronic and progressive. It was called a mixed connective tissue disease. In addition, I was diagnosed with scleroderma, which causes thickening or hardening of the skin, the blood vessels, and various internal organs. I also had digestive problems due to esophageal reflux. In addition, I had rheumatoid arthritis and Raynaud's phenomenon. The symptoms of all these include joint stiffness and swelling, general body pain, fatigue, and fever.

Due to all the complicated health issues, I was put on a regimen of drugs that included forty milligrams of prednisone (side effects: hypertension, elevated blood sugar, osteoporosis, osteonecrosis, myopathy, cataracts, weight gain, acne, and hair loss; Feldene (a drug that is not prescribed anymore for arthritis because of serious side effects); colchicine; calcium; vitamin D; potassium chloride; and Plaquenil (side effects: anemia, heart problems, weight loss, and muscle paralysis). For years, I was on different medications. The sad thing was that I wasn't getting any better. Even with all those medications, I was frequently having to see a doctor with one thing or the other. The only solution they had was to add to or adjust my many medications. I was taking all of those medications with their numerous side effects. How was I going to get well?

I Believe in Divine Healing

So much has been said about divine healing. There are those who say it's not for today—that you really shouldn't expect the Lord to heal you—but I differ in my belief!

Sixty times in the Old Testament alone, God introduces Himself as healer. In His earthly ministry, Jesus went about healing all kinds of sicknesses and diseases. If the Word of God is true, and if we believe Hebrews 13:8 (NIV) "Jesus Christ is the same yesterday, today, and forever," then He is still a healer, and His healing is for today. The very fact that I am standing here before you is proof that God still heals.

The Bible clearly teaches us that sicknesses do not come from God. Sicknesses are from Satan, and Christ came to destroy Satan's work and give us life. John 10:10 (NIV) says, "The thief comes only to steal and to kill and to destroy [our health]: I have come that they may have life, and have it to the full." Being sickly is not living life to the full. If God wants us sick, why would He say He's our healer? Why did Jesus go about healing all kinds of sickness?

Much prayer has gone forth for my healing. Friends and family knew I was not well so they fasted and prayed. My husband, a man who prays a lot, would on many occasions just kneel beside me and pray. I often wondered why I wasn't healed. I was just sick and tired of being ill. I was sick and tired of medications that were not really helping me. My esophagus was also really beginning to bother me, and it was difficult to swallow. I kept explaining to the doctor how I felt, but he seemed helpless. I kept throwing up anything I tried to eat. Watching me eat was awful. I had to struggle to get anything down, and whatever I managed to get down would often end up coming out.

A Decision to Trust God

At the beginning of 2005, the church began our second twenty-one-day fast. In the previous years, whenever there was fasting, I would take my medications at the end of the day. This time though, I decided I would not take any more medications (not for everyone to do). On January 2 when the fast started, I weighed 110 pounds. As the days went on without medication, things got really bad. You know medications are OK—great for pain—and that was what I quickly discovered. I had made up my mind though that I was so sick of being sick and needed God to heal me. I had made my decision, and nothing was going to stop me from getting healed. In my own spirit, I knew I was ready for healing.

Things got so bad that I could barely move. I couldn't eat or drink. I just got weaker and weaker. Taking care of our household was a real challenge. Friends had to cook for us. One sister did our laundry and came by the house almost every day to clean.

> I had made my decision, and nothing was going to stop me from getting healed. In my own spirit, I knew I was ready for healing.

I just couldn't do anything. Every movement in my body hurt, but I had made up my mind and told the Lord that He had to heal me. Sometimes my husband had to carry me downstairs. I couldn't turn in bed. I needed help to sit and stand. My husband had to wash and clothe me. I couldn't drive because I couldn't turn my neck.

We continued to pray. I had made the decision to stand on God's Word concerning healing, and I was not backing down. Around that time also, my husband printed out about ten scriptures on healing, and every morning we would pray those scriptures. We each had our own copies, including the children, and we would read them and pray them out. But things just got worse. The one thing the children heard all the time was that Mummy was hurting.

My wonderful praying husband begged me to take my medications, so that at least we would have a life. I said, "How will I know I have been healed if I take my medications?" Somehow deep down in my spirit I knew God was about to do something. Two ladies began praying with me every Wednesday. We would read and pray through scriptures on healing.

Around February 2005, I decided to try alternative medicine. I went to see a doctor at a place for integrated health. That didn't go too well. In fact, he told me on one visit that I had to gain some weight because my weight loss was critical; otherwise, he couldn't help me. The nutritionist suggested soups and protein shakes and some health foods. I changed my diet and started cutting out sugar and eating a lot more wholesome foods, but nothing seemed to be working. I stopped seeing the doctor, but I kept up the diet changes.

Here Comes My Healing

About that time, I weighed ninety-four pounds. For someone who used to be a size 10, I had to shop for size 2 pants! The church saw us go through all of this and continued to pray. They even declared some days of fasting just for my healing. The interesting thing was that I never missed a service. Sometimes, my husband had to carry me into the service or help me walk, but I was always there. Somehow, I had this faith that something had to happen and that God had to come through. I was going to stand on God's Word no matter what. I believed that if I stayed off all those medications, which were not helping anyway and had terrible side effects, and stood on God's Word by faith, I would be healed. I believe there are two ways God allows divine healing: it could be instant or in some cases over a period of time. Sometimes it's a battle.

We had to stand on God's Word without wavering. And so, we simply continued to confess the scriptures. The more we read and spoke out the scriptures, the more my faith increased concerning divine healing. The Bible says that faith comes by hearing the Word of God (Romans 10:17 NIV).

The Bible also says in Proverbs 4:20-22 (NIV), "My son, pay attention to what I say; turn your ear to my words. Do not let them out of your sight, keep them within your heart; for they are life to those who find them and health to one's whole body." We are also told in Isaiah 53:5 (NIV) that Jesus was "pierced for our transgressions, he was crushed for our iniquities; the punishment that brought us peace was upon Him and by his wounds we are healed." Psalm 103:3 (NIV) also declares that God "forgives all your sins and heals all your diseases." If I can believe Him to forgive my sins because He says so, then I can believe Him to heal all my diseases, because He says so too!
"By your stripes I'm healed!"

Around the third week in July 2005, I was simply standing in the shower with the water just running down my body and crying out to God because I was in so much pain—that is what I did when my husband wasn't around to wash me—and suddenly I found myself saying, "By your stripes I'm healed" over and over again. I knew that those words just came alive for me that day. I had been confessing words on healing for months, but that day, I knew I was healed, and I accepted my healing. The pain was still there when I got out of the shower, but deep within me, I felt that the Word had become life to me. From that day, I confessed the word with more excitement and enthusiasm.

One morning in August, just a few weeks afterward, I woke up and suddenly realized that the pain was not as bad. I was so excited I simply lay in bed. For about thirty minutes, all I could say was "Thank You, Lord!" over and over again. Healing had come.

> I believe with all my heart that there are three keys to divine healing: God's Word, God's Word, and God's Word!

After that, the whole issue with my inability to keep food down was also resolved. I was out one afternoon, and as I tried to drink some water, I started throwing up. Immediately I felt the need to call my doctor and ask for a referral for some sort of x-ray. I just knew that if they could look inside my gut at that exact time, they could find what the issue was. I was able to go straight in and get a barium swallow test done. It was discovered that I had a severe narrowing in my lower esophagus. I had an endoscopy to take care of that. After that, I started eating well again, and now I'm a well-nourished lady. I have no doubt that my decision to call the doctor at the time I did was part of God moving on my behalf to restore my health. It was part of the journey toward my healing. God is the source of all knowledge, including medical knowledge. God can show you what you need to know and what you should do about it. He can use any means He chooses to bring you healing.

I believe with all my heart that there are three keys to divine healing: God's Word, God's Word, and God's Word! Healing begins with the absolute acceptance of and obedience to the Word of God. The Word of God heals. Confessing it activates the healing power of God. Have faith in God and in His Word.

Begin to speak God's Word of healing every day, and faith will build up in your heart. Walk in love. Don't harbor any unforgiveness.

Surround yourself with people who say pleasant words. Proverbs 16:24 (KJV) says, "Pleasant words are a honeycomb, sweet to the soul and healing to the bones." Laugh a lot; a cheerful heart is good medicine. Words are important. Even our minds are controlled by the words we hear and speak. It's important that we speak God's Word aloud because it will change our thinking and cause faith to rise up within us for healing.

I was once at a business motivational seminar when one of the speakers made a comment that stuck with me. He suggested that we focus on the outcome we desire concerning our businesses and to speak out specifically what we want. That just made sense to me even in the area of healing. If we continually believe that by the stripes of Jesus we are healed, our whole mind and body will be aligned toward receiving our healing. God's Word is quick and powerful (Hebrews 4:12 KJV). God's Word does not return empty to Him, but it always accomplishes the purpose for which God sends it (Isaiah 55:11 NIV). When we speak various scriptures of healing over our sick bodies, they will activate our faith to expect and receive our healing.

My healing was not instant. I still struggle sometimes with some aches and pains, and I still will take Aleve or something for the pain, but ultimately, I believe I am healed. By the way, I weigh 120 pounds now, but I think I want to stay there. I eat well, and I feel good.

To God be the glory!

CHAPTER 11

A HUSBAND'S REFLECTIONS

ANGIE'S TESTIMONY IN CHAPTER 10 was part of a talk on healing she gave a few years ago. Now let me continue telling the story from the perspective of a husband and caretaker.

For thirty years, I endured the agony of watching my wife go through the pain and suffering of a disease—multiple diseases. When she was diagnosed two years into our marriage with lupus, the doctor made it clear that there was no cure for the disease. Lupus could attack any organ in the body and destroy it. She had lost two sisters to the same disease, so there was a vivid reminder of what the outcome could be. There was a real possibility that she could lose her life. In fact, her younger sister who passed away lived with us and attended the University of Maryland. She was only a few months from graduation when she passed away, so the university decided to award her a posthumous degree. I remember when things were very difficult and the possibility of her death began to loom larger and larger every day. I remember the pain on my wife's face as she asked me in bed one night, "Honey, what if Emelia dies?" The only answer I could give her was "Honey, let's continue to trust the Lord." When she passed away, I conducted the service and the burial. The title of the message I preached was "The Unanswered Questions of Life." So was my wife also going to die like her two sisters? Was God going to answer our prayers and spare her life? Was she going to defy the odds and live?

When my wife came home with the initial diagnosis from the doctor, I went before the Lord and offered this audacious prayer: "Lord, please let Angie see her children's children." We had no children at the time. I have maintained that prayer over the years. I have even said it publicly in sermons, that I am believing that my wife will see her children's children. Heaven will answer.

Over the years, I watched helplessly as my wife writhed with uncontrollable pain. Once when she got very ill, we went to the specialist's office, and he said these chilling words: "There is nothing else we can do for her." Those were traumatic words to hear. They weighed especially heavy on me because I was about to travel on a trip outside the country. I simply said to the doctor, "I know someone who can do something about the situation." That was over twenty years ago as of the time of this writing. I believed that Jesus would heal her, and Jesus has kept her for over thirty years now. Look what God has done! God does answer prayer.

> When my wife came home with the initial diagnosis from the doctor, I went before the Lord and offered this audacious prayer: "Lord, please let Angie see her children's children." We had no children at the time.

I remember when our children were just two years old and we were in the thick of planting Renewal Christian Center. I had the stress of caring for two toddlers, a wife who had gotten very sick, studying for my doctoral program, preaching and teaching, counseling, training ministry workers, and running the church! Things were so hectic that one of my friends advised me to drop the doctoral studies, but I did not. The Lord gave me the grace and strength to press on. My wife was often so sick that she even joked about the kind of woman she wanted me to marry if the Lord were to take her home. She thought she would die! She went through a lot of suffering.

I remember when she had to crawl up the stairs because she was too weak to walk up those stairs. I remember times when I had to carry her up the stairs. I remember when I would drive to the entrance of the church and carry her in my arms because she was too weak to walk on her own.

I remember when the disease began attacking her fingers, and one of them had to be partly amputated. I remember when she went from a 130-pound robust size 10 to a 90-pound size 2! I remember the day she cried out in faith for fifteen minutes in the shower, "By the stripes of Jesus I am healed! By the stripes of Jesus, I am healed! By the stripes of Jesus, I am healed! (Isaiah 53:5 NKJV)."

All through her pain and suffering, Angie never missed church or slowed down in her responsibilities as a mother, wife, and servant of God. She handled all the administrative issues of the church and had oversight of several ministries. She remained a strong and determined fighter! In fact, I am convinced that one of the reasons God has kept her alive is because she has been so faithful in committing her time, talents, and treasures to the work of God. She is a wonderful inspiration to many. She has been the wind beneath my sails. I love her dearly.

It is important to ask ourselves *why* we want the Lord to grant us another day, another week, another month, or another year of life.

It is important to ask ourselves *why* we want the Lord to grant us another day, another week, another month, or another year of life. I believe such introspection will help us remember that each day of our lives is a gift that must bear fruit to bring pleasure to the heart of God, touch other lives, and advance the agenda of God's kingdom. The words of Paul to the Philippian church speak eloquently to this:

For I fully expect and hope that I will never be ashamed, but that I will continue to be bold for Christ, as I have been in the past. And I trust that my life will bring honor to Christ, whether I live or die. For, to me, living means living for Christ, and dying is even better. But if I live, I can do more fruitful work for Christ. So I really don't know which is better. I'm torn between two desires: I long to go and be with Christ, which would be far better for me. But for your sakes, it is better that I continue to live. (Philippians 1:20–24 NLT)

Paul wanted to live long for purely altruistic reasons. He wanted to pour his years into the lives of others. He wanted others to benefit from the gifts and talents God had given him. He would have liked to depart the earth and be with Jesus in heaven because that would have ushered him into a life of bliss devoid of all the hunger, pain, beatings, and imprisonments he was experiencing on earth. Yet he chose to continue suffering on earth for the benefit of other people. He knew his life was making a difference and enriching God's kingdom.

So a good point of reflection is to ask ourselves periodically, "Why do we want God to continue blessing us with more years?" Is it just so we can live, acquire more stuff, and selfishly enjoy the pleasures of life on earth? Or is it to serve the bigger purpose of making a difference in the lives of others by serving God's kingdom purposes even as we enjoy all the blessings God has so graciously bestowed upon us? God has made a promise that if we seek first His kingdom and His righteousness, He will add all other things unto us (Matthew 6:33 KJV). Our priorities must be right if our lives are to be meaningful and fulfilling. We must not just desire long lives for the sake of just living. We must desire a long life in order to serve the purposes of God for our lives.

I am convinced that what we give to God by way of our time, talents, and treasures testifies for us in heaven when prayers are offered on our behalf. Cornelius received an angelic visitation with these words: "Your prayers and gifts to the poor have been received by God as an offering" (Acts 10:4 NIV). God saw the prayers and offerings of Cornelius as a testimony before Him in heaven and answered his desire to know God by sending Peter to lead him to Christ and true fellowship with the Living God. If we live purposely to accomplish God's design for our lives, He will add all other things unto us, including a long life.

Crisis: A Collapse at Church; Healing Continues

A little over two years ago, my wife collapsed in church and almost died. This chapter is the story of her having to undergo *three* open-heart surgeries!

Angie had not been feeling well all week, so I asked her to stay behind that morning while the children and I went to church. She agreed, but minutes before we left, she suddenly decided to come with us. She could not be dissuaded. It turned out to be a divine prompting. As usual, she stayed in the children's Sunday school area to help monitor activities. I was in church, worshipping, when one of the ushers tapped me on my shoulder and asked if I could step out of the sanctuary. I walked into the hallway to find my wife on the floor being feverishly prayed over by some of the ushers. She was flat on her back, and her eyes were rolling as if she was in the throes of death. She had lost consciousness. An ambulance had already been called before I got there. I continued to pray over her, asking God to revive her and spare her life. Within minutes, the ambulance came. They worked for about fifteen minutes to revive her. I stood right there by the ambulance and kept praying. Finally, she came around. She opened her eyes and asked, "What happened?' I said it was all well. The ambulance then whisked her off to the hospital. The question was "What if she had not insisted on coming with us to church and had collapsed at home with no one around?" Our God is truly awesome! His eyes are continually upon His children.

I was scheduled to preach and did not want to throw the church into speculation and confusion by going off with the ambulance, so I asked one of our deacons to accompany her to the hospital. I went back into the service and preached. My rationale for not going with the ambulance was that the Lord was watching over her, so I could get back into the service and watch over the flock of God. God was doing His part. I had to do my part! I was not disturbed at all. When we do what is humanly possible, God will do the humanly impossible. I was confident that God was going to pull her through. I am thankful for very diligent and trained leaders. When one of our ministers saw that I had been called out and was delayed in returning to the sanctuary, she stepped right in to minister when it was time to preach. I just took over and delivered the Word of God. At the end of the service, I explained what had happened and asked the church to continue praying for her.

> I was confident that God was going to pull her through.

I went over to the hospital with our children and spent several hours with Angie. The deacon took our children out to lunch so I could have time to focus on my wife. I learned from the doctors that they almost lost her and had to shock her back to life twice! Later, she was transferred to Johns Hopkins Hospital in Baltimore where her doctors are, and which is also one of the premier hospitals in the United States. The Lord had it all under control. The interesting thing is that because lupus can affect any organ including the heart, my wife's rheumatologist at Hopkins had opted her into a study being conducted at the hospital. So they already had data on her heart condition and were actually in the process of making some surgical recommendations. If my wife had not been part of that study at Hopkins, the dangerous condition of her heart would never have come to light. As it was, God had it all figured out well in advance!

Angie's cardiologist at Hopkins recommended a very specialized surgical procedure. He said he wasn't comfortable doing it at Hopkins but would highly recommend a world-renowned heart surgeon at the Mayo Clinic in Rochester, Minnesota. He knew the surgeon personally and would do everything he could to make it happen. The surgeon at Mayo Clinic was a very busy doctor, so we had to pray for divine favor. Fortunately, he agreed to do the procedure on December 22,

2016. The condition of my wife's heart was diagnosed as hypertrophic cardiomyopathy. This involved a thickening of the heart muscles to the point where the flow of blood into the heart was highly constricted and therefore could cause heart failure.

The procedure involved an open-heart surgery to cut out some of the muscles from the walls of the heart to enlarge the opening within and thereby ensure a more efficient blood flow. There was also a need to cut off a portion at the bottom of her heart and repair it. As one can imagine, this was a very delicate and risky procedure and had to involve a highly skilled surgeon.

We went to Minnesota for ten days to get the procedure done. We met with the surgeon who was reputed to be the leading heart surgeon at the Mayo Clinic and one of the best in the world. He had been practicing for thirty years. He went through Angie's medical history and remarked bluntly that Angie had real serious issues. I joked that we were also told that he was the best heart surgeon in the country. He humbly deflected the compliment and simply said, "You are in the best hospital in the country."

He was very humble, gracious, and professional. He explained the procedure in detail and mentioned that there was a 1 to 2 percent chance of death associated with the procedure, but that was most unlikely. The procedure was called a "transapical myectomy." This involved cutting away thickened muscles from the heart to relieve the pressure buildup. He likened the condition of her heart to stepping on a garden hose and preventing the water from flowing through it. Cutting away the thickened muscles in the heart would reduce constriction and create more space for blood to flow freely to the heart. Additionally, he was going to cut away a pocket that had developed at the bottom of Angie's heart. Those conditions had created excessive

I had been fasting since the morning. I was in prayer when I heard the Holy Spirit saying to me, "It is OK. Go and get something to eat. She is fine."

pressure on the heart, causing it to overwork. All that had resulted in the various cardiac arrests.

Thus, the surgeons went to work on Angie. After the procedure, she was brought up to recovery, and I was allowed into her room with numerous doctors and nurses attending to her. They seemed quite pleased. Suddenly though, everything changed! My wife started bleeding, and her pressure started dropping. Nothing seemed to be working right. The doctors asked me to step out so they could attend to her. I was pacing the hallway in prayer when one of the nurses came to talk to me. She said that my wife needed to go back into surgery for the doctors to rectify the problem. Fortunately, the doctor who performed the procedure was still on the premises, so any delay was minimized.

They reopened her heart, corrected the source of the bleeding, and stitched her back up. When the nurse initially told me about the need to open her up again, I asked her where the prayer room was and went there to pray. I had been fasting since the morning. I was in prayer when I felt the Holy Spirit alerting me, "It is OK. Go and get something to eat. She is fine." So I got up and went to the cafeteria. I was there having some soup when my phone rang. It was the surgeon. He said everything had been corrected, and my wife was OK. God had intervened again.

I went upstairs to be with Angie. Prayer had played a major role in all this. Our wonderful intercessors, deacons, and ministers were all in fervent prayer—as was the church as a whole! There in Minneapolis, we spent Christmas away from our children for the first time in their lives. A very wonderful family friend took care of them during our absence. We came back just in time for me to prepare for the New Year's Eve service. Fresh from surgery, my wife insisted on coming to the service, and she did. She is one tough nut to crack. God does answer prayer, but the battle was not over!

A few months later, Angie's doctor noticed that the patch beneath her heart was bleeding and needed to be repaired and restitched. This meant another open-heart surgery, the third in five months. The doctor assured her that it could be done at Johns Hopkins and there was no need to travel to Minnesota. So right after the Mother's Day service in

2017, we checked back into the hospital for the procedure. The Lord was very gracious, and it was successful.

My wife is a very active person. Staying home for weeks to recover from open-heart surgery—*thrice*—without being able to move around was like a prison sentence to her and mentally excruciating. Angie shared her depressive thoughts and feelings with the church later. The next chapter concludes the story in her own words.

CHAPTER 12

REFLECTIONS FROM A HEALED WOMAN: ANGIE'S CONTINUED STORY

MY SPIRITUAL JOURNEY LITERALLY STARTED at birth. I was born to Christian parents who were actively involved in their church's young adult activities. Belonging to an active church family, church services, and other spiritual activities were just the norm for me.

My elementary, middle, and high school education was all in boarding schools where church services were mandated. By the time I was in college, my love for God and His kingdom work was a major part of who I was. There were a couple of songs I loved to sing in my college days. One of them was written by Robert Cull.

> Open my eyes, Lord, I want to see Jesus, to reach out and touch Him and say that I love Him. Open my ears, Lord, and help me to listen. Open my eyes, Lord, I want to see Jesus.

My desire to be used by God has always been a guiding passion in my life. Yet when God called us into full-time ministry, saying yes was not easy. After college, I was active in church and held leadership positions in children, youth, and women's ministries.

When I first met my husband, ABK as he's fondly known, after a New Year's Eve service almost thirty-nine years ago, I could never have believed we would be where we are in ministry.

We both thought the other person was interesting during that meeting. To me, he was this quiet gentleman who was not saying much as my sister, I, and a mutual friend stayed after the service to catch up on our Sunday school days.

In writing this reflection chapter, I reached out to a friend from high school to ask whether she thought I would be the girl who would end up married to a pastor and become a pastor myself. This was her response:

> I would not have thought of you as pastor's wife or pastor material in a million years. You know, Angie, you were so outspoken and rather self-confident. I think there is a real miracle here. Never in a million years would I have said you would be a pastor.

Our relationship grew out of respect for each other because, though ABK was not a follower of Christ Jesus, he agreed to go with me to a church service. The Lord saved him a few months later, and he never looked back. I admired his quiet and gentle spirit. He didn't talk much, though I was constantly loud and outspoken. My parents' slight hesitation to our marriage was if he could "handle" me.

I watched as God reached and transformed him and how his love for godliness increased. By the time he asked me to be his wife after five years of being good friends, I just knew he was God's pick for me. I recall him telling our pastor, on our wedding day, that we were committed to God's kingdom work. His prayer back then and now is that we would build a household of faith. God has answered that prayer. I thought I knew the direction I wanted our marriage to go. I have had to face what God wanted for us, and that was way off my plans.

My dream was to start our family of maybe three children, two years into our marriage. Seventeen years passed before God blessed us with our twins by adoption. Those were difficult times not only emotionally but physically. I was diagnosed with lupus and battled through years of infertility. We were separated for three years while my husband went to further his studies in Missouri for training into full-time ministry.

I wondered whether our marriage would survive. I remember in the summer of 1993 when he broke the news to me. My shock and displeasure with the whole idea were clearly expressed to him. He was surprised about my reaction because we were both actively serving in our local church. I remember his response to me. "Angie, I know God has called, and unless we respond, we will be a very miserable couple." That statement from him changed my attitude.

It has taken courage, perseverance, faith, and totally trusting in God's Holy Word and His love against all odds. As I reflect on these things, I come to the conclusion that when God allows you by His grace to break through many of life's challenges and painful experiences, you emerge stronger, and you only trust Him more. The years my husband was away in seminary were the best years of spiritual growth that prepared me for the years to follow. I spent more time in prayer and the Word than ever before.

I felt unqualified for the task though I can now see that God was only waiting for me to say yes. He wanted me to follow Him into the darkness, to show His power in my own life and the lives to be changed around me. Over and over again, He has healed my body. I have learned that God can do all things (Matthew 19:26 NIV). I have learned to trust Him. God has shamed me on numerous occasions when I thought a situation was impossible. Truly with God *all* things are possible. I agree with the words of the writer of this song:

> We've come this far by faith
> Leaning on the LORD
> Trusting in His Holy Word
> He never failed me yet …
> Don't be discouraged
> when trouble comes into your life
> He will bear your burdens
> And remove all our misery and strife. (Albert Goodson)

The lyrics to the above hymn best describe my Christian journey. There have been many challenges and experiences. God has borne my every burden and turned every night into a bright day. God is faithful.

My father, who stayed with us the first couple of days after we got married, had my husband and me promise to pray together every day, a practice I was raised in and still do today thirty-four years later. As a family, prayer is as the air we breathe, both in the good and the bad times. I remember the early years of dealing with lupus and all the related health issues and the many hours my husband spent praying. I am grateful for a praying husband—a man who prayed night and day, the many times when we were not sure whether I would make it. I feel grateful that I am surrounded by a church family that fasted and prayed, brothers and sisters who called their own times of prayer for my healing.

When I think about my blessings, I think about those who made sure there was always food in our home, those who took time to travel from out of state and overseas to come and stay with us to help out. There were those who stayed with the twins when we had to travel— including those who took time to transport them to and from school, keeping them occupied during long hospital stays after open-heart surgeries. And there were many others willing to give of their time and resources.

God is faithful.
His goodness and grace followed me
through years of sickness, cardiac arrests,
and three open-heart surgeries.

I can only conclude that God is faithful. His goodness and grace followed me through years of sickness, cardiac arrests, and three open-heart surgeries. I remember how He stood by me and held my hand in His and told me He was holding me safe. I remember when I was in deep depression and how He reached deep down and literally pulled me out of that dark pit.

Truly I have come this far by faith, leaning on the Lord, trusting in His Holy Word. He never failed me yet. God never fails! He is a prayer-answering God.

CHAPTER 13

CAN GOD TRUST YOU WITH SUFFERING?

AS I SAT IN THE cafeteria of the Mayo Clinic having the soup to break the fast, my spirit was suddenly gripped with a question. "Can God trust you with suffering?"

As I reflected over it, I soon realized it wasn't just a thought. It was the Holy Spirit communicating to me the reality of seeking to walk with God in spirit and in truth and the attendant challenges to be expected. So can God trust you with suffering?

We may not always know what God is up to, but we know He is always up to something beautiful in our lives. The assurance from Scripture is this: "'For I know the plans I have for you,' declares the Lord, 'They are plans for good and not for disaster, to give you a future and a hope'" (Jeremiah 29:11 NLT). The truth, however, is that the journey to that good, divine future can take us on paths that might seem disastrous to us. Those "treacherous paths" may sometimes cause us to question whether the Lord really has good plans for us, but if we hang in long enough with God, we will surely come to that desired future. God uses trials and different kinds of suffering to prepare our lives for what He desires to accomplish through us. Suffering when we know we are walking with God to the best of our abilities is never a wasted thing. It is part of the curriculum in God's school of divinity.

I was convinced that the Holy Spirit was asking me to reflect over my current experiences in terms of my walk with God.

All through Scripture, we see how some of God's choicest servants were tested with suffering. Job is probably the most prominent example of suffering in the Bible. Satan told God that Job was only serving Him because he had been so blessed and protected by God. Satan was confident that if Job encountered any suffering, he would curse God to His face. So God trusted Job and allowed Satan to attack him. In just one day, Job lost everything he had—his livestock, his houses, his servants, and all his children. As if that was not enough, Satan attacked Job with terrible boils from head to toe. Things were so bad that Job's wife said to him, "Are you still maintaining your integrity? Curse God and die" (Job 2:9 NIV).

> God always wins, so be patient and trusting as you journey with Him into your divinely appointed destiny. Press on and battle through your trials. God will see you through the journey. Hold on to the Word of God and never give up, no matter what. Purpose in your heart that you will persevere through your situation because God is faithful, and He will not disappoint you.

Job suffered, but his faith was remarkable. He said in Job 23:10 (NIV), "But He knows the way I take. When He has tested me, I will come forth as gold." God trusted Job with suffering, and then God elevated him to the status of gold! You see, the end result of God trusting you with suffering is that you will come forth as pure gold—gold that has been purified in the fire and cleansed of all impurities! That's when you become ready for God to showcase you! So can God trust you with suffering?

How about Joseph? The Bible tells the story of how he was so hated by his brothers because of his dreams that they sold him to foreigners who took him to Egypt and sold him into slavery. Imagine the feeling of shock as he was initially thrown by his brothers into the pit to die before they actually decided it was more profitable to sell him off.

Imagine the harshness of the moment when the traders counted the money into the hands of Joseph's brothers as the price for him! Imagine the psychological pain Joseph endured as a seventeen-year-old boy on the journey to Egypt, yanked away from the love of his father!

Imagine the pain of being falsely accused of attempted rape by his master's wife! Imagine Joseph's shock when the master's wife presented Joseph's coat as evidence against him when in fact Joseph had actually run off and left his coat behind to escape from Mrs. Potiphar, who was trying to force Joseph into bed with her! Imagine the traumatic feeling of languishing in jail for years because of that false accusation! Imagine the moment when Joseph broke down in that jail cell and said, "I have not done anything to deserve being in this dungeon" (Genesis 40:15 NIV). But God finally took him out of prison and made him the prime minister of Egypt, the very land in which he had first entered as a slave. He entered as a slave, but he exited at the time of his death at the very top of the social ladder. You see, in the end, God always wins, so be patient and trusting as you journey with Him into your divinely appointed destiny. Press on and battle through your trials. God will see you through the journey. Hold on to the Word of God and never give up, no matter what. Purpose in your heart that you will persevere through your situation because God is faithful, and He will not disappoint you.

The words of the prophet Isaiah are comforting.

> Sing for joy, O heavens! Rejoice, O earth! Burst into song, O mountains! For the LORD has comforted His people and will have compassion on them in their suffering. Yet Jerusalem says, "The LORD has deserted us; the LORD has forgotten us." "Never! Can a mother forget her nursing child? Can she feel no love for the child she has borne? But even if that were possible, I would not forget you! See, I have written your names on the palms of my hands ... Those who trust in me will never be put to shame." (Isaiah 49:13–16; 23 NIV)

Our challenges are designed by God to bring us to a fruitful end like Job experienced. I believe there are two important things God has to be able to trust us with in order to fully elevate us to where He wants to place us and what He wants to use us for.

The first is praise. How we handle ourselves when we are being praised for our accomplishments is a strong determinant of how high God will elevate us. The Bible makes an interesting statement in this regard. "Fire tests the purity of silver and gold, but a person is tested by being praised" (Proverbs 27:21 NLT). Praise is an important test of the purity of a person's heart and motives. If we are able to remain humble and focused in the midst of being praised for our accomplishments, giftedness, and talents, God can trust us with more.

If, however, we become proud and puffed up by a little praise, God will not elevate us to higher heights. Many have missed great elevations of blessings because they became proud and could not handle the test of praise. They couldn't manage the blessings of praise that come with accomplishments!

I am also convinced that if God can trust us with the test of suffering, then He can trust us with great elevations of blessings because suffering reveals the strength of our character and our ability to stand under pressure when confronted with adversity. The truth is that life has more valley experiences than mountaintop experiences. Character is built more in the valley experiences of life than in the exhilarations of our mountaintop experiences. Life has more suffering than bliss. Suffering ensures that we can handle things for the long haul and not buckle under pressure. If God can trust you with suffering, He will also trust you with uncommon blessings to bring forth His agenda.

> If God can trust us with the test of suffering, then He can trust us with great elevations of blessings because suffering reveals the strength of our character and our ability to stand under pressure when confronted with adversity.

I like to equate suffering with what a seed goes through in the natural realm before germinating to become a fruitful tree or plant. Jesus reminds us that "unless a kernel of wheat is planted in the soil and dies, it remains alone. But its death will produce many new kernels—a plentiful harvest of new lives" (John 12:24 NLT).

I believe this applies to the spirit realm as well. Unless we die to all our private desires, aspirations, and worldly cravings and place ourselves as true and living sacrifices before God, it will be difficult for God to use us. Just as in the natural realm a seed must first die before it produces fruit, so it is in the spirit realm. In the spirit realm, life is always preceded by death! The spiritual seed must first rot and die before it becomes fruitful.

The testimonies of some of God's choicest servants bear this out. The apostle Paul exemplifies this. Jesus said something remarkable about Paul's calling. "This man is my chosen instrument to proclaim my name to the Gentiles and their kings and to the people of Israel. I will show him how much he must suffer for my name" (Acts 9:15–16 NIV). Paul was greatly used by God, but he also suffered greatly. He attests to this in the letter he wrote to the church at Corinth.

> Five different times the Jewish leaders gave me thirty-nine lashes. Three times I was beaten with rods. Once I was stoned. Three times I was shipwrecked. Once I spent a whole night and a day adrift at sea. I have traveled on many long journeys. I have faced danger from rivers and robbers. I have faced danger from my own people, the Jews, as well as the Gentiles. I have faced danger in the cities, in the deserts, and on the seas. And I have faced danger from men who claimed to be believers but are not.

> I have worked hard and long, enduring many sleepless nights. I have been hungry and thirsty and have often gone without food. I have shivered in the cold without enough clothing to keep me warm. Then, besides all

this, I have the daily burden of my concern for all the churches ...

When I was in Damascus, the governor under King Aretas kept guards at the city gates to catch me. I had to be lowered in a basket through a window in the city wall to escape from him. (2 Corinthians 11:24–28 NLT)

God used Paul to establish churches and spread the gospel, but Paul also suffered greatly. As if the beatings, imprisonments, stoning, hunger, and shipwrecks were not enough, God also gave Paul a thorn in his flesh to keep him humble because of all the wonderful spiritual knowledge and revelations he was receiving. Paul protested. He asked God to relieve him from that burden, but Jesus simply said, "My grace is sufficient for you. My power works best in weakness" (2 Corinthians 12:9 NLT).

Paul came to understand that suffering for the cause of Christ attracts the grace and power of God. Many of us are praying for God to use us, and God desires to do so. But can God trust you with suffering?

If God is going to use you to touch suffering humanity, then He has to prepare you through suffering. You must be able to identify with the suffering of others. People will listen to you if they know you have been through what they are going through.

I am convinced that we cannot experience true elevation from God without passing the test of suffering. Why? Because we live in a world that is full of suffering. So if God is going to use you to touch suffering humanity, then He has to prepare you through suffering. You must be able to identify with the suffering of others. People will listen to you if they know you have been through what they are going through.

Suffering is God's way of pruning you so you can be more fruitful and useful. In fact, the Bible says in 1 Peter 1:22 (NIV), "To this you were called; because Christ suffered for you, leaving you an example, that you should follow in His steps."

Hebrews 5:8–9 (NLT) tells us,

> Even though Jesus was God's Son, He learned obedience from the things He suffered. In this way, God qualified Him as a High Priest, and He became the source of eternal salvation for all those who obey Him.

It is rather interesting to note that the suffering of Jesus helped Him to learn obedience and it helped Him to qualify as the One who could advocate for us before our heavenly Father.

The writer of Hebrews drives it home even further with these words: "For we do not have a high priest who is unable to empathize with our weakness; but we have one who has been tempted in every way—yet He did not sin" (Hebrews 4:15 NIV). Jesus is able to empathize with us because He has already experienced what we are going through!

Suffering has a valuable impact on our ability to help others with their own challenges.

Do you really want God to use you? If your answer is yes, then can God trust you with suffering?

Ponder this poem from an anonymous writer:

When God Wants to Drill a Man

When God wants to mold a man to play the noblest part ...

How He ruthlessly perfects
Whom He royally elects!
How He hammers him and hurts him,
And with mighty blows convert him ...
Only God understands ...

How He bends but never breaks ...
God knows what He is doing.

Absolutely! God knows what He is doing! Let Him finish perfecting you for the purpose He has in mind for your life. He allows suffering for a reason!

CHAPTER 14

THE MARKS ON MY BODY

Audacious Prayer: Oh Lord, Please Heal Me

NOT ONLY CAN I TESTIFY about my wife and God's gracious healing touch upon her body, but I can also testify about my own healing. Jesus heals! Every time I preach or give a talk, I make it a point to declare to my listeners that Jesus heals and Jesus saves. I do that to fulfill a promise I made to the Lord several years ago when He graciously healed me.

The scripture I find most appropriate because of what God has allowed me to so humbly experience is Galatians 6:14 and 17 (NKJV).

> But God forbid that I should boast except in the cross of our LORD Jesus Christ, by whom the world has been crucified to me, and I to the world … From now on, let no one trouble me, for I bear in my body the marks of the LORD Jesus.

I was fortunate to have journaled my experiences as they occurred over the course of my sickness, so I will be sharing quite a bit from my journal.

In March 2010, I went to Ghana, West Africa, to bury my dear mother. Soon after my return to the United States, I started feeling a strange back pain. I mentioned it to my wife and attributed it to the rather hard mattress I slept on in Ghana! The pain wasn't very severe, so I decided to monitor it. I traveled to Haiti on a missions trip in June and saw my doctor shortly after that because the pain was increasing. The doctor did a urine test for kidney stones and wrote a prescription for some muscle relaxers. Since the result of the urinalysis was negative, she concluded that the pain might be due to a strained muscle. She said, "This is possible especially since you drive an SUV. I have seen patients experience muscle pulls from trying to enter their SUVs."

After a week of taking muscle relaxers and using a heating pad, I reported to her that the pain wasn't getting any better. She seemed rather irritated by my insistence that her approach was not resolving the issue. She referred me to an orthopedic doctor.

An interesting thing is that a physician friend of mine had been expressing dissatisfaction with the slow pace at which my primary physician was managing my case. He was of the opinion that a more aggressive approach involving x-rays and MRIs should have been used already. At his urging, I went to an urgent care clinic since I was in severe pain. I was examined and x-rayed, and the physician mentioned that she saw nothing abnormal.

My appointment with the orthopedic surgeon took place the following week. She looked at the x-rays, did a physical examination, and decided to put me on some painkillers and stronger muscle relaxers. She also scheduled me for physical therapy as well as some back-stretching exercises. I wasn't really convinced that the therapy was going to be helpful.

Since I was traveling out of the country the following week, I decided to hold off on the therapy until I returned. I left for Germany, ministered for a whole week, and returned to the United States. I was in pain, but it was bearable.

More Medical Examinations

In September, I went for a follow-up visit with the orthopedic doctor. I explained that the pain had definitely gotten worse. She scheduled an MRI, which I insisted on doing the same day. After the MRI, I asked the technician who had a rather uncomfortable look on his face, "Does everything look OK?" He responded, "The quality of the film looks fine, but I am not a doctor, so I cannot really interpret the film for you." He sent the films off to the orthopedic surgeon. I thanked him and took the original films with me.

The next day, the phone rang as soon as I stepped into my office. My primary physician was on the line, and she explained that the MRI revealed a tumor in my spine that needed to be attended to immediately. She explained that it looked cancerous and that she had made an appointment for me to see a spine specialist. She said I needed to call the doctor urgently.

Since I had someone waiting to see me at my office, I went ahead to see that person and then scheduled the visit with the spine specialist. I was shocked but not alarmed. I felt a certain peace in my spirit. My wife was working upstairs in the church office. I mentioned to her that my primary physician had called and wanted me to see a specialist the next day. I didn't want to alarm or bother her with any further details. I didn't even talk about the possibility of cancer. We drove home together and had a regular family evening and dinner with our children.

The next morning, after our quiet time, I mentioned to her that my primary physician had said that the tumor appeared to be cancerous. Not surprisingly, always the rock she is, she took the news very well and remarked that we needed to fight hard. Interestingly, prior to all this, I asked a few of the prayer warriors to join me in a time of fasting and prayer. So all this rapid cancer development came right in the middle of our time of fasting and prayer. In fact, some of our other intercessors were aware that I had been experiencing some back pains, and they had already taken it upon themselves to fast and pray.

The spine specialist was very gracious. He showed me the tumor on the computer and explained that we were dealing with something potentially very serious.

He immediately ordered some blood work, urine work, and a CT scan to ensure that nothing else was happening in any other part of my body. I did all those things over the next two days. He also went ahead and scheduled an appointment with an oncologist, Dr. Meisenberg, to ensure that all bases were covered. I came home and reported everything to Angie. She was very calm and said, "Honey, we will fight this."

She said what came into her spirit were the words of Jesus in John 9:3 (NIV). "Neither this man nor his parents sinned, but that the work of God might be displayed in his life." What a word! It doesn't get any better than that. God was about to display His work in my life. Angie and I both knew that we were in a serious "warfare situation," especially with the capital campaign work going on to raise funds to build our church campus.

> I knew my faith was being tested and I had to be strong for the church, for my wife and children, and for myself.

I knew my faith was being tested and I had to be strong for the church, for my wife and children, and for myself. I went through all my daily responsibilities with the news of the possibility of cancer hanging over my head. The following Monday, the spine specialist called while Angie and I were driving home from the office. He gave us the results of the blood and urine work he had ordered. He said the blood work was OK, the urinalysis was fine, and there were no abnormalities in either the urine or blood. The tumor did not appear to be cancerous. He said the growth could be treated with medication without surgery. However, he mentioned that the lab had recommended one more urine test.

Later that week, I had my appointment with the oncologist. He also examined the result of both the blood and urine work and concluded they were normal. However, he was insistent that he suspected either multiple myeloma or plasmacytoma, which were both types of cancer. He mentioned that he needed one more type of urine analysis to help him draw a conclusion. Along with that, he ordered a full-body skeletal x-ray and some more blood work for further analysis. That full-body skeletal x-ray proved to be a lifesaver! The skeletal survey was to help him uncover any systemic evidence of multiple myeloma. These were all very expensive tests. He also wanted to do a bone marrow biopsy to detect any chromosomal abnormalities. Finally, he also ordered a needle biopsy of the spine to test the tumor itself.

All through this sudden barrage of hectic testing and difficult news, my spirit remained undaunted. Angie and I were both confident God would show His hand. That Sunday, we had a guest minister, and there was a wonderful presence of the Lord. Close to the end of the service, the guest speaker turned privately to me and said,

> Man of God, I see blood, and I see something like hemorrhoids, but Jesus is saying He is your healer. Don't worry. You will live to fulfill your destiny. God is about to take the church to a new level. All the opposing forces have now been destroyed.

I believe in the operation of the gifts of the Holy Spirit. I believe that God speaks and reveals things to His children. The guest minister had absolutely no idea I was going through some health challenges, but God revealed it to him. I believe that what he saw as hemorrhoids was actually the tumor in my body.

I went to see the spine specialist the following Monday after he made an unexpected appointment for me. He said he had bad news after the last urine test. The test had revealed myeloma of the bones. He had discussed my case with a team of doctors, and they all concluded that I needed to undergo surgery as soon as possible. He also added that I needed a new CT scan of the neck because the full-body x-ray I had done the previous week revealed that a portion of my neck bone was under attack—C6 to be precise. I wasn't surprised because I remember the x-ray technician pausing for a rather long time after he had x-rayed my neck.

I took all this in quietly and continued to believe that God would glorify Himself. I skipped our intercessory prayer service that evening to have a quiet time of prayer at home.

One of our deacons called on my way home to encourage me with Psalm 138:8 (NIV). "The Lord will fulfill His purpose for me. For your love, O Lord, endures forever. Do not abandon the works of your hands."

As I was putting my daughter to bed that night, she suddenly started crying and said, "Daddy, I'm praying for your back. I have two feelings. One part of me feels your back will get worse. But another part of me feels good that it will get better." I said, "Let's go with the good feeling and trust God to heal Daddy." My daughter and I are particularly close. She was seven at the time.

In my quiet time, I had been encouraged by the word that my wife received from the Lord when I first told her about the doctor's report. She received John 9:3 (NIV). "Neither this man nor his parents sinned, said Jesus, but this happened so that the work of God might be displayed in his life." I believed I was going to see the works of God displayed in my life through healing.

Angie and I went to see the oncologist the following Thursday. The front desk nurse, Elaine, lit up when she saw me and mentioned my name. My wife joked, "I wonder if it's a good thing when everyone knows your name at a clinic." The oncology nurse, Judie, came out full of smiles. Later, the oncologist also came out full of smiles and asked us to wait for a few extra minutes.

He took us in and explained that even though my blood work seemed normal for the most part, he suspected I had a rare form of myeloma that was usually very difficult to detect.

He explained it quite well and pointed out the positive aspects of my situation. He proceeded to do a bone marrow biopsy. My wife stayed and prayed all through the procedure. It was very comforting to have my best friend and wife with me. I was wondering how she actually felt as she watched the doctor poke me with that long needle. We went to do another MRI and CT scan. I had stood with her through her health challenges over the years, and now she was my caretaker!

We spent the next day together at the church office. On our way home, Dr. Faust, the spine surgeon, personally called with urgent news. He said the surgery had to be done immediately because the latest MRI and CT scan had revealed an even worse condition in my neck that needed to be tackled immediately to avoid "imminent collapse and disaster." Those were his exact words!

He wanted to see us the next day to discuss the surgery. He said he had already cleared his schedule and penciled me in for surgery on Monday. To him, the neck problem was more urgent than the original lower spinal growth, which had triggered the entire crisis. We made a 3:00 p.m. appointment for the next day, which also happened to be my birthday. Angie and I went home, and she went off with the kids to their math tutorials class and then to Bible studies. I stayed home for some quiet meditation and prayer. Before Angie left with the kids, we went to our bedroom to pray. For the first time in all this unfolding health drama, she shed tears as we prayed. We both reminded the Lord in our prayer that we were trusting Him to see us through.

As Angie was driving off with the kids, she said, "Don't think you are going anywhere yet; remember you have young children." She meant that death was not an option for me!

I said, "Honey, don't worry. It's all going to be fine. I will live to write all the books I have to write and also make sure that you have a million dollars in the bank before I leave for heaven."

She said, "You better decide to live and take care of your children."

I said, "I will." Then off she went with the kids. My heart was filled with joy and contentment as I stood outside the garage and waved them goodbye. Faith does amazing things to your spirit. It gives you peace, joy, and a sense of humor even in the most daunting situations.

I went to my study for quiet meditation and prayer. As I began to pray, I remembered that one of the things I had meant to do was to buy some Communion juice so we could have Communion together and pray as a family. So off I went to get some juice at the grocery store and went back home to pray. During my prayer time, I lifted all the copies of the MRIs, x-rays, and CT scans before the Lord and said, "Lord, when I give my testimony after all this crisis, I promise to tell the story of my healing every time You give me the opportunity to preach. No matter where I am in the world, I will always have a copy of the x-ray as a memorial to testify of Your healing power and to glorify Your name. I will even frame a copy of it.

I meditated and prayed on Psalm 118:17–18 (NKJV).

> I shall not die but live and declare the works of the Lord. The Lord has chastened me severely, but He has not given me over to death.

I wrestled in prayer. Angie and the kids came home around 9:30 p.m. I took the juice I had blessed in my prayer time, got some crackers, prayed with the family, and we had Communion together. We believed God for my healing. I tucked the kids into bed, and Angie and I had dinner.

She remarked during dinner that one of the intercessors came to her after the service and said, "I have never seen a church pray so hard for their pastor." It was encouraging for me to know that the saints were crying out in prayer. God was preparing a powerful testimony through this trial. He would certainly be glorified.

Our appointment with the surgeon the next day was also my birthday. I woke up around 3:00 a.m. with a song in my heart as I went to my study to pray. The song was "Glory be to God in the Highest." It was raining heavily, and I remember remarking to myself that those were showers of blessing.

Angie and I went to see the spine surgeon in the afternoon. He explained that I had suffered a very bad bone erosion in my neck. He wanted me to be very cautious. He cautioned me not to drive around and not to lift anything heavier than half a gallon of milk. He explained that any trauma to my neck could cause the "sliver of bone" left to break, and I could be paralyzed from the neck down. What a way to spend my birthday!

The next day, we went for the pre-op tests, and I came home to finish preparing Sunday's sermon for the kickoff of our building fund campaign. It had been very hectic, especially for Angie as she helped to handle all the preparations for the campaign as well as the ups and downs of preparing for my unexpected major surgery.

After the sermon, I announced to the church that I had been scheduled for surgery the next day. I asked everyone who could to fast and pray for me on that day. The church was shocked, but there was a strong response of prayer.

There were two very good doctors involved in the surgery. The procedure took six hours, and the doctors were very pleased. A bone was replaced in my neck.

But Jesus, the Great Physician and my Healer, healed me by His stripes. I had to go through both chemotherapy and radiation treatment to ensure that my body had no residue of any active cancerous cells. God gave me grace throughout the entire ordeal, and I knew I had to be strong for the church, for my family, and for myself.

Exactly a month after the first surgery, the doctors decided to do a second procedure in my lower spine

> Exactly a month after the first surgery, the doctors decided to do a second procedure in my lower spine area. The procedure took five hours and was very successful as well. It was a very delicate surgery because it involved my spine and nerves. Another bone was replaced in my spine. The doctors were concerned about my ability to regain my full mobility skills because, in their words, "Your nerves had taken a beating from the tumor."
> "Your body is completely normal. There is no sign of cancer in you!"

area. The procedure took five hours and was very successful as well. It was a very delicate surgery because it involved my spine and nerves. Another bone was replaced in my spine. The doctors were concerned about my ability to regain my full mobility skills because, in their words, "Your nerves had taken a beating from the tumor."

Until you have been through radiation and chemotherapy, you will never have an idea what the body goes through. It was only by God's grace that I stood to preach and lead the church week after week while undergoing weekly chemotherapy treatment.

Exactly seven months after the discovery of the tumor, the doctors did every test imaginable and said, "Your body is completely normal. There is no sign of cancer in you!"

CHAPTER 15

LESSONS LEARNED

LET ME SHARE A FEW of the lessons I learned during my illness.

Lesson 1: The Power of Prayer

Prayer is the one thing that changes everything. God's hand is moved when His children pray. The enemy's hand is kept away when prayer is released to heaven. The Bible says in Matthew 18:19 (NIV), "If two of you on earth agree about anything you ask for, it will be done for you by my Father in Heaven." The Bible also says in Psalm 50:15 (NIV), "Call upon me in your day of trouble; I will deliver you and you will honor me."

I believe God touched me because the saints were praying. There are people in the church who genuinely love my family and continually pray for us. I am eternally indebted to them.

Lesson 2: The Power of Love

I can't thank God enough for the love of my wife and children all through this ordeal. They stood by me with care and kindness. They nurtured me with love. There were also people God touched to extend extra support and love specifically for the ordeal. The power of love can never be underestimated. It is more potent than any medicine given to the human body. I believe that medical care is expedited in its effectiveness when the sick person is surrounded by bountiful love. I can't thank God enough for the love of my family and church.

I remember a text I received once from one of our members who had suffered a massive stroke. I went to see her in the hospital, and many of the members visited and loved her through the situation. Some offered all kinds of help and even cooked meals for her family. Her recovery was quick and complete. She sent me a text message saying, "Pastor, I believe I was healed more by the love I received than the medications the doctors gave me." She later shared that with the church.

Lesson 3: The Power of Faith

The Bible records an interesting incident that Ahaz, the king of Judah, faced. The Bible says in Isaiah 7:3–9 (NIV),

> Then the LORD said to Isaiah, "Go out, you and your son Shear—Jashub [which means: a remnant will return] to meet Ahaz at the end of the aqueduct of the Upper Pool, on the road to the Washerman's Field. Say to him, 'Be careful, keep calm, and don't be afraid. Do not lose heart because of these smoldering stubs of firewood—because of the fierce anger of Rezin and Aram and of the son of Remaliah. Aram, Ephraim and Ramaliah's son have plotted your ruin, saying, "Let us invade Judah; let us tear it apart and divide it among ourselves, and make the son of Tabeel king over it." Yet, this is what the Sovereign LORD says: "'It will not take place; it will not happen, for the head of Aram is Damascus, and the head of Damascus is only Rezin. Within sixty-five years Ephraim will be too shattered to be a people. The head of Ephraim is Samaria and the head of Samaria is only Remaliah's son (But I am your

head). If you do not stand firm in your faith, you will
not stand at all.'"

What grabs my attention is the last sentence. "If you do not stand
firm in your faith, you will not stand at all." Satanic plots and attacks
against God's children are very real, but the assurance of divine victory
is even greater. If you do not stand firm in your faith, however, you
will not receive the victory. God has made numerous promises in the
Bible concerning our healing, but we must have faith in God. We must
believe God's Word. Faith is the substance of things hoped for, the
evidence of things not seen (Hebrews 11:1 NKJV). If you don't believe,
you won't receive. You must believe to receive your victory. You must
believe to receive your healing.

Lesson 4: You Must Be a Strong Leader

The attack on my body came at a time when we were busy preparing
for the building fund campaign. I had to undergo sudden spinal surgery
the very week we were kicking off the campaign. If I was down, the
whole church would have been discouraged.

In fact, the day after my doctor had called me with the bad news
about the tumor, someone called early in the morning while sobbing.
She said, "Pastor, my whole world is falling apart." Her husband had
been unfaithful, and she had just found out. She needed some strength
and comfort from the counsel of her pastor! She didn't know what I
was going through myself. I felt the anointing of God in a very special
way as I counseled and prayed with her over the phone. Later, I must
confess that I burst into laughter in my office, saying, "If only she knew
what her pastor was dealing with." It's good to have a sense of humor.
It's good for the soul!

I also remember having to do a three-day fast with someone who
was going through some serious legal problems at the same time. This
was during my numerous trips for doctors' appointments and various
required tests! Later, when I announced the surgery, the person was

totally surprised. He said, "Pastor, how could you counsel, fast, and pray with me when you were going through such difficulties yourself?"

It is interesting that during my time of recovery, radiation, chemotherapy, and preoccupation with the building fund campaign that I also began experiencing all kinds of other challenging leadership issues and distractions in the church. The enemy was attacking on all fronts, but I prayed my way through. I kept pressing on toward our vision.

The promise of God is that His strength is perfected in our weakness. Be strong, no matter how difficult the situation might be. Stand steadfastly upon the Word of God. Your weeping may endure for a night, but joy will come forth in the morning (Psalm 30:5 NKJV).

Lesson 5: The Power of Grace

Another vital lesson through my medical trials was that I became more cognizant of the grace of God. God is too good to be unkind to you and too wise to make a mistake, as one songwriter so eloquently puts it. God will never give you more than you can handle. He will never take you to a place where His grace will not sustain you. If He allows the enemy to strike you with sickness, don't panic; His grace will see you through. If you are financially faithful to God, and your business, job, or finances come under attack, don't worry. His grace is sufficient for you. Even if He allows people you trust to turn their backs on you, don't worry. He will raise up new people to stand with you.

God has sufficient grace for every situation you encounter. Be strong in the grace that is available to you in Christ. The Bible tells us that "out of His fullness we have already received grace in place of grace already given" (John 1:16 NIV). This means the favor of God upon our lives is unfathomable! Grace on top of grace! There is always new grace in place of grace already given in Christ! It is interesting that the apostle Paul always wished the grace of God upon the churches and the recipients of his letters. A classic example is what he said to Timothy. "You then, my son, be strong in the grace that is in Christ Jesus" (2 Timothy 2:1 NIV). The writer of Hebrews actually refers to the throne of God as the "throne of grace." He invites us to "approach

God's throne of grace with confidence, so that we may receive mercy and find grace to help us in our time of need" (Hebrews 4:16 NIV).

Jesus was once a man. He knows what you are going through. He has already provided you with grace to sustain you through every conceivable challenge or trial, including sicknesses and diseases. Your responsibility is to appropriate that grace in your situation. God's grace is always sufficient to see us through any challenges.

Lesson 6: Protect Your Leader

No organization, business, company, nation, or church can survive without good leadership. Israel had many kings, but very few of them loved God and had the true welfare of the people at heart. Many of their leaders did evil in the eyes of God and led God's people astray. They were not good leaders.

The truth is that the spiritual landscape of today has many selfish spiritual leaders who make merchandise of God's people—pastors who tell people what their itching ears want to hear. The apostle Paul warned Timothy about this.

> Preach the word of God. Be prepared, whether the time is favorable or not. Patiently correct, rebuke and encourage your people with good teaching. For the time is coming when people will no longer listen to sound and wholesome teaching. They will follow their own desires and will look for teachers who will tell them what their itching ears want to hear. They will reject the truth and chase after myths. (2 Timothy 4:2–4 NLT)

We live in times when Bible-based preaching and teaching are becoming extinct. Some pastors are preaching motivational messages aimed at retaining their audience but not equipping them to love God or live for Jesus as true disciples. Many congregations are not being challenged and built up with the power that comes from the preaching and teaching of God's pure and unadulterated Word, which alone has the power to transform the wicked human heart. This has done and continues to do damage to the body of Christ.

The psalmist describes the power, usefulness, and relevance of God's Word in these words: "By your words I can see where I am going; they throw a beam of light on my dark path" (Psalm 119:105 the Message Bible). The application is clear: without God's Word, we walk in darkness and uncertainty.

So when Satan finds a genuine man or woman of God who truly has the interest of God's people at heart, and who purposes to teach them God's Word and lead them to paths of righteousness, He will do everything to strike them down.

When I recovered from the illness and returned to the pulpit, I asked the congregation the following questions in a sermon:

- Do you think Satan is happy that, in these days when some pastors are divorcing their wives, Angie and I have just celebrated twenty-five years of marriage?
- Do you think he is happy that we have set the example that in sickness and in health, in riches and in poverty, in childlessness and trials, we will still glorify God with our marriage?
- Do you think Satan is happy that we have labored to teach the unadulterated truth of God's Word for the past ten years?
- Do you think he is happy that by prayer, godly counseling, and example we are preventing marriages and homes from breaking up?
- Do you think that Satan is happy that we have raised this church up to be a praying church?
- Do you think Satan is happy that we are teaching people to reach their full potential for Christ?
- Do you think Satan is happy that we are leading the church to be a "spiritual hospital" where the lost will come to Christ and the wounded, the battered, the broken, the sick, and the afflicted will all receive healing from Jesus?

I said that to the church to encourage them to continually hold us up in prayer. Satan's sole goal is to steal, kill, and destroy (John 10:10 NIV). So when Satan finds leaders who are genuinely raising up people for God, he will do everything to attack them. The Bible says when you strike the shepherd, the sheep will scatter (Zechariah 13:7 NIV). When the leaders of God's church are struck by the enemy, there is usually a scattering of the people. That is why Satan always attacks genuine men and women of God. Sometimes, he attacks through people—sometimes through close people.

The Bible is full of many such examples.

In Numbers 12, we read the story of how Miriam and Aaron, Moses's own siblings, rose up to attack and criticize Moses because of his marriage to a foreigner. They said, "Has the LORD only spoken through Moses? Hasn't he also spoken through us?" (Numbers 12:2 NIV). God was so angry that He punished Miriam by making her leprous. It is interesting that the compassion of Moses is what caused him to plead with God on behalf of Miriam. God healed Miriam. But what if Moses was not a caring and compassionate leader? We must always pray for our leaders so they will respond compassionately even when they are severely attacked.

In Numbers 16, we see another attack against Moses and Aaron. The Bible says,

> Korah, son of Izhar, the son of Levi, and certain Reubenites—Dathan and Abiram, sons of Eliab, and On son of Peleth—became insolent and rose up against Moses. With them were 250 Israelite men, well known community leaders who had been appointed members of the council. They came as a group to oppose Moses and Aaron and said to them, "You have gone too far! The whole community is holy, every one of them, and the LORD is with them. Why then do you set yourselves up above the LORD's assembly?" (Numbers 16:1–3 NIV)

Here we see some of the foremost leaders among the people attacking the authority of Moses. The result of this was that God brought judgment. God caused the earth to open up, and all the dissenters and their families were swallowed up.

Every true servant of God is bound to go through some form of attack from Satan. That is an inevitable part of the spiritual landscape. Paul reminded Timothy that "everyone who wants to live a godly life in Christ Jesus will be persecuted" (2 Timothy 3:12 NIV).

It could be sickness, attacks against your family, or people rising up against you due to their own hidden selfish ambitions. That is why Paul said to Timothy,

> Don't have anything to do with foolish and stupid arguments, because you know they produce quarrels. And the LORD's servant must not quarrel; instead, he must be kind to everyone, able to teach, not resentful. Those who oppose him he must gently instruct, in the hope that God will grant them repentance leading them to a knowledge of the truth, and that they will come to their senses and escape from the trap of the devil, who has taken them captive to do his will. (2 Timothy 2:23–26 NIV)

Satan loves to take people captive to do his will. He uses people to oppose God's servants and to create confusion. Satan's goal is always to strike the shepherd and scatter the flock. I have a good friend whose vibrant church came under attack. Some leaders rose up against him, resulting in an actual fist fight in church among the leadership. The police had to be called in! Today, the church he pastors is only a shadow of what it used to be, and those who caused the confusion have all left the church. His family was almost destroyed in the process.

Stand with, pray for, and support the pastor and
vision carrier God has appointed to lead His flock.

Our responsibility as Christians is to stand with, pray for, and support the pastor and vision carrier God has appointed to lead His flock and not to join Satan in his work of striking the shepherd. If we strongly disagree with a pastor or the leadership, the most responsible thing to do is pray and leave the church if need be. We should never be the instigators of division and confusion in the church. It is a dangerous thing to do because God is not the author of confusion or division. Scripture actually tells us to warn divisive people and not to associate with them if they persist in their divisive ways (Romans 16:17 NIV).

Protect God's appointed servants with fervent prayers because they have put themselves and their families on the line for the sake of God's children and God's work.

Scripture speaks quite strongly against divisiveness, so don't assist Satan by attacking the leadership. The devil can do his own work. He doesn't need any more advocates to aid him. Satan's goal is to attack every genuine man or woman of God with everything he can lay hands on from within and without the church. As members of God's church, we have a responsibility to protect God's appointed servants with fervent prayers because they have put themselves and their families on the line for the sake of God's children and God's work. I am grateful that our church prays for us on a daily basis and our leaders are very protective of our well-being. That is certainly one of the greatest blessings a servant of God could receive in ministry.

Lesson 7: God Can't Use You until You Are Marked

A couple of years ago, I felt convicted while reading Galatians 6:17 (NIV). "From now on, let no one cause me trouble." The question I was confronted with, which changed my spiritual understanding and caused me to weep brokenly for over an hour, was this: "ABK, what marks do you bear for Jesus?" It was a sobering, revealing, and even frightening question—a time of personal spiritual reckoning!

I am convinced that God wants to use our lives in extraordinary ways, but He can't use us unless we first allow Him to leave a mark on us. When God leaves a mark on you, your appetites and desires will change. Your life will be focused on seeking Him first, and in the process, all other things will be added to you. God can't use you unless He first leaves a mark on you. God leaves a mark when you have a personal encounter with Him that leaves you broken and helpless. Such encounters give you a deeper desire to be dependent upon God alone because you realize your utter helplessness without God. So are you prepared for God to leave a mark on you?

Paul had marks all over his body. He records these words in 2 Corinthians 12:7–10 (NIV).

> To keep me from becoming conceited because of these surpassingly great revelations, there was given me a thorn in my flesh, a messenger of Satan to torment me. Three times, I pleaded with the Lord to take it away from me. But He said to me, "My grace is sufficient for you and my power is made perfect in weakness. Therefore, I will boast all the more gladly about my weaknesses, so that Christ's power may rest on me."

God's mark on your body is a sign of your human weakness, and it compels God to release His strength and grace to sustain you. Sometimes, the mark comes in the form of a severe trial that keeps you on your knees for the rest of your life. The experience humbles you and leaves you in total awe of God's sustaining power. It drives the roots of your life deeper into God.

When God leaves a mark on you, even demons will take notice. They will know you by your spiritual marks. They will know that you are not an imposter. They will not ask you what they asked the fraudulent sons of the Jewish chief priest. "Jesus I know, and Paul I know; but who are you?" (Acts 19:15 NIV). They will recognize that you have also been with Jesus!

Paul had his mark: his beatings, his imprisonments, his hard work, his sleepless nights, his hunger, his false accusers, the 195 lashes on his body, his marks from being beaten three times with rods, his three shipwrecks on the open sea, and his death threats—all for a man who is said to have been only four feet and six inches tall!

Jesus also had His marks from all the attacks, anger, and opposition He encountered from the religious leaders of the day. He was even called a devil! Moses had his marks of forty long, difficult years as a fugitive in the desert. Joseph had his marks of the hatred he encountered from his own family and the lies against him that landed him in jail for years. Abraham had his marks of waiting twenty-five years before the birth of the promised child, Isaac. Jacob had his marks when he had an encounter with God, and his hip was disjointed as he struggled with God for a blessing. He was left with a limp for life!

> Are you really willing for Jesus to leave a mark on you so He can truly use you?

It is easy to overlook the story of Mary, the mother of Jesus. Mary also bore a mark. The social shame of being supernaturally pregnant before her marriage with Joseph was consummated must not have been an easy mark to bear. One can imagine all the stares and gossip she must have quietly endured for nine months! Sarah also bore the mark of over two decades of painful childlessness waiting for the promised child, Isaac, to be born. She was old, wrinkled, and beyond the natural age of childbearing, but she waited! Each of these servants was greatly used by God after they had been marked.

Are you really willing for Jesus to leave a mark on you so He can truly use you?

I remember a statement a pastor friend of mine made to me as I was seeing him off after stopping by my office one day. He said, "Dr. ABK, God has really blessed you. You don't ever seem to have any problems." Then he apologized and said, "I shouldn't say that. Your wife has been through a lot." Little did I know that there were even more marks to come for me personally!

We increase in usefulness and effectiveness the more we are broken up by God. We increase with brokenness. The most powerful servants of God are the ones who were thoroughly broken by God before being used on divine missions.

Brokenness has value. If we want God to use us, then we have to allow Him to break us! Until He breaks us up, He cannot multiply us to bless others. Jesus broke up the five loaves of bread before they were multiplied to feed the five thousand. In fact, the multiplication happened as the loaves were being broken up. We increase in usefulness and effectiveness the more we are broken up by God. We increase with brokenness. The most powerful servants of God are the ones who were thoroughly broken by God before being used on divine missions. Abraham was a broken man—twenty-five years of barrenness, waiting for the fulfillment of God's promise. Moses was a broken man—forty years in the wilderness. Joseph was a broken man—many years of slavery and imprisonment. David was a broken man—many years in caves and on the run. Hannah was also marked by brokenness as she waited on the Lord to be blessed with a child. It was that brokenness of heart that caused her to give Samuel back to the service of God in the priesthood. The fact that she so passionately prayed at the altar was a sign of her brokenness and willingness to be used by God.

I believe the reason David became the greatest songwriter and comforter the world has ever known was because of the sufferings he went through. We see his suffering and brokenness through the numerous psalms he wrote. David did not write Psalm 23 from the comfort of the palace in Jerusalem. He wrote it from his experiences in the valley of the shadow of death. His pain, sufferings, and brokenness are now a source of comfort for you and me.

Paul was a broken man. He was broken by the Lord on the Road to Damascus. He was broken by imprisonments and shipwrecks. Humbled and broken by pain, God gave Paul spiritual insight that is sustaining the church today!

I love these words by Gene Edwards in his book *A Tale of Three Kings*:

> God has a university. It's a small school. Few enroll; even fewer graduate. Very, very few indeed. God has this school because He does not have broken men and women. Instead, He has several other types of people. He has people who claim to have God's authority ... and don't—people who claim to be broken ... and aren't. And people who do have God's authority, but who are mad and unbroken. And He has, regretfully, a great mixture of everything in between. All of these He has in abundance, but broken men and women, hardly at all. In God's sacred school of submission and brokenness, why are there so few students? Because all students in this school must suffer much pain.[4]

If you want to be a person God uses, then you must allow Him to painfully break you.

Our church believes that God has called us to be a "spiritual hospital." One day, a question popped into my mind that I believe was the Lord communicating to me.

> Do you know what it means to be a spiritual hospital where the lost come to Christ and the sick, wounded, battered, and broken all receive healing? Do you know

why I have allowed you to experience so much suffering and pain over the past few years? Because I want you to know what it means to be sick, wounded, battered, broken—and then be healed! Your love will be tested through the trials you will go through as you serve My people.

CHAPTER 16

OH LORD, NOT AGAIN!

I WAS BACK IN THE full swing of my ministerial and family life. Everything was going quite well with my health. I was very grateful. However, things were soon to change.

Four years after I had been completely cleared of any trace of cancer in my body, I suddenly started feeling a strange twitch under my tongue. I noticed it one Sunday while speaking in church. It felt as if my tongue was getting tied up! Very soon, I started experiencing excruciating headaches. That was very unusual because I rarely have headaches. The constant twitching right under my tongue was also getting increasingly painful. I called my oncologist. After various tests, he discovered a tumor at the base of my skull, and it was affecting my nerves. Hence, the terrible pain and headaches. We had to cancel a scheduled family cruise, which we had been looking forward to for a while.

Things were rapidly going downhill. I woke up one Saturday morning with a complete inability to articulate my words. I was scheduled to preach on Sunday, and it was too late to arrange for a replacement. That afternoon, my wife had to step in my place to speak at a meeting just so I could rest my tongue! Speaking in church the next day proved to be rather challenging. My words were slurred and dragging, but I pressed through. I still can't picture how the congregation sat through that sermon and what was running through their minds. Was the pastor OK? Was he going to be OK?

My tongue had actually been twisted to one side and the oncologist explained that I had suffered a mild stroke and that my nerve was quite damaged. He mentioned that the nerve damage could take several months to repair itself and that my speech was going to be affected for a while. He knew I was a pastor, and he felt sorry that I couldn't articulate my words properly. I went through radiation and chemotherapy without drawing any attention to it at all.

> God gave me strength to carry out all my responsibilities as a pastor. The church had no idea that I was going through such a difficult time.

Perhaps the most frustrating thing for me was how much of my time was consumed by the numerous trips to the hospital for the chemotherapy and radiation treatments. All through the treatment, I would dutifully teach Bible studies every Wednesday and preach every Sunday. The grace of God was simply amazing. I did not publicize my treatment in any way. I felt the Lord wanted me to handle things without alarming the church. The grace of God upon my life through this period was simply amazing. God gave me strength to carry out all my responsibilities as a pastor. The church had no idea that I was going through such a difficult time. Somehow, I felt that was the best way to handle it. My board members knew I was going through treatment. As usual, they were very prayerful and extremely supportive.

It Is Time for a Bone Marrow Transplant

Soon after my initial diagnosis of multiple myeloma, my oncologist connected me with a renowned oncologist at Johns Hopkins Hospital in Baltimore, Maryland. They weighed the possibility of a bone marrow transplant, but it was never conclusive because I was healthy and in remission. The doctor at Hopkins was not convinced it would be beneficial at the time. I remained healthy, and life went on.

I had returned from a trip to Israel when I suddenly started experiencing severe pains in my right shoulder and the left part of my rib cage. I went through another bout of radiation and chemotherapy for several weeks. Again, I quietly endured the pain without publicizing it. I simply asked God for grace to endure it. The comfort, satisfaction, and encouragement I had was that the church was fervently praying for my family and me on a daily basis without even knowing about my new health challenges. I never slowed down on what I had to do. I even went on a scheduled trip to Morocco a month after returning from Israel. My conviction is that as long as I am taking care of myself spiritually, physically, and medically, God will always give me the grace to function in every expected way. My responsibility is to do whatever needs to be done to take care of my body, continue to pray, and leave the rest to God! Scripture makes it clear that the eyes of the Lord are upon the righteous! That is my comfort and stance when it comes to life in general! I do my part and trust Him to take care of things. Life is already a challenge, so why exacerbate things by worrying about what only God can control?

> Life is already a challenge, so why exacerbate things by worrying about what only God can control?

My doctor at Hopkins was now convinced that it was time to reevaluate me for a stem cell transplant. He scheduled me for one. I had no doubt that the timing was right and that everything would go well. I believed the timing was right because I had asked God at the beginning of the year to perfect that which concerned my life so that I could focus on His work. Every January, our church goes through twenty-one days of fasting and prayer to prepare us spiritually for the year ahead. Typically, we would have a theme for the year, and our fasting and prayer would revolve around the theme during those twenty-one days and all through the year. The theme is usually the basis of my sermon during the last night of December as we pray our way into the new year. During the fast, we also encourage everyone to personalize the theme and make their requests with the theme in mind. Our theme for that year was "Oh Lord, perfect that which concerns me." This was based on Psalm 138:8 (NKJV), which says, "The LORD will perfect that which concerns me; Your mercy, O LORD, endures forever; Do not forsake the work of your hands."

During the fast in January, one of my personal requests was for the Lord to perfect everything concerning my health. I did not want to be distracted by any medical issues. I wanted to remain healthy and focus on the vision God had given us for His church.

Without knowing that I was going to be scheduled for a transplant, I was listening to a sermon on the radio a couple of weeks before the doctor's call and the speaker mentioned how the Lord used a stem cell transplant to cure him of myeloma. This happened to be the same disease I had been battling. My interest was obviously piqued. So when the doctor called to suggest and discuss the transplant, my spirit was already prepared to receive it. I am a firm believer in the fact that because we live in Jesus and move in Him and have our being in Him, He will always direct and instruct us in the way we should go at every point in time. Scripture attests to this. "I will instruct you and teach you in the way you should go; I will counsel you with my loving eye on you" (Psalm 32:8 NIV). We also have the assurance that "the LORD directs the steps of the godly. He delights in every detail of their lives" (Psalm 37:23 NLT). That being the case, knowing what to do at every point in time should not be a hand-wringing thing. Since the Lord delights in us, we should be confident—and not afraid—knowing that He will always direct us appropriately.

I believe that the supernatural should be part of the natural for God's children. Our very lives should be an intertwining of the natural and supernatural. This conviction is based on the biblical assurance that we are seated with Christ in the heavenly realms (Ephesians 2:6 NIV) and that God's Spirit dwells in us (Romans 8:9 NIV). So at any point in time, we are functioning both in the natural and supernatural because our lives are in Christ and in the Spirit of God. We should, therefore, never be afraid of what is ahead of us because Jesus and the Holy Spirit of

God will never misdirect us. We get misdirected when we do not truly cultivate our relationship with God through knowledge and obedience to His Word and communion with His Spirit.

> The supernatural should be part of the natural for God's children. Our very lives should be an intertwining of the natural and supernatural.

The call from my oncologist was in November, close to the end of the year, but I felt it was an answer to my prayer for the Lord to perfect everything concerning my health. I felt the transplant was an answer to that prayer, so I was very receptive to it. I explained to our church congregation that my doctors had recommended a transplant. On December 9, I said goodbye to the church and went through a barrage of tests and procedures to get ready for the transplant.

A bone marrow transplant is risky and involving. I had a central line put into my body. I was injected with growth hormones to increase my bone marrow, which was later harvested to be transplanted. We made several visits to the hospital, a three-hour daily drive in and out. The procedure itself involves being given a heavy dose of chemotherapy, which wipes out your entire immune system. Your harvested, cleaned, and stored bone marrow is then transplanted into your body. You become completely weak and subject to infection because you have no natural capacity to fight off any disease. Because your immune system is wiped out, you have to protect yourself carefully against any possible infection. You are continually nauseous, you lose your appetite, you lose a lot of weight, and you lose your hair on top of it all!

The transplant was done on Christmas Eve, December 24. The Lord was gracious, and the procedure went very well. It takes about three to six months to rebuild your immune system after the stem cell transplant, so I stayed out of church for three months. To protect myself from any possible infection, I slept in our guest room for several weeks and wore a mask at home for a while. It also takes time to regain your appetite, energy, and weight. In fact, several months after the transplant, I had still not regained my weight—not that I needed to lose any weight in the first place!

Angels for the Journey

The grace of God will always be sufficient for whatever challenges you go through. God will bring you angels in the form of people to stand with you in every trial. His promise in Isaiah is the following:

> When you go through deep waters, I will be with you. When you go through rivers of difficulty, you will not drown. When you walk through the fire of oppression, you will not be burned up; the flames will not consume you … because you are precious to me. You are honored and I love you. Do not be afraid for I am with you. (Isaiah 43:2–5 NLT)

Sometimes, the presence of God is with us through the people He surrounds our lives with, especially in difficult times. I see those individuals as angels placed in our lives by God to minister to us. We are not islands unto ourselves. We were created as relational beings dependent on one another. We need the love and support of others, and I thank God for blessing my life with many remarkably loving and supportive people. They are ministering angels sent by God.

Angela

My first angel was my wife. Never in a million years could I have imagined that the shoe was going to be on the other foot and that my wife whom I had supported and taken care of for over thirty years through her health challenges was now going to be my caretaker! She did a splendid job! God gave her strength and grace to be my caretaker all through the transplant procedure and recovery. She drove tirelessly back and forth to the hospital. She stayed with me for the month we relocated for proximity to the hospital. She took care of me with excellence. Her love and strength were remarkable. Incidentally, her name, Angela, means angel! She was my angel.

Our Twins

My next angel came as twins—our twin children! In the past, we would arrange for someone to be with them at home anytime we traveled, but now they were sixteen and old enough to be by themselves at home. They assured us that they needed no supervision and that they would act responsibly—and they did. They took care all their school assignments responsibly. They handled their responsibilities both at church and at home with admirable diligence. They were at home for a whole month without Mom and Dad. I learned a valuable lesson. The training you give your children doesn't really surface until you find yourself away from them. That is when their true sense of responsibility kicks in. Almost without fail, I would say to them whenever I dropped them off at school, "You are too gifted and too blessed not to be the best, so go for the gold." I have said that to them for years, and now we were seeing the best out of them. They rose to the occasion and made us proud. They went for the gold!

Our Church Family

Other angels came in the form of our church family. The love, prayers, and practical support were varied and endless. The board set up a time to pray for me every day. One of our deacons dropped off and picked up our children to and from school every day. He ensured that they were present at their numerous school and church activities. All this was possible because he had recently retired from his job. What divine timing! A family friend took the children in for the Christmas holidays. Another church leader ensured that they were treated to lunch at a restaurant every Sunday after service, something we did not do that often!

For an entire month, my wife and I were away from the church, but attendance remained strong. Our leaders stepped into their assigned roles, and the church functioned seamlessly! Even after my wife went back to church, I had to stay and recover for several more weeks. One thing I have always believed in is the importance of proper training to enable others to use their gifts, talents, and skills to serve alongside the pastor or leader of the organization. It is very important to intentionally train and give people the opportunity to handle different aspects of the ministry so that in the absence of the leader, the church or organization does not fall apart. That builds strength into the church and empowers people to serve wholeheartedly.

> Intentionally train and give people the opportunity to handle different aspects of the ministry so that in the absence of the leader, the church or organization does not fall apart.

I am an avid believer in frequent meetings and training for organizational leaders. One of my favorite things is to take a leader out for a one-on-one lunch. It gives me the opportunity not just to hear their concerns about the ministry but also to know the state of their lives and to encourage and minister to them. I frequently meet with different ministry leaders and also with our entire leadership team on a quarterly basis as much as possible. We go through different facets of leadership and pray for the church and ourselves. I even bring in individuals who I see as potential leaders into those meetings as well. This acquaints them with my heart and vision and enables us to function in unity. This is quite time-consuming, but I believe the value of investing in your core leadership is incalculable. Sometimes I would simply call and pray with them over the phone. When leaders pray together, they stay together! Our leaders became my angels in my long absence. They preached, taught, served, and directed the affairs of the church for several months without any schisms! They were my angels!

My Neighbor

My neighbor was another angel. She is a trained nurse, and she put her professional skills to work on my behalf. Before the procedure, she would come in, do the required injections, and take care of the central line that had been put in me for the transplant. She was an angel.

My Doctors

My medical doctors were also angels. They took care of me from the time of the initial diagnosis through the transplant and after. They were professional, understanding, and meticulous. They explained every detail and examined all options with me.

They followed up on me with great care. I believe the knowledge and abilities the medical profession has garnered to help humanity is a gift from God. It is mind-boggling to reflect on the advances of medicine. Even with the limited knowledge available about the complex human body, the ability available in medicine to treat diseases is nothing short of amazing. Complex procedures on the human heart, the eye, the intestines, the brain, the bones, the cells, and various parts of the human body should cause us to give thanks to our Creator God who makes all this possible!

I believe it is also important to pray for the physicians who take care of us. Without the grace of God, things could go massively wrong, as happens from time to time. Prayer invites the hand of God into every medical situation and procedure. Take time to pray for your medical providers. Build a personal relationship with them. Let them know that you care about their personal well-being. Ask about their families when you go to receive care from them. Let them know you are praying for them. Very few people will object to the fact that you are praying for them. I personally know the family situations of all my medical providers.

One nurse practitioner once told me she and her husband have been praying for children, and I began praying with her. She got pregnant and later had a miscarriage, but I am believing that God will honor her request. One of my doctors has a daughter living outside the country, and I make it a point to follow up on her well-being through her father. Another nurse navigator has a daughter who lives in Chicago and serves the youth in a church.

I always pray with her and keep abreast of her progress and challenges. Recently, one of my physicians mentioned that he was going on a medical leave. There was a tumor that needed to be removed from his brain. My immediate reaction was to pray for the procedure to go well for him. I called his nurse practitioner to inform her that I was praying for the doctor. The doctor underwent the operation on his brain successfully. Thankfully, it was not cancerous. When we first met after the procedure, we exchanged notes and were both thankful to be alive. He reminded me that it could have been otherwise. Things could have turned out quite differently, he said. It really could have been otherwise! And then he reminded me of one of his favorite poems, which simply says, "One day, it will be otherwise." We should, therefore, make the most of life until it becomes otherwise! He thanked me for my love and prayers, and I responded that I had no choice but to pray for him to be alive for a long time so he could continue to take care of me. God is the repository of all knowledge. It is important to pray for our medical providers because they need divine guidance to make the right diagnosis, prescribe the right medications, and successfully undertake complex procedures. We can't afford to take any procedure for granted. It always helps to bathe everything in prayer. Prayer will release divine guidance to your doctor.

My Pastor Friends

Finally, my pastor friends with whom I shared my situation stood prayerfully with me throughout the procedure. They were also my angels. It is a blessing when people follow through with their promise to uphold you in prayer. The truth is not everyone who promises to pray for you will do so. Many simply don't set time aside to pray. In fact, many don't even have time to pray for themselves because of the busyness of life! It is, therefore, vitally important that you only share crucial prayer requests with those who are truly committed intercessors. Some would just listen to your request as a news item without doing anything about it.

Because of the necessity and power of prayer, it is critical to have a circle of people you can truly depend on when things are critical. Remember that Jesus was counting on His disciples to hold Him up in prayer only to find them sound asleep! The biblical account is quite interesting.

> Then Jesus went with His disciples to a place called Gethsemane, and He said to them, "Sit here while I go over there and pray" … Then He said to them, "My soul is overwhelmed with sorrow to the point of death. Stay here and keep watch with me." Going a little farther, He fell with His face to the ground and prayed … Then He returned to His disciples and found them sleeping. "Couldn't you men keep watch with me for an hour?" he asked Peter. (Matthew 26:36–40 NIV)

In Jesus's critical hour of need, when His soul was overwhelmed with sorrow, the most trusted people around Him could not be counted on to stand with Him in prayer. They were sound asleep! The truth is we cannot entrust our critical prayer needs to those who would be sleeping soundly and sending snores instead of prayers to heaven on our behalf. Having prayer partners who we can count on is a true blessing. Faithful intercessors help you persevere through trials. Prayer does work, but it is also hard work!

I am grateful for the wonderful prayer partners who stood with me in my time of need.

Satan and Diseases

One reason it is important to pray against sickness is that sicknesses and diseases are not from God. They came as a result of the sin that fell on the human race through Adam and Eve. With the fall of humanity, our perfect bodies became subjected to the imperfections that affected creation. Even the careless and greedy practices of humans that affect the environment we live in make us liable to sickness. It is, therefore, important to pray for God to protect us from sicknesses and diseases that have become a part of our existence. In fact, Scripture makes it clear that God's desire is to heal us from sicknesses and diseases. The Bible says of Jesus,

> Surely He took up our pain and bore our suffering, yet we considered Him punished by God, stricken by Him and afflicted. But He was pierced for our transgressions, He was crushed for our iniquities; the punishment that brought us peace was upon Him and by His wounds, we are healed. (Isaiah 53:4–5 NIV)

We can make the point that part of the blessing of Jesus coming to die on the cross was to bring us healing through His stripes.

I also believe that because Satan's goal is to "steal, kill, and destroy" (John 10:10 NIV), he attacks humanity with sicknesses and diseases. In the book of Job, Satan is seen actively eyeing Job for an opportunity to attack and destroy him. One of the things he did when God granted him the permission was to attack Job's body with boils. The glee Satan had in doing this is nauseating. He said,

> "Skin for skin! A man will give up everything he has to save his life. But reach out and take away his health, and he will surely curse you to your face" ... [When God gave him the permission] Satan left the LORD's presence, and struck Job with terrible boils from head to toe. (Job 2:4–7 NLT)

It is evident that sickness is a choice weapon of Satan because he knows it renders us helpless and could cause us to question the faithfulness and love of God. He was confident that attacking Job's health could tempt Job to turn his back on God and even curse God!

Sickness can be devastating. It leaves us helpless and dependent on others. Sickness can leave people in such physical and emotional pain that it can lead to bitterness in one's very soul. The helplessness unleashed by sickness could even leave one wishing for death. Satan knows it is one of the things people fear the most. A sick person would spend whatever it costs or do whatever it takes to get well. Satan was well aware of this, so he attacked Job's health in a bid to finally turn him against God. But even in poor health, Job held unto his faith in God.

One day, the Lord gave me an interesting insight into Isaiah 54:17. That passage says, "No weapon forged against you will prevail, and you will refute every tongue that accuses you. This is the heritage of the servants of the LORD, and this is their vindication from Me" (Isaiah 54:17 NIV). I was getting ready for service one Sunday morning when my understanding of that passage was quickened in a totally different way. I was planning on praying for the sick in the service, and the insight I received was that sicknesses and diseases were weapons that the enemy forges against God's children to destroy them just like he hoped to destroy Job.

A few weeks later, I was preparing to enter the sanctuary for the Sunday morning service when I felt the prompting to pray "a hedge of health" around the church (see Job 1:10 NIV). I was a bit puzzled by the wording "Pray for a hedge of health around the church."

I made that word known to the church. I was obedient and did exactly that during the time of worship. Shortly after that, I felt the prompting to pray Isaiah 33:24 (NIV) over the congregation. "No one living in Zion will say, 'I am ill,' and the sins of those who dwell there will be forgiven." Again, I was obedient and encouraged the congregation to receive that word and believe it. Only a few weeks later, the COVID-19 pandemic struck rather viciously and changed virtually every society on earth. I reminded the congregation about the "hedge of health" we had prayed over the church and encouraged everyone to believe the Lord for protection, especially since we had numerous health care workers in the church.

> Only a few weeks later, the COVID-19
> pandemic struck rather viciously and
> changed virtually every society on earth.

I believe it is God's desire to bring healing to His children when our bodies are struck with diseases. Exodus 23:25 (NIV) gives us this assurance: "Worship the LORD your God, and His blessing will be on your food and water. I will take away sickness from among you."

When Satan attacks our health, his sole goal is to put our faith into crisis, discourage us, wear us out, and cause us to turn our backs on God. We must therefore fight off sicknesses and diseases with every spiritual weapon we have as we undertake all necessary medical steps as well.

Sure, not every ailment is of satanic origin; nonetheless, we cannot rule out the hand of Satan as we battle diseases. All through the Gospels, we see the numerous times that Jesus dealt with demonic involvement when healing people. A classic illustration is this account in Matthew:

> And when they had come to the multitude, a man came to Him, kneeling down to Him and saying, "Lord, have mercy on my son, for he is an epileptic and suffers severely; for he often falls into the fire and often into the water. So I brought him to your disciples, but they could not cure him." Then Jesus answered and said, "O faithless and perverse generation, how long shall I be with you? How long shall I bear with you? Bring him here to me." And Jesus rebuked the demon, and it came out of him; and the child was cured from that very hour. Then the disciples came to Jesus privately and said, "Why could we not cast it out?" So Jesus said to them, "Because of your unbelief; for assuredly, I say to you, if you have faith as a mustard seed, you will

say to this mountain, 'Move from here to there,' and it will move; and nothing will be impossible for you. However, this kind does not go out except by prayer and fasting." (Matthew 17:14–21 NKJV)

Jesus was teaching His disciples the valuable spiritual lesson that there were certain diseases that needed to be tackled with fasting and prayer because of strong demonic involvement.

We see another interesting example in Luke 13. This involved a woman who had been oppressed with an infirmity by Satan for eighteen years. The story is quite fascinating. The account says,

> One Sabbath day as Jesus began teaching in a synagogue, He saw a woman who had been crippled by an evil spirit. She had been bent double for eighteen years and was unable to stand up straight. When Jesus saw her, He called her over and said, "Dear Woman, you are healed of your sickness!" Then He touched her, and instantly she could stand straight. How she praised God! But the leader in charge of the Synagogue was indignant that Jesus had healed her on the Sabbath day. "There are six days of the week for working," he said to the crowd. "Come on those days to be healed, not on the Sabbath." But the Lord replied, "You hypocrites! Each of you works on the Sabbath day! Don't you untie your ox or your donkey from its stall on the Sabbath and lead it for water? This dear woman, a daughter of Abraham, has been held in bondage by Satan for eighteen years. Isn't it right that she be released even on the Sabbath?" (Luke 13:10–16 NLT)

In this particular situation, Jesus was pointing out the connection between the woman's illness and Satan. She had been bound by Satan with that illness for eighteen years! Jesus set her free from that demonic oppression! The truth is God needs our healthy physical bodies to undertake the assignments He has for our lives. Sickness slows us down and consumes our valuable time, energy, and resources that could otherwise be profitably expended in God's kingdom. It is in Satan's interest to attack our bodies and prevent us from pursuing our divine destinies and vision. We must understand this and fight off those attacks with every weapon at our disposal.

Not every sickness or disease is of demonic origin, but it is clear from Scripture that there are times when the enemy attacks people with illnesses and diseases. As part of our regular prayers, we must continually pray to prevent the enemy from targeting our bodies with sickness and disease. It is a worthwhile spiritual undertaking because as Scripture reminds us, our struggle is not against flesh and blood but against spiritual forces of evil in the spirit realm. Therefore, it is imperative that we put on the full armor of God (Ephesians 6:11 NIV).

> Not every sickness or disease is of demonic origin, but it is clear from scripture that there are times when the enemy attacks people with illnesses and diseases.

Sickness brings a lot of suffering, but we can be sure that our suffering is not pointless. Why does God allow His children to go through times of testing and suffering? Is our suffering in vain? The answer is no! God does not waste any experience He allows us to go through. God often uses our trials as launching pads to move us to new levels of understanding, service, and blessings. Our sufferings lead us to new elevations that we could never have attained otherwise. God does not allow trials without a beneficial goal in mind. Every servant of God used mightily in the scriptures went through painful trials and suffering. That is what caused them to grow into "spiritual oaks," which are strong and able to withstand the tremendous challenges encountered as part of being greatly used by God to touch needy humanity.

Spiritual Oaks versus Spiritual Mushrooms

God cannot use "spiritual mushrooms" to do the work of "spiritual oaks." Spiritual oaks are developed and tested by God—sometimes over several years! Trials are necessary if we are to become spiritual oaks strong enough to be used extensively by God. We are reminded in James that trials test our faith and help us to develop perseverance and maturity, making us complete (James 1:2–4 NIV). Without the testing of our faith, we would only grow as spiritual mushrooms that cannot last in the face of adversity.

Wild mushrooms seem to appear overnight, and they grow and expand quite rapidly. They just seem to pop up from nowhere and usually last for a day, a week, or maybe a month. They are easily destroyed. A spiritual mushroom is no match against the attacks of Satan and his vicious demons!

Oaks, on the other hand, take years to grow and develop. Oaks grow from acorns. The process of growing and developing an oak tree is quite fascinating. Here's an account:

> When the acorn is ripe, it falls from the mother tree to the ground. Very few acorns survive to sprout and produce a new oak tree because of hungry animals and human activity and having to bounce or roll to where they can grow. It's a risky process; only a tiny proportion of acorns make the transformation from seedling to mature oak tree … If the seedling is not eaten or destroyed, it gradually grows and develops into a sapling tree after four to five years. The sapling then grows into a small tree that flowers and produces its own acorns.
>
> Every tree of reproductive age, about twenty years old, is capable of producing acorns. Peak acorn production occurs from 50 to 80 years … Over the next hundred years, the young tree matures into a majestic adult. Oak trees can live for hundreds or a thousand years, fruiting

new acorns every summer ... Over its lifespan, an oak tree can produce as many as 10 million acorns, which some will grow into a new generation of oak trees.[5]

As James says, diverse trials help us to develop perseverance, maturity, and completeness. A person who cannot persevere through challenges cannot be looked upon as a role model to help others through the challenges of life. Life is full of trials, and if God is to use us effectively to help others, then it is imperative that we ourselves are tested through trials. Trials mature us into spiritual oaks who cannot be easily knocked down and who can contribute effectively to God's kingdom for years, just as oaks do in the natural.

May God use your suffering as a catalyst for your growth, expansion, and multiplication. May you become a spiritual oak that produces other oaks through the numerous acorns you produce over many years of steadfast service in God's kingdom. May God turn what the enemy meant for evil into a blessing that will affect many lives for His glory. Let me encourage you with these words from the prophet Isaiah:

Lord, by such things men live and my spirit finds life in them too.

You restored me to health and let me live.

Surely, it was for my benefit that I suffered such anguish. In your love, you kept me from the pit of destruction; you have put all my sins behind your back.

For the grave cannot praise you, death cannot sing your praise. Those who go down to the pit cannot hope for your faithfulness. The living, the living praise you; as I am doing today.

Fathers tell their children about your faithfulness.

The LORD will save me and we will sing with stringed instruments all the days of our lives in the temple of the LORD. (Isaiah 38:17–20 NIV)

May God bring you healing in every area of your life: mental, emotional, physical, and spiritual.

May your adversities turn your life into a testimony to honor God and encourage others. May God restore you and let you live. Amen!

CHAPTER 17

THE NEED FOR PRAYER

PRAYER IS SIMPLY COMMUNICATING WITH God and listening to hear back from Him. It is not just talking to God in a one-sided manner but a two-way communication in which we speak to God and expect to hear from Him. Prayer is humans speaking to God and waiting to hear back from Him. Communicating with God through prayer can be verbal or nonverbal. In 1 Samuel 1, there is the story of a barren woman, Hannah, broken by her barrenness. The Bible tells us, "Hannah was praying in her heart and her lips were moving but her voice was not heard" (1 Samuel 1:13 NIV). In fact, Eli, the priest, after observing her for a while at the altar, actually mistook her for a drunken woman! When he found out that Hannah was in sincere prayers to God for a child, Eli wished her well and believed with her for a child from God. The answer to that nonverbal prayer was the birth of the prophet Samuel.

Scripture also tells us, "While Jesus was here on earth, He offered prayers and pleadings, with a loud cry and tears, to the one who could rescue Him from death. And God heard His prayers

> Prayer is humans speaking to God and waiting to hear back from Him.

because of His deep reverence for God" (Hebrews 5:7 NLT). Those were loud, verbal prayers! So God hears and answers prayer—verbal or nonverbal, quiet or loud!

Paul also tells us that there are times when our prayers take the form of groans. He records this in Romans.

> And the Holy Spirit helps us in our weakness. For example, we don't know what God wants us to pray for. But the Holy Spirit prays for us with groanings that cannot be expressed in words. And the Father who knows all hearts, knows what the Spirit is saying, for The Spirit pleads for us believers in harmony with God's own will. (Romans 8:26–27 NLT)

If we are to pray without ceasing as scripture tells us to, then it is obvious that some of our prayers may often be nonverbal. We can sit in the train and be in fervent prayer without anyone knowing. We can communicate with God at a very deep level in public or in the presence of others without attracting attention. Nehemiah seems to have prayed a very quick but effective nonverbal prayer when he communicated with the king about the ruins in Jerusalem.

> So the King asked me, "Why are you looking so sad? You don't look sick to me. You must be deeply troubled." Then I was terrified, but I replied, "Long live the King! How can I not be sad? For the city where my ancestors are buried is in ruins, and the gates have been destroyed with fire." The King asked, "Well, how can I help you?" With a prayer to the God of heaven, I replied, "If it pleases the King, and if you are pleased with me, your servant, send me to Judah to rebuild the city where my ancestors are buried." (Nehemiah 2:2–5 NLT)

God answered the request, and Nehemiah was granted permission to go and rebuild the wall of Jerusalem. That quick nonverbal prayer in addition to all the other preparatory prayers Nehemiah had offered to God prior to appearing before the king secured him an immediate answer.

We can weave prayer into every situation without drawing the slightest attention to the fact that we are calling upon the God of heaven! We can pray with open or closed eyes depending on the circumstances we find ourselves in. The condition of our hearts and our spiritual focus and reverence for God are what count the most and not necessarily our outward posture!

Pray without Ceasing

If we desire for God to use us in any significant way, then we must endeavor to become persons of fervent prayer. Prayer should be our business as Christians. Prayer invites God to move on our behalf. If we continually kneel before God, we will have the strength and courage to withstand any situation and stand with boldness before any person.

> Is there good news? Keep on praying.
> Is there bad news? Keep on praying.
> Do you have a job? Keep on praying.
> Are you jobless? Keep on praying.
> Is it well? Keep on praying.
> Is it not so well? Keep on praying.
> Are you healthy? Keep on praying.
> Are you sick? Keep on praying.
> Is there money in the bank?
> Keep on praying.
> Is the bank account empty?
> Keep on praying. Pray without ceasing.

Prayer is so critical to the Christian journey that the apostle Paul enjoins us to "pray without ceasing" (1 Thessalonians 5:17 NLT). This means that our prayer life must not be contingent upon what is happening or not happening in our lives. So is there good news? Keep on praying. Is there bad news? Keep on praying. Do you have a job? Keep on praying. Are you jobless? Keep on praying. Is it well? Keep on praying. Is it not so well? Keep on praying. Are you healthy? Keep on praying. Are you sick? Keep on praying. Is there money in the bank? Keep on praying. Is the bank account empty? Keep on praying. Pray without ceasing. Your Father in heaven has His eyes on you, and His ears are open to your cry! Don't stop praying!

Just as we breathe continually to stay alive physically, we must also pray continually to stay alive spiritually. We don't breathe only when we feel like breathing, so we should not pray only when we feel like praying. We should pray continually just as we breathe continually.

Prayer must not be relegated to a five-minute routine in our lives. It is certainly important to set aside specific times to pray on a daily basis, but the biblical injunction to pray without ceasing means we must weave prayer into the mundane activities of life. We can pray in the shower, pray when cooking in the kitchen, pray when driving, pray when mowing the lawn, or pray when standing in the queue at the bank or at the checkout stand in the supermarket. We can take the opportunity to pray while waiting for our car to be serviced instead of chatting endlessly on the phone, texting away our lives, or plainly wasting valuable time surfing the internet and social media! We must pray without ceasing.

The truth is communicating with God continually can be quite tasking to us. Our flesh may not necessarily feel excited about setting time aside to pray, but prayer is essential because it helps us to maintain a rich relationship with God. A strong relationship with God does not just happen. It takes effort and intentionality. Prayer is a vital part of that effort. It requires commitment. We must also understand that the enemy of our soul, Satan, would do everything possible to keep us from committed prayers. That is why prayer is so difficult for many Christians, but we must pray nonetheless because prayer is one of our most effective weapons in our battle against Satan and his demons!

Prayer is so essential to the well-being of God's children that the prophet Samuel said to the Israelites, "As for me, far be it from me that I should sin against the LORD by failing to pray for you" (1 Samuel 12:23 NIV). Even though the Israelites had sinned by rejecting both God and Samuel and asking for an earthly king instead of God, Samuel knew he had to continue praying for them. Prayer is critical to the life of the believer, and it is vitally important that God's servants spend time to bring His children before the throne of grace in constant prayer. God expects that!

A Man Who Depended on Prayer

The story is told of five Bible college students who visited London to hear some of the great preachers of their day. They visited the church of Charles Surgeon, one of the greatest preachers of all time. It was a hot summer day, and as they waited outside for the doors of the church to be opened, a stranger approached them and said, "While you are waiting, would you like to see the heating apparatus of this church?" The students agreed, so the stranger took them downstairs to the basement of the church. He then pointed to about seven hundred people who were bowed down in prayer for the impending service and said, "This is our heating apparatus; this is what heats up this place!" What the students found out later was that that strange guide who showed them around was Spurgeon himself, the pastor of the church! There were seven hundred people praying for the church service! No wonder Charles Spurgeon's ministry and great sermons impacted so many lives. Charles Spurgeon stated, "Whenever God determines to do a great work, He first sets His people to pray."[6]

> Every mighty move of God is preceded by intensive prayers.

Every mighty move of God is preceded by intensive prayers. The Day of Pentecost is an eloquent illustration of this. A hundred and twenty people gathered in prayer in an upper room in obedience to the command of Jesus (Acts 1:13 NKJV) and continually devoted themselves to prayer (Acts 1:14 NKJV). When the Day of Pentecost came, the Holy Spirit fell on them. The power of God that they experienced is what caused three thousand people to come to Christ in one day as Jews gathered in Jerusalem from all over the Diaspora to celebrate this important harvest festival of Shavuot. This outpouring of the Spirit caused an immediate explosion of growth—a harvest—in the early church. It all started with prayer as they gathered in obedience to Jesus's command to wait for what God had promised (Acts 1:5 NIV).

In Acts 13, we also see that God called out Barnabas and Saul and commissioned them into ministry out of a prayer meeting. This happened at the church in Antioch. The biblical account says,

> While they were worshipping the Lord and fasting, the Holy Spirit said, "Set apart for me Barnabas and Saul for the work to which I have called them." So after they had fasted and prayed, they placed their hands on them and sent them off. (Acts 13:2–3 NIV)

The mighty ministry undertaken by Paul and Barnabas was born out of a prayer meeting. God has plans to use us, but those plans come to fruition when we draw them out of heaven through fervent prayers. God has designated His church to be "a house of prayer for all nations" (Isaiah 56:7 NKJV).

When the house of God on earth is busily engaged in prayer, then the hand of God gets busy in heaven to release blessings to the earth.

We must pray without ceasing because Jesus Himself is at the right hand of God praying without ceasing. Scripture tells us, "Christ Jesus who died—more than that who was raised from the dead—is at the right hand of God and is also interceding for us" (Romans 8:34 NIV). The early church followed the example of Jesus by being committed to prayer. This is captured in a statement in Acts 2:42 (NIV). "They devoted themselves to the apostles' teaching, to the breaking of bread and to fellowship and to prayer."

The word *devoted* relates to focus, passion, and intensity. In the Greek, the picture that comes to mind is that of a wild animal focused on its prey, ready to devour it. That is how intensively the early church prayed. In fact, the reason the apostles selected deacons in the early church was because they deemed it critical to focus on prayer and the teaching of God's Word. With the rapid growth of the church, complaints began surfacing about the distribution of food to care for widows in the church. Deacons were appointed to resolve that situation. Scripture says,

> So the Twelve called a meeting of all the believers. They said, "We apostles should spend our time teaching the word of God, not running a food program. And so, brothers, select seven men who are well respected and are full of the Spirit and wisdom. We will give them this responsibility. Then we apostles can spend our time in prayer and teaching the word." (Acts 6:2–4 NLT)

Why We Should Pray without Ceasing

So why should we pray without ceasing? Why should prayer be a lifestyle for a Christian? Numerous reasons could be given for this, but I would like to mention two.

First, Spiritual Warfare

We should pray without ceasing because we are engaged in spiritual warfare. Spiritual warfare refers to the fact that there is a war being waged against God's children from the invisible spiritual realm by Satan and his demonic spirits. We cannot afford to be ignorant of that. Life is a warfare. The forces are invisible, but the results of the conflict are visibly manifest for all to see. We do not physically see evil beings, but they are real nonetheless. They function just like terrorists who secretly plan their attacks unnoticed until they strike with deadly results. The Bible makes it clear that "the thief comes only to steal and kill and destroy" (John 10:10 NIV). We do not physically see Satan because he is a spirit being, but we see the results of his destructive works all around us—killings, mass shootings, addictions that destroy people's potential, broken homes and destroyed families, divisiveness and confusion, hatred, jealousy, greed, and lies. All these are contrary to the workings of God's Spirit, and they originate from hell. We are locked in a real battle with Satan and his demonic agents, so we have to pray continually.

The Bible reminds us of the reality of this warfare in Ephesians.

> Finally, be strong in the Lord and in His mighty power. Put on the full armor of God so that you can take your stand against the devil's schemes. For our struggle is not against flesh and blood, but against the rulers, against the authorities, against the powers of this dark world and against the spiritual forces of evil in the heavenly realms. Therefore, put on the full armor of God so that when the day of evil comes, you may be able to stand your ground and after you have done everything to stand. (Ephesians 6:10–13 NIV)

In other words, if you don't fortify yourself proactively, you can fall to pieces when the enemy attacks. Soldiers constantly prepare themselves for battle even when there is no battle looming on the horizon. This readies them for when an enemy does mount an unexpected attack. They are always in a state of preparedness even in times of peace! This applies to spiritual warfare as well. We must proactively put on the full armor of God so we can stand and not fall on the day of evil. Prayer is one of our most effective weapons of fortification against the enemy. This is underscored in the same sixth chapter of Ephesians. "And pray in the Spirit on all occasions with all kinds of prayers and requests. With this in mind, be alert and always keep on praying for all the Lord's people" (Ephesians 6:18 NIV). Three times in this single verse there is an emphasis on prayer!

> If you don't fortify yourself proactively, you can fall to pieces when the enemy attacks.

So how real is spiritual warfare? Peter helps us with an answer. "Stay alert! Watch out for your great enemy, the devil. He prowls around like a roaring lion looking for someone to devour" (1 Peter 5:8 NLT). I often joke that Satan is always hungry and constantly looking for breakfast, lunch, and dinner—and he wouldn't mind some dessert after the main course! So let's be alert so we do not end up on Satan's plate to be devoured.

There is far more to life than we see with our physical eyes. The invisible spiritual world is as real as the physical world in which we live. Things that happen on earth have a spiritual correlation in the heavenly realms. This is attested to by the experience of the prophet Daniel. Daniel's prayer was blocked by the prince of Persia for three weeks because of spiritual warfare in the heavenlies. That prince of Persia was a demonic spirit. When the demonic resistance was finally broken, this is what the angel told Daniel:

> Do not be afraid, Daniel, since the first day that you set your mind to gain understanding and to humble yourself before your God, your words were heard, and I have come in response to them. But the Prince of the Persian Kingdom resisted me for twenty-one days. Then Michael, one of the chief angels, came to help me, because I was detained there with the King of Persia. (Daniel 10:12–13 NIV)

The truth is sometimes we may be waiting on God for some answers, and it seems to take forever. The reason could be demonic opposition. Satan does not give up easily, but if we persist, we will receive our answers because God has the power to send reinforcements from heaven just as He did for Daniel.

That is why Jesus tells us to always pray and not give up (Luke 18:1 NIV). Our objective should always be to *pray until something happens* (PUSH). If we pray and do not give up, something is bound to happen sooner or later because God does answer prayer. Sometimes God may say yes almost immediately. Sometimes He may say no. Other times

He may say yes, but demonic opposition can cause a delay in the manifestation of the answer. The forces of opposition are real, but our victory is assured! Scripture reminds us, "Having disarmed the powers and authorities, he (Jesus) made a public spectacle of them, triumphing over them by the cross (Colossians 2:15 NIV). That is why the Bible describes us as being more than conquerors. God's children are not destitute people. We fight from a position of victory, not defeat. The enemy is already disarmed, and our victory has been secured through our Lord and Savior Jesus Christ.

The assurances in Psalm 91 should bring peace to our hearts. The psalmist declares,

> If you make the Most High your dwelling—even the Lord who is my refuge—Then no harm will befall you, no disaster will come near your tent. For He will command His angels concerning you to guard you in all your ways. They will lift you up in their hands so that you will not strike your foot against a stone. You will tread upon the lion and the adder; you will trample the great lion and the serpent. Because he loves me, says the Lord, I will rescue him. I will protect him, for he acknowledges my name. (Psalm 91:9–14 NIV)

He who lives in you is greater than he that lives in the world. Satanic attacks are bound to come, but your responsibility is to put on the whole armor of God so you can stand when the day of evil comes.

Several years ago, I was on a plane from Geneva to London in transit to the United States. I was reading a book when suddenly the Holy Spirit alerted me to some developments that were ahead of me. He alerted me to a particular way in which the enemy was operating in our church. I was stunned and puzzled because the situation became immediately clear to me. Frankly, I did not know how to solve it. I decided to pray intensively about it. It was such a sensitive situation that I did not even feel comfortable involving others in the prayer. It was a very uncomfortable and potentially destructive thing if left to fester.

About three years after that revelation from the Holy Spirit, a friend of mine flew into town so we could spend a couple of days in prayer. On the way home from the airport, he told me the exact thing I had heard on the plane three years earlier! It was quite unnerving. At great cost and with much pain, I made a bold move and dealt with the situation. If I had waited any longer and not dealt with it, the consequences would have been much more costly. In fact, the moment I took that step, the door opened for the fulfillment of a request we had been praying about. The Lord blessed the church with a piece of land in a very strategic location. The hindrance had been dealt with. The demonic stronghold was broken.

We must understand that we are engaged in a nonphysical conflict. People are not the enemy, but Satan uses people as instruments just like God uses people to accomplish His purposes. Satan can take people captive to do his will when their hearts are unguarded. We must have a strong spirit of discernment at all times! Sometimes, for no apparent reason, people may change their attitude toward you or even rise up against you. It can happen on the job or even in the church, and you are left wondering, *What in the world is going on?* We cannot be *ignorant* about the reality of spiritual warfare. All that glitters is not gold. We must discern the spirit behind the actions of people. Judas was described as a devil even though he functioned as the treasurer on Jesus's ministry team. The words of Jesus in John 6 must serve as an eye-opener for us. "Have I not chosen you, the Twelve? Yet one of you is a devil!" (He meant Judas, the son of Simon Iscariot, who was later to betray Him. (John 6:70 NIV). If Satan was able to enter the heart of one of the twelve disciples, then we must be cognizant of the fact that he can take anyone captive to do his will!

It is Satan who incites people to steal, kill, and destroy, so don't fight people; otherwise, you will destroy many valuable relationships around you. Fight Satan, the instigator. Fight Satan with prayer. Fight the powers behind the scenes. That is why Jesus said to his closest ally, Peter, "Get behind me, Satan! You are a stumbling block to me; you do not have in mind the concerns of God, but merely human concerns" (Matthew 16:23 NIV). This happened when Peter took Jesus aside and rebuked Him for talking to them about His impending death and resurrection. Peter wanted to dissuade Jesus from undertaking the assignment which His Father had sent Him to accomplish on earth. Jesus discerned that Satan was the instigator behind the words of Peter. Hence the direct rebuke of Satan. Jesus did not rebuke Peter; he rebuked Satan.

The spiritual warfare Satan was waging through Peter was not yet over. Jesus also said to Peter in Luke 22, "Simon, Simon, Satan has asked to sift all of you as wheat. But I have prayed for you, Simon, that your faith may not fail. And when you have turned back, strengthen your brothers" (Luke 22:31–32 NIV). Satan was out to derail Peter's assigned destiny. Jesus saw that in the spirit realm and placed a covering of prayer over Peter and His disciples.

> Learn to pray a covering over your life, children, spouse, family, marriage, health, destiny, relationships, job, business, finances, ministry, and church.

Pray without ceasing because prayer will quench all the fiery darts of Satan and his demonic agents! Learn to pray a covering over your life, children, spouse, family, marriage, health, destiny, relationships, job, business, finances, ministry, and church. Prayer is an effective weapon against satanic attacks, so pray without ceasing!

Second, God Moves When We Pray

The second reason we should pray without ceasing is because God moves when we pray. For reasons that can never be adequately explained, God depends on our prayers to get His work done and to bless His people. The authority we have through prayer is mind-boggling. God is looking for prayer warriors who will cry out on behalf of His people and plead for them!

The prophet Joel speaks to this.

Let the priests who minister before the LORD, weep between the temple porch and altar. Let them say, "spare your people O LORD. Do not make your inheritance an object of scorn, a byword among the nations. Why should they say among the peoples, where is their God?" (Joel 2:17 NIV)

The prophet Ezekiel also reminds us of the difference that one praying person can make before God.

I looked for someone among them who would build up the wall and stand before me in the gap on behalf of the land so that I would not have to destroy it, but I found no one. (Ezekiel 22:30 NIV)

> God was looking for one intercessor ... but He found none.

God was looking for one intercessor whose prayers would have stayed His hand from bringing judgment on the land, but He found none. I am convinced that Satan trembles when he sees one righteous person on his or her knees because he knows that the prayer of a righteous person is powerful and effective. One praying person can change the destiny of another human being, a family, a nation, or a church. God is looking for prayer warriors who will help facilitate His kingdom agenda on this earth.

One of the most insightful statements about the power of prayer was made by God Himself to King Solomon at the dedication of the opulent temple in Jerusalem. God said to Solomon,

When I shut up the heavens so that there is no rain, or command locusts to devour the land or send a plague among my people, if my people, who are called by my name, will humble themselves and pray and seek my face and turn from their wicked ways, then I will hear

from heaven, and I will forgive their sin and will heal
their land. (2 Chronicles 7:13–14 NIV)

This assurance from God gives us insight into how prayer paves the
way for God to act graciously and mercifully even when His deepest
anger has been aroused by sin. Prayer and repentance have the power
to cause astonishing things to happen that cannot be accomplished any
other way!

We can't explain it all, but the God who created the vast universe
and controls all things has given us the privilege and authority to pray
so He will move to get His work done and bless His people. Prayer is
a divinely bestowed power and privilege that unnerves the devil, and
that is why he stops at nothing to keep God's children from spending
time on their knees. Nothing scares Satan more than a righteous heart
and knees bent before the throne of God. You will have to fight off
some discouraging thoughts when it is time to pray. "You are too tired
to pray. You don't really need to pray. Your prayers make no difference.
God will not hear you. It's OK if you don't show up for that prayer
meeting; not many will be there anyway. Your needs have been met,
so what's the point in praying any further?" You might be tempted to
stay at home to watch TV and eat some ice cream instead of going to
church and joining a prayer meeting or turning off the TV and spending
time on your knees before God.

Prayer puts us in a position to experience the blessings of God. The
Bible tells us in Ephesians 1:3, "Praise be to the God and Father of our
Lord Jesus Christ, who has blessed us in the heavenly realms with every
spiritual blessing in Christ." (NIV). This means we have already been
blessed with all conceivable blessings in the heavenly realms. Scripture
also assures us that God shall supply all our needs according to His
glorious riches in Christ Jesus (Philippians 4:19 NIV). The problem
is we live on earth so those blessings in the heavenly realms are of no
good to us if we cannot experience them in the earthly realm! Our
prayers have the power to cause those heavenly blessings to be released
to affect our situations on earth! Prayer is what "moves" the hand of
God to release those blessings from the spiritual realm in Christ to the

earthly realm, where His children live and need those blessings. Prayer positions us to receive from God.

The power of prayer is a mystery you and I can never fully understand. We simply have to accept it by faith and use it. The biblical injunction is that God expects us to pray for His will to be accomplished on earth. The prophet Isaiah records these words in connection with prayer:

> I have posted watchmen on your walls, O Jerusalem, they will never be silent day and night. You who call upon the LORD, give yourselves no rest. And give Him no rest till He establishes Jerusalem and makes her the praise of the earth. (Isaiah 62:6–7 NIV)

We are to call upon the Lord unceasingly until that which He has purposed to do for us is accomplished. We are to give ourselves no rest in prayer and to give God no rest in reminding Him to move on our behalf.

God wants us to approach the throne of grace with boldness so we can receive mercy and grace to help us in our time of need (Hebrews 4:16 NKJV).

So pray until that door is opened. Pray until that legal case is settled. Pray until that bondage is broken. Pray until that healing appears. Pray until that home is restored. Pray until that husband or wife lives up to godly expectations. Pray until that blessing is released. Pray until God moves in His church. Pray until revival breaks out. Pray because Jesus will answer! Pray because our Lord and Savior Jesus Christ modeled prayer Himself.

CHAPTER 18

THE PRAYER LIFE OF JESUS

PERHAPS NOTHING UNDERSCORES THE IMPORTANCE of prayer more than the fact that Jesus, the Son of God, was a man of prayer. In fact, the Bible tells us that Jesus is currently seated at the right hand of God interceding for us. Jesus is still praying in heaven for us. After His earthly life prayer was over, Jesus assumed a new prayer life in heaven! This is a mystery we can never fully understand!

This should wake us up to the necessity of prayer. Scripture tells us that Jesus was often in prayer. He prayed with intensity. Prayer was an integral part of who Jesus was and what He did. We often see Jesus slipping away from the crowd to spend time in prayer. The Gospel of Luke is particularly helpful in highlighting the prayer life of Jesus.

Jesus Prays at His Baptism

At the baptism of Jesus, the heavens opened and the Spirit of God descended upon Jesus as He was praying.

> When all the people were being baptized, Jesus was baptized too. And as He was praying, heaven was opened, and the Holy Spirit descended on Him in

bodily form like a dove. And a voice came from heaven: "You are my beloved Son, whom I love; with you I am well pleased." (Luke 3:21–22 NIV)

It is significant that Jesus did not just get baptized and walk away. He saw the significance of communing with His Father at that crucial event in His life. I believe Jesus was letting the Father know that He had humbled Himself and been obedient to fulfill all righteousness. God was pleased, and He validated Jesus by sending the Holy Spirit to descend on Him in the form of a dove and speaking directly from heaven to endorse Jesus as His beloved Son. This was a public prayer that drew a public response from heaven. It is significant that Jesus invited the presence of His Father into His baptism through prayer. The heavenly validation came as Jesus was praying. Nothing should be done outside of communing with our heavenly Father. We are to pray without ceasing!

Jesus Prays before Choosing the Twelve

Another interesting example of Jesus in prayer is found in Luke 6. Here the record indicates that Jesus spent an entire night in prayer prior to choosing His twelve disciples. At this point, Jesus had many followers, and He had to select twelve to be designated as apostles. Jesus bathed the selection of His ministry team in prayer. He separated Himself from the busyness of ministry and prayed all night long! Luke writes,

One of those days Jesus went out to a mountainside to pray, and spent the night praying to God. When morning came, He called His disciples to Him and chose twelve of them, whom He also designated as apostles. (Luke 6:12–13 NIV)

The importance of this prayer cannot be glossed over. Jesus selected His twelve disciples after a long and intensive time of prayer, which lasted all night long! He knew the important role the twelve were going to play so He sought guidance from His Father to select the right individuals.

I wonder how many terrible outcomes we have reaped simply because we rushed and appointed people into positions without seeking God about those choices! How many marriages should never have been entered into because no divine approval was sought through prayer? How many business partnerships have been entered outside God's will? How many career choices have been made without divine input? The truth is there are many crucial decisions we make without seeking divine input. The result is often one of tears, regret, and chaos. Prayer should be a necessary thing in any decision we make. Prayer would open us up to divine wisdom, guidance, and input. We must constantly seek divine guidance through prayer.

> Prayer should be a necessary thing in any decision we make. Prayer would open us up to divine wisdom, guidance, and input.

It is interesting that when Solomon was given the opportunity to ask God for anything he wanted, he asked for wisdom to govern God's people. He asked God for the ability to distinguish between right and wrong (1 Kings 3:9 NIV). That is the value of seeking God in prayer prior to making crucial decisions. Prayer opens us up to divine guidance to help us distinguish what is right from that which is wrong. It helps us distinguish what might be lawful but not necessarily expedient from that which is truly expedient. Proverbs tells us that there is a way that seems right to a man, but in the end, it leads to death (Proverbs 14:12 NIV). There are many death traps in life. Prayer helps to expose them so that we can avoid them.

It is also important to note that after Jesus had come down from His all-night prayer time, Luke records that many came to Him and were healed. This is worth digesting.

> He went down with them and stood on a level place. A large crowd of His disciples were there and a great number of people from all over Judea, from Jerusalem and from the coastal region around Tyre and Sidon, who came to hear Him and to be healed of their diseases. Those troubled by impure spirits were cured, and the people all tried to touch Him, because power was coming from Him and healing them all. (Luke 6:17–19 NIV)

The people saw that power was exuding from Jesus to cure their diseases and to drive out impure spirits, so they all tried to touch Him. It is evident that the all-night prayer Jesus had on the mountain clothed Him in the power of God's Spirit to minister to the crowd. If we are to experience the manifest power of God to set people free from illnesses and demonic oppression, then we must of necessity spend extensive time in prayer as Jesus did.

Jesus Prays regarding His Ministry Itinerary

Mark also tells a story that seems to indicate that Jesus planned His ministry activities and itinerary after much prayer. Mark writes this account:

> Very early in the morning, while it was still dark, Jesus got up, left the house and went off to a solitary place where He prayed. Simon and His companions went to look for Him, and when they found Him, they exclaimed: "everyone is looking for you!" Jesus replied, "Let us go somewhere else—to the nearby villages—so I can preach there also. That is why I have come." So He traveled throughout Galilee, preaching in their synagogues and driving out demons. (Mark 1:35–39 NIV)

It appears that Jesus got a sense of direction for where to minister after He had spent the early morning in solitary prayer. Peter was expecting Jesus to minister to the waiting crowd, but Jesus gave him a completely new plan, "Let us go somewhere else … so I can preach there also" (v. 38 NIV).

The Bible declares, "The LORD directs the steps of the godly. He delights in every detail of their lives (Psalm 37:23 NLT). He also assures us, "I will guide you along the best pathway for your life. I will advise you and watch over you" (Psalm 32:8 NLT). Prayer should undergird every course of action we pursue. Prayer helps us to receive instructions from God concerning all our activities. God takes pleasure in directing His children to discover His plans for them. I once heard someone make a statement the Lord dropped in his heart when he was wondering about a new direction God had thrust upon him. "It is not up to you to determine your destiny; it is up to you to discover it." I believe prayer helps us discover God's destiny for our lives because, as David says in Psalm 139, "Your eyes saw my unformed body; all the days ordained for me were written in your book before one of them came to be" (Psalm 139:16 NIV). Prayer will help us discover what God has ordained for us during our days on earth.

Jesus Prays before Feeding the Five Thousand

Another fascinating example of Jesus in prayer is seen during the feeding of the five thousand. Luke tells us that after teaching the multitudes about the kingdom of God and healing the sick, the disciples urged Jesus to send the crowd away to the surrounding villages so they could buy some food and secure some lodging since Jesus had been ministering to them in a remote location. But Jesus simply replied, "You give them something to eat" (Luke 9:13 NIV). The disciples responded that it was an impossible task because all they had on hand were five loaves of bread and two fish. Luke records these words:

> (About five thousand men were there.) But He said to His disciples, "Have them sit down in groups of about fifty." The disciples did so and everyone sat down. Taking the five loaves and the two fish and looking up

to heaven, He gave thanks and broke them. Then He gave them to the disciples to distribute to the people. They all ate and were satisfied, and the disciples picked up twelve basketfuls of broken pieces that were left over. (Luke 9:14–17 NIV)

The fascinating thing about this miracle is that John tells us in his account of this story (John 6:6 NIV) that Jesus knew what He was going to do even before He asked the disciples to find some food for the hungry crowd. So what was the essence of Jesus offering the thanksgiving prayer? I believe that Jesus prayed a prayer of gratitude because He knew that His heavenly Father had already made provision for the need at hand! His prayer was simply linking the resources of heaven with the need He and His disciples were encountering on earth. It was a rather short prayer of faith and gratitude for God's provision. I believe there are times when our faith in God's ability to provide should simply cause us to offer prayers of thanksgiving knowing that we have already been blessed with all spiritual blessings in the heavenly realms and that God has promised to supply all our needs according to His riches in glory by Christ Jesus. A prayer of gratitude brings joy to our Father's heart because it underscores our faith in His goodness, faithfulness, and ability to take care of us!

Mark's account of Jesus's time in prayer after feeding the five thousand gives us another insight into the power of prayer. Mark tells us,

After leaving them, He went up on a mountainside to pray. Later that night, the boat was in the middle of the lake, and He was alone on the land. He saw the disciples straining at the oars, because the wind was against them. Shortly before dawn, He went out to them, walking on the lake ... They cried out because they all saw Him and were terrified. Immediately He spoke to them and said, "Take courage! It is I. Don't be afraid." Then He climbed into the boat with them and

the wind died down. They were completely amazed.
(Mark 6:46–51 NIV)

A wonderful insight from Mark's account is the fact that Jesus saw the dire situation of the disciples while He was in prayer on the land and the disciples were in the boat on the lake. When we spend time in prayer, God will cause us to see distressing situations that need our attention and intervention. He can reveal things to us and move us to act when we spend time in His presence. Jesus reached out to save the disciples out of their calamity because it was revealed to Him in prayer.

Jesus Prays Alone

It is also interesting to note that Jesus went off to the mountain to spend some time in solitary prayer right after this! Mark's account tells us, "Immediately, Jesus made His disciples get into the boat ahead of Him to Bethsaida, while He dismissed the crowd. After leaving them, He went up on a mountainside to pray" (Mark 6:46 NIV).

> After this wonderful miracle, Jesus ... went off on a prayer retreat!

After this wonderful miracle, Jesus did not take a victory lap by relaxing and savoring the moment with His disciples. He went off on a prayer retreat! What a powerful lesson! Oftentimes, our tendency is to relax and throw a party after God has blessed us with a very successful outcome. But the truth is those are the very moments the enemy could take us unawares and attack! Taking a cue from Jesus, times of great accomplishments should be followed by times of prayer. We should pray to thank God for the grace bestowed. We should ask God to protect the gains accomplished. We should pray to be bestowed with even greater successes. We should pray to protect what is ahead. We should pray that we would continue in humility and not be puffed up with pride because of what we have just accomplished! We should pray for God to use us in an even greater dimension. We should pray without ceasing!

Jesus Prays at His Transfiguration

Another arresting moment of Jesus in prayer is found during His transfiguration on the mountain. Here we see Jesus modeling His prayer life right before His disciples. Jesus had times of solitary prayer, but He also taught and allowed the disciples to see Him in prayer. This is what transpired from Luke's account:

> Jesus ... took Peter, John, and James with Him and went up onto a mountain to pray. As He was praying, the appearance of His face changed, and His clothes became as bright as lightning. Two men, Moses and Elijah, appeared in glorious splendor, talking with Jesus. They spoke about His departure, which He was about to bring to fulfillment in Jerusalem. Peter and His companions were very sleepy, but when they became fully awake, they saw His glory and the two men standing with Him. As the men were leaving Jesus, Peter said to Him, "Master, it is good for us to be here. Let us put up three shelters—one for you, one for Moses and one for Elijah" ... While he was speaking, a cloud appeared and covered them, and they were afraid as they entered the cloud. A voice came from the cloud saying, "This is my Son whom I have chosen; listen to Him." (Luke 9:28–35 NIV)

There are some interesting lessons to glean from this particular prayer. First, Moses and Elijah appeared to Jesus during His time of prayer to discuss His impending departure from the earth. This tells us that it appears the great cloud of witnesses in heaven is privy to the responsibilities God has given us on earth, and our intensive times of prayer can cause them to "get in" on what we have been assigned to do. The faithful departed patriarchs of our faith are rooting for us to finish our assignments well.

Second, the account tells us that Jesus's appearance was transformed, and His clothes became as radiant as lightning. This is a reminder that there is a deep spiritual transformation and radiance that engulfs us when we enter the presence of our heavenly Father in prayer. This is buttressed by the fact that Moses also experienced a transformed appearance when he spent time on Mount Sinai to receive the Ten Commandments from the Lord. The Bible says,

> When Moses came down from Mount Sinai with the two tablets of the covenant law in his hands, he was not aware that his face was radiant because he had spoken with the LORD. When Aaron and all the Israelites saw Moses, his face was radiant, and they were afraid to come near him. (Exodus 34:29–30 NIV)

There is obviously a deep spiritual radiance that glows from us when we spend time in the presence of God. Prayer causes us to glow with divine radiance. Our intensive times of prayer would cause people to see the presence of God over us. We experience transformation when we spend time in intensive prayer before the throne of God. That transformation is an attestation that we have been with the Lord. It causes us to walk in favor before God and before people.

Third, the account of the transfiguration also tells us that God validated Jesus by declaring, "This is my Son whom I have chosen; listen to Him" (Luke 9:35 NIV). So prayer is never an exercise in futility. Prayer is hard work, but it yields the validation of God on our lives and causes us to glow with the very presence of God. We must pray continually and intensively. Jesus spent extensive time in prayer and so should we, especially those who have spiritual oversight in God's kingdom. We must intentionally model prayer before those who have been entrusted into our spiritual care—our family and those we influence spiritually in God's church.

Jesus Prays in the Garden

The life of Jesus is an amazing example of a life clothed in prayer. Perhaps the most arresting example of Jesus in prayer is what happened in the Garden of Gethsemane prior to His arrest and subsequent crucifixion.

Jesus needed strength to fulfill His mission. He was struggling in His flesh. Intensive prayer is what saw Him through His struggles. Luke tells us,

> Jesus went out as usual to the Mount of Olives, and His disciples followed Him. On reaching the place, He said to them, "pray that you will not fall into temptation." He withdrew about a stone's throw beyond them, knelt down and prayed, "Father, if you are willing, take this cup from me; yet not my will, but yours be done." An angel from heaven appeared to Him and strengthened Him. And being in anguish, He prayed more earnestly, and His sweat was like drops of blood falling to the ground. When He rose from prayer and went back to His disciples, He found them asleep, exhausted from sorrow. "Why are you sleeping?" He asked them, "Get up and pray so that you will not fall into temptation." (Luke 22:39–46 NLT)

There is so much to glean from this account of Jesus in prayer. First, we see that *Jesus seemed to have a favorite place of prayer*—the Mount of Olives—because Luke tells us that Jesus went there as usual. While we must continually pray no matter where we are, it is also helpful to have a "prayer closet" where we can quietly retreat to commune with God. A familiar place for regular prayer gives us the exciting anticipation that we are going to meet with God. It gives us a sense of joy and fulfillment to know that God is there with us in that sacred place. Personally, my study at home is my sacred place of prayer. The family knows that I am usually in prayer, studying, or meditating when I am down there.

I will always remember when my son came one day looking for me in the basement. He was about six years old at the time. He found me on my face on the floor in prayer. Without saying a word, he quietly took the same posture and stayed there with me for quite a while. I hugged him after I got up and thanked him for joining me in prayer. I wonder what joy my heavenly Father must have felt, seeing my son taking after his earthly father in a prayer posture!

Second, *Jesus withdrew from the disciples*, went a bit further by Himself, and called upon the Father in prayer. This tells us that in our deepest times of need, as important as it is to have others supporting us in prayer, it is critical that we carry our own prayer burden with deep passion. No human being can petition God about your situation better than you.

Third, *God sent an angel to strengthen Jesus*. Luke says, "An angel from heaven appeared to him and strengthened him. And being in anguish, he prayed more earnestly, and his sweat was like drops of blood falling to the ground." Luke 22:43-44NIV). Just picture that! The spiritual struggle was so intense that His tiny blood vessels started to burst under the pressure and intensity of prayer. Jesus prayed in anguish. The truth is: Trials and temptations make us weak and vulnerable. Jesus desired to do the Father's will, but His flesh was under attack from Satan. His human will struggled against the divine will, but God the Father sent an angel to strengthen Him to persevere in the divine will.

Prayer brings us angelic assistance to help us overcome the weakness of our flesh so that we don't give in to temptation. That is why Jesus told the disciples to get up and pray so they would not fall into temptation because even though the spirit may be willing, the weakness of the flesh can cause us to succumb to its dictates. We must pray without ceasing so we do not fall into temptation. Prayer kept Jesus on track, and prayer will keep us on track. When we call upon God in our time of distress, He will answer our cry. He will uphold us. He can even send an angel to strengthen us!

> Prayer brings us angelic assistance to help us overcome the weakness of our flesh so that we don't give in to temptation.

Jesus Prays the Lord's Prayer

So did the extensive prayer life of Jesus have any effect on His disciples? The answer is yes because scripture tells us that the disciples were so affected that they asked Jesus to teach them to pray. They wanted to emulate the Master. The Bible tells us,

> One day Jesus was praying in a certain place. When He finished, one of His disciples said to Him, "Lord, teach us to pray, just as John taught his disciples."
> He said to them, "When you pray, say:
> 'Our Father in heaven,
> Hallowed be your name.
> Your Kingdom come.
> Your will be done
> On earth as it is in heaven.
> Give us each day our daily bread.
> And forgive us our sins,
> For we also forgive everyone who sins against us.
> And lead us not into temptation.'"
> (Luke 11:2–4 NIV)

Jesus answered the desire of the disciples by teaching them the Lord's Prayer as a model guide in praying. It is possible that the disciples had requested to be taught to pray because they had observed the enormous time Jesus had been spending in prayer and realized they needed to be like Him. There seems to be a connection between their request to be taught to pray and the admirable prayer life of Jesus. They had seen demons subdued in the presence of Jesus. They had seen the blind regain sight. They had seen lepers healed and the lame resume walking. They had seen the power of His words. They had seen the boldness and wisdom with which Jesus had withstood the hypocritical religious leaders. Possibly they had surmised that all this was happening because of Jesus's life of intense prayer. They wanted to pray like Jesus. May those under our care and leadership be so encouraged by our personal prayer lives that they would desire to pray just like us!

I still recall our seminary class on the theology of prayer. I remember my summary notes.

> Jesus prayed with great regularity in His time on earth. Jesus varied His prayer times—morning, noon, and night. Jesus varied the length of His prayers. Jesus sought the guidance of the Father in prayer at key points in His ministry. Jesus knew the power of prayer. Hence, the vast amounts of time He spent in prayer. Jesus sought the help of His Father in prayer to be able to do the Father's will. The prayer life of Jesus so impacted the lives of His disciples that they asked Him to teach them to pray.

If Jesus the Son of God was so dependent on prayer, then I must do likewise. The prayer life of Jesus along with the prayer life of one of my mentors encouraged me greatly to become dependent on prayer. My wife would probably not be alive today but for the power of prayer. I would probably not be alive today but for the power of prayer. Our church would definitely not have survived all the demonic resistance we have experienced to date but for the power of prayer. We must pray without ceasing. God hears and answers when we cry out to Him in prayer.

CHAPTER 19

JESUS WANTS US TO PRAY AUDACIOUSLY

SEVERAL YEARS AGO, MY NEIGHBOR stopped by to help me winterize our home. It was a rather cold night so I made him a cup of tea. My son, who was just seven years old, came and whispered in my ear, "Daddy, ask him if he wants some croissants too."

I said to my son, "You ask him yourself." He did, so we added some croissants to the tea.

When my wife came home, I narrated the story to her. She laughed and said, "Well, your son is just like you. He will give the shirt off his back to a total stranger—like father, like son."

At that moment, many thoughts started flooding my mind. I recalled the numerous times I had reached out to help others, sometimes at great sacrifices to the family, causing my wife to panic.

I recalled the time I borrowed money from my retirement account to help prevent a foreclosure on a friend's home. I recalled selling off some stocks to help a family out of a financial crisis. I recalled the time when I loaned out $7,000 to a family that was in a financial crisis. They only paid back $2,000. We never got the rest back. I also recalled the morning a friend called from out of town asking desperately for help with his son's tuition. This was a good friend who had been kind to me in the past. I loaned him some money with the promise that it would be repaid back after he had cashed a soon-to-mature certificate of deposit. When the time came for repayment, he sent me less than half of the money and said he had decided to reinvest his money. After a few weeks, I called and told him not to worry about the rest of the money. I felt it was better to write it off than dwell on it. So my wife was right in remarking that I will give the shirt off my back to a total stranger!

As I reflected over those things, I said to myself, "But God gave us more than the shirt on His back!" The Bible tells us, "For God so loved the world that He gave us His only Son that whoever believes in Him should not die but have everlasting life" (John 3:16 NKJV).

The love God has for His children is far beyond anything we can imagine. The Bible assures us, "For the sake of His great name, the Lord will not reject His people; because the Lord was pleased to make you His own" (1 Samuel 12:22 NIV). Think about that! God has chosen you, and He will never reject you. Scripture also says in Romans 8:32 (NIV), "He who did not spare His own Son, but gave Him up for us all—how will He not also, along with Him graciously give us all things?" Not just some things but all things! We serve a giving and gracious God who is rich enough to give us all things because He owns everything! In fact, the Bible says in Job 41:11 (NIV), "Who has a claim against me that I must pay? Everything under heaven belongs to me."

Based upon the vastness of His power and riches, God throws us an open invitation in John 15:7 (NIV). "If you remain in me and my words remain in you, ask whatever you wish. And it will be done for you."

God is daring us to be audacious in the things we ask of Him. He is saying to us, "No matter how wide you open your mouth, no matter how huge your request, I have the resources to do it!"

Ask for whatever you wish! This means there is no limit to what God expects us to ask from Him; nor is there a limit on what He is prepared to do for us as long as our desires are embedded in His plans for us! Ask for whatever you want Him to do in accordance with His will, and it will be done for you!

In fact, the Bible tells us in Jeremiah 33:3 (NKJV), "Call to Me, and I will answer you, and show you great and mighty things which you do not know." God wants to show us great and mighty things beyond what we know—great things that we should be asking Him to do! I believe that God wants to do far more than we can ever ask of Him. There are great things He wants us to pursue for His glory. Scripture reminds us that God "is able to do exceedingly abundantly above all that we can ever ask or think according to His power that is at work in us" (Ephesians 3:20 NKJV). The promises of God are mind-boggling! Paul tells us, "No eye has seen, no ear has heard and no mind has imagined what God has prepared for those who love Him" (1 Corinthians 2:9 NIV). And then in Psalm 81:10 (NIV), the Bible says, "I am the LORD your God who brought you out of the land of Egypt; open your mouth wide and I will fill it."

God is daring us to be audacious in the things we ask of Him. He is saying to us, "No matter how wide you open your mouth, no matter how huge your request, I have the resources to do it!" So clearly, God expects us not to be timid when we come asking! God expects us to ask with boldness and audacity!

God Wants Us to Ask with Audacity

God expects us to pray audaciously. He expects us to ask audaciously and believe Him to grant our requests. As mentioned earlier, the word *audacious* means bold, daring, and fearless. So audacious prayers are bold, daring, and fearless prayers. I believe that until we have the spiritual courage to pray audacious prayers, we will never undertake audacious things for the kingdom of God because an audacious vision must be backed by audacious prayers.

Several years ago, I read a book called *Built to Last*. In it, the authors

201

describe numerous factors they believe are responsible for the success of some of the world's most outstanding corporations. One of the things they mentioned was that the most successful corporations often pursued what they termed "Big Hairy Audacious Goals" (BHAGs).

An audacious goal is simply one that is so bold and fearless that it even seems risky to pursue it. An example of such a goal was when President J. F. Kennedy said in 1961 that America must land a man on the moon and bring him back to the earth before the decade of the 1960s was over. This was an audacious goal. Most scientists believed it only had a 50 percent chance of success but because the president believed in that vision, the United States Congress funded it, and in 1969 Neil Armstrong became the first man to walk on the moon and return safely to the earth. That was a very audacious goal. It was bold and fearless.

> What Goliath
> are you facing?

Also, a few years ago, a thirty-four-year-old man named Nik Wallenda walked on a two-inch steel cable for about a quarter of a mile across a portion of the Grand Canyon for twenty-two minutes. He experienced thirty-mile-per-hour winds. The steel cable on which he was walking swayed constantly, and his contact lenses became dusty. He had no safety harness so one slip could send him to a harsh death on the rocks below. But he pressed on. He prayed audibly all through the walk. "Thank You, God, for calming the cable. I love You, Jesus. Father, please calm the winds." He had been dreaming of doing this since he was a teenager, and he did it! A year prior to that, he had also walked successfully across Niagara Falls! Those were audacious feats. Wallenda believed it was all to the glory of God, and God helped him accomplish those audacious dreams. I sincerely believe that God wants us to pray audaciously and undertake audacious things so the world can see the manifestation of His power and glory through His children.

David was audacious when he faced Goliath. He said to him, "I'll strike you down and cut off your head … I will give the carcasses of the Philistine army to the birds and the wild animals" (1 Samuel 17:46

NIV). Goliath was a nine-foot-tall giant with many years of battle experience, but David was only a teenager with no fighting experience against such a formidable opponent. Nonetheless, David was audacious. He was bold and fearless because he knew the Lord was with him.

So what Goliath are you facing? A health Goliath? A Goliath on the job? A financial Goliath? A legal Goliath? A Goliath in your marriage? A Goliath in the form of a son or daughter whose life needs to be turned around? A Goliath in the form of a seemingly impossible dream or vision? Would you be audacious enough to pray and believe God to help you defeat that Goliath? You see, with God, all things are possible!

Jesus Expects Us to Be Audacious

Jesus wants us to ask from the Father with audacity. This is illustrated by a story He told His disciples in one teaching session. Luke's account is as follows:

> Then Jesus said to them, "Suppose you have a friend and you go to him at midnight and say, 'Friend, lend me three loaves of bread; a friend of mine on a journey has come to me, and I have no food to offer him.' And suppose the one inside answers, 'Don't bother me. The door is already locked, and my children are in bed. I can't get up and give you anything.' I tell you, even though he will not get up and give you the bread because of friendship, yet because of your shameless audacity, he will surely get up and give you as much as you need.
>
> So I say to you: Ask and it will be given to you; seek and you will find; knock and the door will be opened to you. For everyone who asks receives; the one who seeks finds; and to the one who knocks, the door will be opened." (Luke 11:5–13 NIV)

Matthew concludes this same story with these words:

> Which of you, if your son asks for bread, will give him a stone? Or if he asks for a fish, will give him a snake? If you, then, though you are evil, know how to give good gifts to your children, how much more will your Father in heaven give good gifts to those who ask Him? (Matthew 7:9–11 NIV)

The language suggests that we should ask and keep asking. Seek and keep seeking. Knock and keep knocking. We should persist in asking shamelessly because we will receive answers to our requests. Jesus is encouraging us to ask from our heavenly Father with audacity!

Three things made the man in the story audacious.

First, *he was bold in his request because he was confident that his friend would not turn him down.* Most good friends can be counted on to help in times of need. True friendships often create a deep bond of loyalty, which gives us the audacity to ask for difficult things. Scripture tells us that there are some friends who are so dependable that they stick closer than brothers (Proverbs 18:24 NKJV). Such friendships undoubtedly can give us the confidence to knock on their doors any time of day.

It is interesting that Jesus actually describes our relationship with Him as one of friendship (John 15:14 NIV). Not only is He our Lord and Savior, but He has also given us the privilege of being His friends. This takes fear out of our relationship with Him and gives us the boldness to approach Him with our needs. Like a true friend, He will always understand our situation.

Second, *the man was audacious in knocking on his friend's door because he was confident his friend had what he needed.* If he was not sure of that, he probably would have gone to someone else. We approach people boldly for help only when we know they are capable of helping us. God created everything, and He owns everything in the world. All the silver and gold belong to Him, and He does whatever He pleases with it. That is why scripture assures us that He is able to do immeasurably more than we can ever ask of Him and that He will supply all our needs according to His riches in glory by Christ Jesus.

Finally, Jesus reminds us that *the man received the bread because of his "shameless audacity."* This is an invitation for us to ask of God with shameless audacity! Jesus underscores the Father's heart to bless us by saying that if we as humans know how to give good gifts to our children, how much more will our Father in heaven give good gifts to those who ask Him?

Another encouragement from Jesus to pray with audacity is seen in Luke 18. Here Jesus tells us to pray and not give up! He encourages us to have audacity of faith when approaching our heavenly Father in prayer. Luke records the story as follows:

> Audacious prayers are persistent in nature and tenacious in faith!

> One day, Jesus told His disciples a story to show that they should always pray and never give up. "There was a judge in a certain city," He said, "who neither feared God nor cared about people. A widow of that city came to him repeatedly, saying, 'Give me justice in this dispute with my enemy.' The judge ignored her for a while, but finally, he said to himself, 'I don't fear God or care about people, but this woman is driving me crazy. I'm going to see that she gets justice, because she is wearing me out with her constant requests!'"

> Then the Lord said, "Learn a lesson from this unjust judge. Even he rendered a just decision in the end. So don't you think God will surely give justice to His chosen people who cry out to Him day and night? Will He keep putting them off? I tell you, He will grant justice to them quickly! But when the Son of Man come returns, how many will he find on earth who have faith?" (Luke 18:1–8 NLT)

Just like the story of the man who went knocking on his friend's door for bread, Jesus is driving home the point that if we are bold enough to ask and believe God for answers, He will surely answer. The woman was not intimidated by the fearsome reputation of the unjust judge. She was a disadvantaged widow who had no lawyer to plead her case before the judge, but she had the audacity to believe that her persistence would pay off, and it did! The odds were against her, but her persistence paid off. Audacious prayers are persistent in nature and tenacious in faith!

CHAPTER 20

SOME AUDACIOUS PRAYERS IN THE BIBLE

THE BIBLE IS REPLETE WITH examples of people who prayed audaciously and received answers! Let's explore a few of them and learn some lessons.

Show Me Your Glory

Moses offered one of the most audacious prayers in the Bible when he asked God to show him His glory. The biblical account says,

> Moses said to the LORD, "You have been telling me, 'Lead these people,' but you have not let me know whom you will send with me. You have said, 'I know you by name and you have found favor with Me.' If you are pleased with me, teach me your ways so I may know you and continue to find favor with you. Remember that this nation is your people."
>
> Then the Lord replied, "My presence will go with you, and I will give you rest."

Then Moses said to Him, "If your presence does not go with us, do not send us up from here. How will anyone know that you are pleased with me and with your people unless you go with us? What else will distinguish me and your people from all the other people on the face of the earth?" And the LORD said to Moses, "I will do the very thing you have asked because I am pleased with you and I know you by name."

Then Moses said, "Now show me your glory."

And the LORD said, "I will cause all my goodness to pass in front of you, and I will proclaim my name, the LORD, in your presence ... But," He said, "you cannot see my face for no one may see me and live." (Exodus 33:12–20 NIV)

Then the LORD came down in the cloud and stood there with him and proclaimed His name, the LORD. And He passed in front of Moses, proclaiming, "The LORD, the LORD, the compassionate and gracious God, slow to anger, abounding in love and faithfulness." (Exodus 34:5–6 NIV)

This is a rather fascinating account. Moses had encountered God in the burning bush. He had seen the amazing miracles of the ten plagues the Lord brought on Egypt. He had seen the parting of the Red Sea and the drowning of the chariots and horses of Pharaoh, but Moses was still hungry for more of God! He wanted to experience not just the continual presence of God but also the glory of God! Moses had become bolder in His relationship with God because he knew he had found favor with God!

It is interesting that when Moses first encountered God in the burning bush, he was afraid to look at God. But with the passing of time, as he walked obediently with God and found favor with Him, Moses became emboldened to ask God to show him His glory!

> When we walk faithfully with God, we will find favor and have the audacity to ask God even for what appears to be the unthinkable!

When we walk faithfully with God, we will find favor and have the audacity to ask God even for what appears to be the unthinkable! May you be so enriched in your faith that you will see the manifest glory of God in unimaginable ways! Be audacious in your hunger to experience God at a deeper level.

Let the Rain Cease!

The prophet Elijah also prayed audaciously and commanded the rain to stop falling, and it ceased for three years. Israel had fallen into idolatry, worshipping the false god Baal. God sent the prophet Elijah to minister to the nation and turn their hearts back to God. Elijah got the attention of the nation through a rather dramatic display of divine power. He boldly declared to King Ahab who had led Israel away from God, "As the LORD, the God of Israel, lives, whom I serve, there will be neither dew nor rain for the next few years except at my word" (1 Kings 17:1 NIV). After three years of drought, God sent Elijah to go back and tell the king that the rain was coming, and it did! Elijah prayed audaciously, and God answered.

The Bible gives us an encouraging reminder that God is ready to answer our own audacious prayers. We are reminded that "the prayer of a righteous person is powerful and effective" (James 5:16 NIV). James tells us further that:

> Elijah was a human being, even as we are. He prayed earnestly that it would not rain, and it did not rain on

the land for three and a half years. Again, he prayed, and the heavens gave rain, and the earth produced its crops. (James 5:17–18 NIV)

The allusion to Elijah's humanity tells us that God is no respecter of persons. Elijah had previously run away from Queen Jezebel out of fear for his life. He had also become so depressed that he actually asked God to take away his life. In spite of all these human failings, God heard Elijah's bold prayers. The lesson here is that God will answer the audacious prayers of any righteous person.

The apostle Paul reminds us that the things in Scripture were written to serve as examples for us (1 Corinthians 10:11 NIV). So just like Elijah, who was as human as we are, the Bible endorses the fact that we can also pray bold and audacious prayers and ask God for impossible things to happen.

So is there something you need to command to *stop* in your life, just as Elijah stopped the rain? Or is there something you need to command to come *into* your life, as Elijah commanded the rain to fall? Is there some rain that needs to fall to end some particular drought in your life? Something to make your life more fertile? You can believe God to answer your big, hairy, audacious prayers! God takes delight in that!

Not Afraid of a Blazing Furnace

King Nebuchadnezzar of Babylon was one of the most powerful kings of the ancient world. Defying his orders meant instant death! The Bible tells us though that three young Hebrew boys had the audacity to defy him because they would rather burn in a fire than disobey the Word of God. The king had made a rather imposing gold statue that measured ninety feet tall and nine feet wide. He set this on a hill in one of the provinces of Babylon. Then the king commanded that everyone was to bow to the statue at the sound of various musical instruments, or they would be thrown into a blazing furnace. The three Jewish young men—Shadrach, Meshach, and Abednego, who were provincial leaders in the kingdom—refused to bow to the gold statue because, as Hebrews, they were cognizant of Yahweh's command not to bow down to or worship any graven image. Their refusal enraged Nebuchadnezzar, who ordered them to be brought before him. His words were straight to the point.

> I will give you one more chance to bow down and worship the statue I have made when you hear the sound of the musical instruments. But if you refuse, you will be thrown immediately into the blazing furnace. And then what god will be able to rescue you from my power? (Daniel 3:15 NLT)

With great audacity of faith, the young men responded to the king,

> O Nebuchadnezzar, we do not need to defend ourselves before you. If we are thrown into the blazing furnace, the God whom we serve is able to save us. He will rescue us from your power, Your Majesty. But even if he doesn't, we want to make it clear to you, Your Majesty, that we will never serve your gods or worship the gold statue you have set up. (Daniel 3:16–18 NLT)

The king was so furious that he gave orders for the furnace to be made seven times hotter than usual, but God rescued them. Even though they were thrown into the fire, they did not lose a single hair on their heads! They simply walked around unharmed in the fire. In fact, the Bible tells us that the heat was so strong that the flames killed the soldiers who threw the three men into the furnace. Seeing the three men unharmed in the fire, the biblical account continues.

> Nebuchadnezzar jumped up in amazement and exclaimed to his advisers, 'Didn't we tie up three men and throw them into the furnace?' 'Yes, Your Majesty, we certainly did,' they replied. Look Nebuchadnezzar shouted. 'I see four men, unbound, walking around in

the fire unharmed! And the fourth looks like a god!'
(Daniel 3:24–25 NLT)

The three men were asked to step out of the fire. They were unscathed, and their bodies did not even smell of smoke!

The conclusion of the story makes risking our lives audaciously for God worth every bit of the effort. The Bible finishes the story this way:

> Then Nebuchadnezzar said, "Praise to the God of Shadrach, Meshach and Abednego! He sent His angel to rescue His servants who trusted in Him. They defied the King's command and were willing to die rather than serve or worship any god except their own God. Therefore, I make this decree: If any people, whatever their race, or nation or language, speak a word against the God of Shadrach, Meshach, and Abednego, they will be torn limb from limb, and their houses will be turned into heaps of rubble. There is no other god who can rescue like this!" Then the King promoted Shadrach, Meshach and Abednego to even higher positions in the province of Babylon. (Daniel 3:28–30 NLT)

Shadrach, Meshach and Abednego believed and declared audaciously that God would rescue them even if they were thrown into the fire—and God did.

Shadrach, Meshach, and Abednego believed and declared audaciously that God would rescue them even if they were thrown into the fire—and God did.

God will not let us down when we take an audacious stand for His name! His promise in Isaiah is "When you walk through the fire of oppression, you will not be burned up; the flames will not consume you" (Isaiah 43:2 NLT). The end of the story brought glory to God. Not only were the three Hebrew men saved, but they were also promoted to higher positions, and God was revered as the "Saving God." If we are willing to pray and believe God for audacious outcomes and dare to put everything on the line for God, He will not disappoint us. He did not disappoint Shadrach, Meshach, and Abednego, and He will stand by us as well!

Would you dare to be audacious for God? Step out audaciously on a mission for God, and watch Him grant you protection in the most unimaginable way! When God puts you on a mission, He stays with you. He will never abandon you! Dare to be audacious for God, and you will see His glory!

You Will Recover All

What would you do if you found everything you owned stripped away by raiders? How would you respond? Would you have the audacity to believe that God can restore it all back to you?

David found himself in just that kind of a situation, and he dared to believe God! During his time in exile when King Saul was feverishly hunting him down to kill and prevent his ascension to the throne, David took refuge at a place called Ziklag in Philistine territory.

One day, David arrived with his men from a trip out of town only to discover that a people called the Amalekites had raided the town in which David and his men lived. They looted the town and burned it to the ground. The worst part was that they carried off the women, children, and everyone else either to be sold off or kept as slaves. It was normal practice in those days. People would attack other nations and carry off whatever they could as loot! That was how they accumulated wealth.

Scripture gives this account:

> When David and his men saw the ruins and realized what had happened to their families, they wept until they could weep no more. David's two wives, Ahinoam from Jezreel and Abigail, the widow of Nabal from Carmel, were among those captured. David was now in

great danger because all his men were very bitter about losing their sons and daughters, and they began to talk about stoning him. But David found strength in the LORD his God … Then David asked the LORD, 'Should I chase after this band of raiders? Will I catch them?' And the LORD told him, 'Yes, go after them. You will surely recover everything that was taken from you!' (1 Samuel 30:1–8 NLT)

With four hundred men out of his group of six hundred, David pursued the raiders. He overtook them and recovered everything. Interestingly, they found the raiders spread out on a field eating, drinking, and enjoying the plunder. David and his men fought hard, defeated them, and recovered everything, including their wives and children. Not a single thing was missing!

There are times in life when we lose just about everything we have. Sometimes we may lose a job, resulting in the loss of much of what we have. Sometimes we fall into hard financial times and lose our cars and even our homes. Some even become homeless because life has taken a very hard turn! Sometimes we lose a loved one—a parent, a child or spouse—and wonder if we will ever recover from it! Sometimes we lose our health and struggle to make it from one day to the next! The truth is life is rather unpredictable.

We never know when adversity may strike, but when it does, we have two options: give up and live in despair perpetually or rise up and find strength in the LORD our God as David did. We can either live in bitterness or have the audacity to believe that our weeping may endure for a night but joy will come forth in the morning. Even though our lost loved one will not come back to life on this earth, God can give us the strength and hope to acknowledge the loss and still see the sufficiency of His grace even in our adversity. Joblessness and financial reversals can leave us in very difficult circumstances, but God is able to reverse our situations and restore our fortunes. The prophet Joel has some comforting words for us. "The LORD says, 'I will give you back what you lost to the swarming locusts, hopping locusts, the stripping locust, and the cutting locusts'" (Joel 2:25 NLT).

It is never easy when we find ourselves stripped of some of the things that make life bearable and enjoyable, but if we dare to believe and pray audaciously, it is not impossible for God to help us to pursue, overtake, and recover all. We must endeavor to find strength in the Lord our God even in the most crushing of adversities. It is important to take time to weep and mourn because we are human, but we must also arise at the end of it all and have the audacity to believe that God is able to reverse our losses and even take us beyond our former situation just as He restored the fortunes of Job.

I Am Tired of Suffering

There was a woman who dared to be audacious in her faith and in her prayer. She is famously known by Christians as "the woman with the issue of blood." This woman had been bleeding for twelve years and had gone from one physician to the next—all to no avail. No specialist could bring her a cure. She had exhausted all possibilities and spent every penny she had looking for that elusive cure. To make matters worse, her condition meant that she lived as an ostracized person because anyone or anything she touched automatically became ceremonially unclean under Jewish religious law. She was a desperate woman who urgently needed relief.

Mark describes her situation as follows:

> She had suffered a great deal under the care of many doctors, and had spent all she had, yet instead of getting better she grew worse. When she heard about Jesus, she came up behind Him in the crowd and touched His

cloak, because she thought, 'If I just touch His clothes, I will be healed.' Immediately her bleeding stopped and she felt in her body that she was freed from her suffering. (Mark 5:26–29 NIV)

Jesus felt the faith of the woman and remarked that someone had touched her out of the crowd in spite of the fact that there were so many people crowding around Him.

He kept looking around the crowd asking, 'Who touched me?' because He felt that power had gone out of Him! Finally, the woman owned up and Jesus said to her, "Daughter, your faith has healed you. Go in peace and be freed from your suffering." (Mark 5:34 NIV

Fear of being rebuked could have kept the woman from receiving her healing, but she found the courage to declare with audacity, "If I touch His clothes, I will be healed" (Mark 5:28 NIV). And she was healed.

The woman was in despair because she had an incurable disease. She was sick and broke, but she had one thing going for her: audacity! She was audacious enough to declare, believe, and receive her healing. The force of her audacity caused power to come out of Jesus and instantly reverse her twelve-year malady! Not only was her physical bleeding stopped, but her financial bleeding of twelve years was stopped as well. She was made whole. Her ostracism also ended!

There are many seemingly incurable situations that we face in life. Sometimes, we might bleed from them for years, but if we do not throw in the towel and if we have the audacity to touch God in our desperation, there is no telling what He will do!

Give Me a Double Portion

The prophet Elisha also prayed one of the most audacious prayers in the Bible. His mentor, Elijah, was about to be taken by God into heaven, and Elisha wanted the power and anointing of Elijah to descend on him as well. He followed Elijah doggedly until Elijah asked him,

> "Tell me, what can I do before I am taken from you?"
>
> "Let me inherit a double portion of your spirit," Elisha replied.
>
> "You have asked a difficult thing," Elijah said, "yet if you see me when I am taken from you, it will be yours—otherwise, it will not." (2 Kings 2:9–10 NIV)

Elisha continued to stick closely to Elijah. The account is quite fascinating.

> As they were walking along, and talking together, suddenly a chariot of fire and horses of fire appeared and separated the two of them, and Elijah went up to heaven in a whirlwind ... Elisha then picked up Elijah's cloak that had fallen from him and went back and stood on the brink of the Jordan. He took the cloak that had fallen from Elijah and struck the water with it. "Where now is the LORD, the God of Elijah?" he asked. When he struck the water, it divided to the right and to the left, and he crossed over. The company of the prophets from Jericho, who were watching, said, "The Spirit of Elijah is resting on Elisha." And they went to meet him and bowed to the ground before him. (2 Kings 2:11–15 NIV)

Elisha's audacious prayers were heard even though Elijah, his mentor, had acknowledged that it was a very difficult request. But God heard him, and Elisha became very anointed in ministry. In fact, the anointing on his life was so strong that even his buried dead bones raised a dead man back to life. The biblical account is rather gripping.

Elisha died and was buried. Now Moabite raiders used to enter the country every spring. Once while some Israelites were burying a man, suddenly they saw a band of raiders; so they threw the man's body into Elisha's tomb. When the body touched Elisha's bones, the man came to life and stood up on his feet. (2 Kings 13:20–21 NIV)

There is an important lesson here. No prayer is too audacious for God to answer if we truly desire to honor His name and accomplish His purposes. Elisha had obviously seen the powerful way in which Elijah's ministry had affected the nation of Israel. He knew how Elijah had commanded the rain to stop. He knew how Elijah had commanded the rain to come back, and it had. He knew that if he himself was going to have any strong impact on the nation, then he needed to be given even more of God's anointing than he saw on Elijah. If our desire is to ask audaciously from God so His purposes will be served, God will surely answer because it is to His glory. God takes delight in answering audacious requests that are meant to bring Him glory.

> No prayer is too audacious for God to answer if we truly desire to honor His name and accomplish His purposes.

This lines up with scripture.

God's purpose in all this was to use the church to display His wisdom in its rich variety to all the unseen rulers and authorities in the heavenly places. This was His eternal plan which He carried out through Christ Jesus our Lord. (Ephesians 3:10–11 NLT)

Audacious feats bring glory to God and cause the powers of darkness to bow in shame at the manifestation of God's power through His children. Be audacious in asking God to use you in extraordinary ways. If your motives are pure, God will answer!

Rectify This Injustice

The Bible tells an interesting story of an audacious request made by five sisters whose father's death had left them in danger of not having an inheritance. Their story is told in Numbers 27.

> The names of the daughters were Mahlah Noah, Hoglah, Milkah, and Tirzah. They came forward and stood before Moses, Eleazar the priest, the leaders and the whole assembly at the entrance to the tent of meeting and said, "Our father died in the wilderness ... Why should our father's name disappear from his clan because he had no son? Give us property among our father's relatives."

> So Moses brought their case before the LORD, and the LORD said to him, "What Zelophehad's daughters are saying is right. You must certainly give them property as an inheritance among their father's relatives and give their father's inheritance to them. "Say to the Israelites, "If a man dies and leaves no son, give his inheritance to his daughter. If he has no daughter, give his inheritance to his brothers. This is to have the force of law for the Israelites as the LORD commanded Moses." (Numbers 27:1–11 NIV)

The daughters of Zelophehad were brave, determined, and wise. According to the extant law of Israel, a man's inheritance could only be passed on to a surviving son. If he had no son, the property was lost to the family forever. But Zelophehad had only daughters and no sons. The family was in danger of having no landed property, which was rather crucial in their agrarian economy. The daughters audaciously approached Moses and made their case for their father's inheritance. God made an exception and changed the law in their favor.

> The daughters audaciously approached Moses and made their case for their father's inheritance. God made an exception and changed the law in their favor.

I often wonder whether we really know, understand, and trust the heart of God. Do we really believe that God will work everything out for our good? Do we really believe that God has our best interest at heart? Do we really believe that God hears and answers our cry? The answer is yes! God will do anything to ensure our well-being.

There are three key things to glean from this audacious request from the daughters of Zelophehad.

First, *our silence in the face of injustice and unfairness can have a detrimental effect on generations to come.* Can you imagine what unborn generations would have lost if the five sisters had not had the audacity to seek redress for their unjust situation? We must be audacious in approaching God on behalf of the underprivileged, and God can cause laws to be changed on their behalf.

Second, *we must be bold in approaching God in any unjust situation we encounter in life because God is ready to hear us and act on our behalf.* God is prepared to change and establish laws if we are bold enough to petition Him! Don't take no for an answer until you have passionately pleaded your case before God!

Third, *have an audacious vision to rectify any form of injustice in society, and God will give you what you need to succeed.* God works through humans. He is waiting for dreamers to approach Him so that He can bring about justice for the voiceless.

I Want to See

What would you do if you had been born blind and reduced to begging for money at the roadside? If you heard of an opportunity to receive your sight, would you be audacious or timid in crying out to be considered?

Bartimaeus was born blind and left to eke out a living by begging for money along the streets of Jericho. One day, sitting by the roadside, he heard a commotion and found through enquiry that Jesus of Nazareth was passing by. Luke tells his story thus:

> He called out, "Jesus, Son of David, have mercy on me!" Those who led the way rebuked him and told him to be quiet, but he shouted all the more, "Son of David, have mercy on me." Jesus stopped and ordered the man to be brought to Him. When he came near, Jesus asked him, "What do you want me to do for you?"
>
> "Lord, I want to see," he replied. Jesus said to him, "Receive your sight; your faith has healed you." Immediately he received his sight and followed Jesus, praising God. When all the people saw it, they also praised God. (Luke 18:38–43 NIV)

Blind Bartimaeus desperately needed to have his sight restored. His blindness had reduced him to a disrespected and undignified wayside beggar. When he heard about Jesus passing by, he knew he had to cry out with great audacity. The people around him shouted him down to remind him that he was being a nuisance, but he was undeterred; his audacity paid off! Jesus honored his boldness. Jesus honored his audacity! Jesus stopped and gave him his sight!

Sometimes, audacious prayers must be offered in the face of tremendous opposition and prevailing negative circumstances, but like blind Bartimaeus, we must cry out in desperation because Jesus can stop and answer our cry. Let nothing discourage your audacity. It will pay off! Jesus will stop for you!

This Food Must Keep Multiplying

When Israel became godless and idolatrous, the prophet Elijah manifested the power of God in amazing ways. One of those was the feeding of the widow at Zarephath. Elijah had prayed audaciously that there would be no rain in the land until he spoke to reverse the situation. God watched over that word, and the land was gripped in the throes of famine.

Elijah himself needed to survive, so God sent him away to a place called Zarephath to be fed by a most unlikely person: a widow who had only one meal left for her household.

Elijah met the widow at the city gate when he arrived and asked her to feed him first with what she had at home and trust God to sustain her whole household through the severe famine.

His declaration to the widow was very audacious.

> Elijah said to her, "Don't be afraid. Go home and do as you have said. But first, make a small loaf of bread for me from what you have and bring it to me and then make something for yourself and your son. For this is what the LORD, the God of Israel says: 'The jar of flour will not be used up and the jug of oil will not run dry until the day the LORD sends rain on the land.'"

> So she went away and did as Elijah had told her. So there was food every day for Elijah and the woman and her family. For the jar of flour was not used up and the jug of oil did not run dry, in keeping with the word of the LORD spoken by Elijah. (1 Kings 17:13–16 NIV)

God honored the bold prayers of Elijah and miraculously multiplied the woman's supply of food through the three-year famine. God is still in the multiplication business. When Jesus needed to feed five thousand hungry people at one of His gatherings, He prayed over five loaves of bread and two fish. God multiplied it to feed those thousands of people with some leftovers as well.

God has not changed. He knows when to multiply whatever little we have at hand to make ends meet. Don't be frazzled by the meager resources you have in hand compared to the enormity of your need. Be audacious in your declaration that the God of multiplication can attach His adequacy to your inadequacy and cause abundance for your situation.

Do the best you can with whatever resources you have in your hand, and trust God to take you through. Let's trust Him to continue manifesting His glory now just as He did in the days of Elijah.

Some Common Threads

An examination of the various audacious prayers in Scripture reveals some common threads that run through them.

Audacious Prayers Were Uttered amid Great Odds

The odds were simply against all those who prayed. The odds did not favor the woman with the issue of blood who had been bleeding for twelve years. How in the world could she have ever hoped to touch Jesus through the thronging crowd? But she went against the odds and pressed on for her healing!

Blind Bartimaeus had everything stacked against him, but he cried out in defiance of his detractors until Jesus stopped for him. David had everything stacked against him at Ziklag. What were the chances that he would successfully overtake the raiders and recover everything he had lost? But he went against the odds and recovered everything.

The daughters of Zelophehad had the laws of the land stacked against them, but they audaciously asked for the law to be changed in their favor and God allowed it to happen. So don't be scared by the fact that the odds are against you. Let it rather spur you on to ask God audaciously for the impossible! The doctor's report may be stacked against you, but believe audaciously that God can turn things around in your favor. The legal

> Believe audaciously that God can turn things around in your favor.

223

situation might be stacked against you, but believe unswervingly that God is able to do all things. The resources at hand might be woefully inadequate, but trust God to multiply it to meet the need at hand.

Faith Runs through the Audacious Prayers in the Bible

The Bible defines faith as "the substance of things hoped for, the evidence of things not seen" (Hebrews 11:1 NKJV). Bold prayers are offered with the confidence that God will answer regardless of the odds. We offer those prayers with an absolute trustworthiness in God's ability to answer. This common thread of faith runs through every audacious prayer in the Bible. In the natural world, audacious prayers would seem rather difficult and impossible. Elijah plainly told Elisha that asking for a double portion of the anointing on his life was a very difficult request, but Elisha persevered in his faith, and the request was granted. The woman with the issue of blood believed fervently that she would be healed, and God answered her prayer. In fact, Jesus's remarks bear this out. "Daughter, your faith has healed you" (Mark 5:34 NIV). Blind Bartimaeus had faith that Jesus would hear his cry and deliver him from blindness, and his faith paid off! Jesus said to him, "Receive your sight; your faith has healed you."

The situation you face may be rather daunting and seemingly hopeless, but remember these words of Jesus: "Everything is possible to the one who believes" (Mark 9:23 NIV).

Audacious requests require audacious faith. God will never turn His back on audacious faith.

CHAPTER 21

SOME PERSONAL AUDACIOUS PRAYERS

Pray Elisha's Prayer

I HAD THE PRIVILEGE OF being blessed with some very good friends during my seminary days. In fact, I still keep in touch and periodically get together with some of them. Those are cherished relationships.

One of those friendships was with a couple who showed me great kindness. I was attending seminary in the Midwest and away from my wife in Maryland. This lovely couple made me feel so much a part of their own family. The man and I were seminary classmates, and his wife was a professional in town. They would often invite me to their home for dinner, and the wife often typed my school papers because my typing skills were dismal. We developed a very good friendship over the three years I was in seminary. They were just a jewel of a couple. After seminary, I moved back to Maryland, and they continued to work in Missouri. Our paths crossed again when I decided to enroll in a doctorate program in the same city they lived in. I would fly into town every few months and take classes for a week before flying back home to Maryland.

My friends decided that they wanted to save me the cost of hotel accommodation and car rental since I frequently flew into town for classes. Every time I arrived, they would give me a room in their home to stay in, a car to drive, and food. This went on during the entire doctoral program. One morning, I was about to fly out of town after staying in their home when the Holy Spirit prompted me to call them together and pray with them. The prompting was based on the prayer of Elisha for the Shunamite woman who had been taking care of him every time he was passing through her town on ministry assignments.

The story is told in 2 Kings.

> One day Elisha went to Shunem. And a well-to-do woman was there, who urged him to stay for a meal. So whenever he came by, he stopped there to eat. She said to her husband, "I know that this man who often comes our way is a holy man of God. Let's make a small room on the roof and put in a bed and a table, a chair and a lamp for him. Then he can stay there whenever he comes to us."
>
> One day when Elisha came, he went up to his room and lay down there. He said to his servant Gehazi, "Call the Shunammite woman." So he called her, and she stood before him. Elisha said to him, "Tell her, 'You have gone to all this trouble for us. Now what can be done for you? Can we speak on your behalf to the king or the commander of the army?'"
>
> She replied, "I have a home among my own people."
>
> "What can be done for her?" Elisha asked.
>
> Gehazi said, "She has no son, and her husband is old."
>
> Then Elisha said, "Call her." So he called her, and she stood in the doorway.

"About this time next year," Elisha said, "you will hold a son in your arms."

"No, my lord!" she objected. "Please, man of God, don't mislead your servant.!"

But the woman became pregnant, and the next year about the same time she gave birth to a son, just as Elisha had said. (2 Kings 4:8–17 NIV)

This is the story the Holy Spirit placed on my heart when I felt prompted to call my friends and pray with them before leaving town that morning. They had been married for several years at the time but had no children. The interesting thing was that in all our years of friendship, I had never asked them about children. However, that morning, the Holy Spirit was about to bless them in a very wonderful way. So I called them into their family room just before leaving their home and told them that I felt a prompting to pray with them for the blessing of children. They acknowledged that they really wanted God to bless them with children. They received the prayer, and I left for the airport.

A few months later, my friend sent me an email announcing that his wife was pregnant. After the birth of a beautiful baby girl, he sent another email and a picture of the new baby. He added, "This blessing is a direct result of the prayers you offered for us."

A few months later, my friend sent me an email announcing that his wife was pregnant. After the birth of a beautiful baby girl, he sent another email and a picture of the new baby. He added, "This blessing is a direct result of the prayers you offered for us." The most interesting thing about all this was what he told me later. He explained to me that the day I prayed with them was a very difficult time for them. Knowing that they had tried unsuccessfully to have children over the years, they had finally decided to adopt. Everything had been arranged, and they were in the process of waiting to adopt a newborn baby from a teenage pregnancy. However, the birth mother changed her mind and decided to keep the baby when she was born! It was quite a painful experience for them since the nursery had already been prepared in their home and friends and family were waiting to rejoice with them! That was the prevailing situation in their lives when I called to pray with them. Of course, I had absolutely no idea that they were experiencing such pain, but the Lord knew! That simple audacious prayer in that living room resulted in a miracle. They were later blessed with another child—a boy! It was so wonderful when we saw the miracle girl in her teens several years later at a conference in Florida. What an awesome God we serve! He is certainly full of surprises. He does answer prayer! Sometimes, an audacious prayer can come to us when we least expect it. God may prompt our hearts to pray over a situation or a circumstance. The Holy Spirit always has a reason for such promptings. It always pays to obey. Never be afraid to pray audaciously when you feel the prompting to do so. God may simply be waiting to use you as an instrument of blessing in somebody's life.

By the Sidewalk in New York City

A very faithful member of our church got married to a beautiful young lady in New York City. Many of us attended the wedding, and I preached the wedding sermon. As I was walking by the sidewalk into the reception hall after the ceremony, I ran into the groom's brother and his wife. His brother used to worship with us until he moved to California and got married there. It was a rather interesting encounter. They were excited to see me because I hadn't seen them in a while. They mentioned they had been planning to come and see me to discuss an issue. I asked them if everything was OK, to which they responded, "Not quite."

I spent a few minutes talking with them about their situation. They informed me that they had been looking forward to having a baby, all to no avail. They had been married for a few years at the time. They wanted to come and see me to pray and believe with them. I told them I was going to pray with them right there on the sidewalk, and I wanted them to believe that God will answer. We joined hands and prayed.

After the prayer I said to them, "Would you promise me one thing? When God answers this prayer, would you fly down from California to have us dedicate this baby at our church in Maryland?" They said yes with a smile. A year later, they flew down from California to Maryland, and I dedicated the baby to the glory of God. Their testimony was a huge encouragement to many. God does answer audacious prayers regardless of where we offer them—even by a sidewalk!

A $20,000 Request

At the height of the economic recession, which resulted in the massive housing market slump, the Lord answered a wonderfully audacious prayer for us. We were purchasing a new home amid the economic gloom. At the completion of the house, the value had fallen so much that it did not make any economic sense to purchase it at the contracted price prior to construction. We renegotiated with the builder, who agreed to sell the house to us at its current market value. We were thrilled with the deal. However, I said to my wife that I wanted to ask for another favor from the builder. I wanted them to waive an extra $20,000 we were to bring to closing on the house. The builders' representative said that he was pretty sure the request would be denied because the house had already been drastically reduced and the builder was taking a loss. However, he recommended that I write a letter for the request if I so desired. He was confident my request would be denied, but I felt otherwise.

So I prayed and sent a letter for the $20,000 waiver, and the request was granted! What I found to be absolutely thrilling was that we had made a $20,000 pledge to our church's building fund, and I had told my wife how wonderful it would be if we could channel the money from the settlement to fulfill that pledge! The Lord answered that bold prayer. No request is too difficult for Him to grant. He answers prayer in amazing ways. To him who believes, all things are possible! It pays to pray and believe audaciously! You never know what surprises the Lord may have in store for you.

May All the Trees Fall Away

The house we live in is heavily surrounded by wood. It is situated in a quiet area on five acres of trees. We enjoy that blessing from the Lord. It is gorgeous in the fall season when all the colors of the leaves are changing. It is beautiful in the spring when it's all green and lush! However, there is also the real danger that any of the trees could fall toward the house when the weather is stormy and winds are severe. When we first moved in several years ago, that possibility was always on my mind, so I said to my wife that I was going to pray over the trees, and I did. My audacious prayer was that I commanded all the trees to remain standing even in the midst of severe weather. I prayed that no tree would ever fall to endanger the house. I prayed that any tree that fell would fall away from the house.

It has been several years now, and no tree has fallen toward the house in spite of the numerous storms we have had. Any tree that has fallen has always been away from the house and posed absolutely no threat. I do not believe this to be a coincidence. I believe that as the Scripture clearly states we can decree a thing and it shall be established (Job 22:28 NIV). I also believe as Scripture teaches that the tongue carries the power of life and death (Proverbs 19:21 NIV)! When we audaciously speak life, we must believe that life will result!

> Sometimes, I pray what I call "fun prayers" ... the truth is that nothing is too big or too small to pray about.

I love plants and have quite a few at home. Sometimes, I am able to nurture and keep the same plants for many years. There was one particular plant that I kept for over fifteen years. It was a wedding gift from my boss at work, and I joked that the plant had to stay alive along with my marriage. Thankfully, my marriage has outlasted the plant. It died after fifteen years, but my marriage continues after three decades!

Sometimes, I pray what I call "fun prayers" because I believe prayers cut across all aspects of life! I remember transplanting a plant once and seeing the life ebbing out of it a couple of days later because of the transplant. I wasn't too thrilled when I saw that my "green thumb" wasn't working its usual "magic"! I joked, "I paid $15 for this beautiful plant and would hate to see the money go to waste!" I just did not want to see that happen! So I prayed over the plant and kept speaking to it day after day. I watered and attended diligently to it. Slowly, the withering leaves started coming back to life, and I was very pleased. I truly believe God answers all kinds of prayers, including a desire to see a beloved plant defy an untimely death—especially when it had cost $15 of His son's (and His) money! This may be a rather funny story, but the truth is that nothing is too big or too small to pray about.

A Man Comes Out of Coma

As I was concluding this book, my very good friend, Pastor Bill, invited me to preach in a healing service at his church. He was getting ready to write the forward to this book and asked if I remembered to include a very audacious prayer that the Lord had answered when we prayed for a man several years ago. I had totally forgotten about the story until he reminded me. Then it all came back to me. I asked him to tell the story in his own words.

> This occurred in the early 2000s. A man was in coma and on a ventilator due to drug addiction overdose. He was pronounced brain-dead in a southern Maryland hospital. Bill and Albert were meeting in Maryland for prayer and planning concerning the future plans for Renewal Christian Center. Bill received a call concerning the young man from a relative who was a member of our church. I told them I would stop by on

my way from the meeting. I asked Pastor Albert if he would join me. Of course, Albert quickly agreed, even though that request required about a forty-five-minute drive to and from. When we arrived at the hospital, we explained who we were and why we were there. The staff graciously led us to his bed, where we saw a man with wires and tubes all over his body. A nurse confirmed that he was brain-dead and not to expect any responses to our voice in prayer.

What happened next was miraculous. As we prayed commanding life to return to his body, he began to jerk, sat up, and opened his eyes. Nurses and a doctor quickly came to the bedside, astonished at what just happened.

It was getting late in the evening and all I could think to say was "See you later" as I began to walk to the exit door of the unit. Suddenly, my cellphone rang, and it was my wife, Mary, who in a panicked voice told me that a couple of minutes ago (the same time the man was raised up) she heard a noise in the basement. She went downstairs, only to find the hot water heater bulging and split open.

Water was running everywhere. I told her how to turn off the water supply and of course there was a mess to clean up. It is my belief that the devil was so upset at what God had just done for the man that he went on the attack in my home.

The man who installed the new water heater said that in thirty years of operating his business, he had never seen anything like that. The water heater had bulged out like someone tried to break out of it.

The repair man heard the story and would not receive anything for the tank or installation. The man who was raised from the dead was saved and began to attend church. God truly does turn around things meant for harm for good for those who love the Lord and who are called according to His purpose (Romans 8:28).

I am so thankful that Pastor Bill reminded me about this miraculous answer to an audacious prayer. May you be encouraged that because Jesus is the same yesterday, today, and forever (Hebrews 13:8). He is perfectly capable of answering any audacious requests you ask of Him. May you experience increased faith.

The Gift of a Classic Car

I admire classic cars. I am always fascinated by them. I think the closest relationship I have had with classic cars is the fact that I like driving my cars until they are no longer drivable. Typically when we need a new car in the family, I take my wife's old car and keep driving it while she gets the new car. I just like maintaining and driving old cars as long as possible until they no longer make economic sense because of frequent repairs.

That aside though, I thoroughly enjoy looking at classics, especially at the annual auto show close to where we live. I even entertained the idea of owning a classic car if we could afford one someday, but I knew it was only a dream because I just couldn't see my wife agreeing with that idea, no matter how much money we had to spare.

One Friday morning, I was driving to the office when I saw a very nice classic car. I thoroughly admired it. On my way back from work, the thought of the classic car came to my mind again, and a bright idea came to me. *Why don't you pray for the Lord to bless you with a classic car since your wife will never agree to your buying one?* I thought that was a great idea, so I prayed audaciously to the Lord.

Lord, You have said You will give us the desires of our hearts. I desire to have a classic car, but You know the chances of that are very slim first because of the money needed and second because Angie will simply not allow it. You are able to do all things, so why don't You touch someone's heart to bless me with a classic car?

Believe it or not, the very next day, I had a call from a young lady I know. She said, "Pastor, I have been praying about this for a while, and I think the Lord wants me to give you my classic car. I have been going back and forth about it and have been discussing it with my mom, and I really feel the Lord wants me to bless you with it." Just unbelievable! Her uncle was a former NFL player who had purchased a Mercedes 560 SL for her grandmother in 1988. For the past ten years, the car had been kept in the garage without being driven! The grandmother had given the car to her. She drove it for a while and decided she wanted to give it to me as a gift! She had been thinking about that for a while. I was so stunned! I think the Lord was simply waiting for me to pray so the young lady could have peace about blessing me with that beautiful classic! Of course, I knew my wife could not object to that blessing! It was completely out of her hands! And best of all, I didn't have to worry about explaining how the pastor got to own a classic car! I could enjoy it with a clean conscience. They brought the car to me a couple of weeks later. God does answer audacious prayers—even to be blessed with a classic!

Weaving Prayer into Life

Prayer must simply be a way of life. The dichotomy between the "spiritual" and the "nonspiritual" must not be drawn too severely. We must always remember that we are not just physical beings. We are body, soul, and spirit. With our spirit, we commune continually with God. The Spirit of God dwells in us, and our spirit bears witness with His Spirit that we are children of God (Romans 8:16 NIV). That being the case, we must live with the understanding that God is so much a part of us that He cares even about the smallest things we encounter in life.

It is not too far-fetched to ask God to bring a dying plant back to life. After all, remember that He asked Adam to take care of the Garden of Eden and care for creation. We are to pray without ceasing because we need God's involvement in everything we do. We must ask for His blessing and involvement in all we do and possess. For instance, I never take our cars for servicing without asking God for favor. First, I ask that the right hands will be assigned to the car. I always ask Him to give wisdom to the mechanic who would be working on the car. I ask that the diagnosis will be truthful and accurate and that I would not have to be overcharged because of unnecessary work. I remind God that the car belongs to Him so He must take care of it. I do the same with anything that has to be repaired in our home as well. I simply ask God to take care of that which He has entrusted into our care! It has always worked! We must learn to cover our entire life with prayer. I think prayer is one of the most underutilized spiritual weapons in the arsenal of Christians. We seem to have relegated prayer to the "big stuff" in life without allowing it to cover the entirety of our living. Life is made of both big and small stuff. It is therefore imperative that we cover all aspects of our life with prayer.

I have a habit that I have gotten away from but which I really need to get back to more regularly. I used to pray before making or receiving any phone call. I would quickly mutter a prayer asking God to give me wisdom as I speak and to make me a blessing to the person I would be speaking to on the phone. This has been particularly helpful because as a pastor, you never know what you may be dealing with when the phone rings. It could be someone with a desperate situation who needs divine wisdom to attend to it.

I remember a desperate phone call I received one January 1 from a mother whose only son suddenly passed away right in her presence at home. This was the very first day of the new year! It was an apparent heart attack. I immediately prayed with her and went over to their house. The family was waiting for me to come. So how do you console such a grieving mother without divine wisdom? What do you say at that moment? A habit of praying before receiving or making calls places your mind and tongue in the hands of God.

> We never know what we may encounter at
> any given time on any given day so we must
> be prayerful at all times. We must continually
> converse with the Spirit of God who lives in us.

I also remember a phone call I once received from a wonderful lady whose husband was temporarily living outside the country. She had to travel back and forth to see him from time to time. Meanwhile, the burden of raising their children was left on her shoulders. Practically, she was functioning as a single mother. One day, I received a phone call from her, and she was totally broken and weeping uncontrollably. She mentioned that her husband was having an affair with another woman. I remember praying before taking the call. I also remember the anointing of God that covered me as I prayed with her at the end of our conversation. I distinctly remember the calmness and relief that came over her as we finished our conversation and as we prayed. The interesting thing was that I was dealing with the diagnosis of multiple myeloma myself when I received that call. It had only been about a few days or so since the doctor gave me the diagnosis. She didn't know what I was going through at the time. She desperately needed the prayer, counseling, and covering of her pastor, and I could not disappoint her, my own challenges notwithstanding!

We must continually walk and breathe prayer. We must pray without ceasing. We never know what we may encounter at any given time on any given day so we must be prayerful at all times. We must continually converse with the Spirit of God who lives in us. He is our paraclete sent by our heavenly Father to walk alongside us in the journey of life. It is also important to rearrange our schedules and shut ourselves away periodically for a time of personal, private fasting and prayer. The benefits of such a discipline are incalculable. Our strength and spirit are renewed as we wait upon the Lord.

CHAPTER 22

THE KEYS TO EFFECTIVE PRAYERS

PRAYER HAS THE POWER TO change everything, so learn to fight your battles on your knees. If you kneel in prayer, you will have the strength to stand in any situation. There is power in righteous prayer. Prayer can cause changes in people's attitudes, hearts, and minds without you ever uttering a word.

David Wilkerson, founder of Teen Challenge Ministries and Times Square Church in New York, talked about praying girlfriends and boyfriends out of his grandchildren's lives. If he was uncomfortable with a boy or girl being dated by one of his grandchildren, he would simply pray them out of their lives. One of his grandchildren once came to him and said, "Grandpa, did you pray away my boyfriend?" It may sound funny, but we can even depend on the power of prayer to end undesirable relationships in the lives of our loved ones! Instead of endless talks and angry outbursts of disapproval, we can resort to prayer even as we talk and counsel. Prayer can turn situations around. We must not underestimate the power of prayer.

So how can we ensure that our prayers are effective? James 5:16

> Learn to fight your battles on your knees.

(NIV) tells us, "The prayer of a righteous man is powerful and effective." The word *effective* as used here means "energy." Effective prayer is prayer that has spiritual power and energy to make things happen. So how can we pray effectively? How can we pray in such a way that things will happen? What gives energy to our prayers?

Six Keys to Effective Prayer

There are certain keys to praying effectively, and if our audacious prayers are to be heard, then those keys cannot be ignored. I want to talk about six of those keys.

Key 1: A Clean Heart

James reminds us, "The prayer of a righteous person is powerful and effective."

The first key to effective prayer is righteousness. A righteous person is someone who lives in obedience to the Word of God.

A righteous person is committed to doing God's will. A righteous person does not live in unconfessed sin. A righteous person does not live in bitterness or harbor unforgiveness.

A righteous person lives in a conscious fear of God. A righteous person is someone whose life is a living sacrifice to God.

A righteous person is not a perfect person but a person who truly desires to live a holy life by ensuring that his or her actions are authentic and pleasing to God.

I like the words of the great English preacher Charles Spurgeon. "If you want that splendid power in prayer, you must remain in loving, living, lasting, conscious, practical abiding union with God."

The Bible makes it clear that God will not hear our prayers if we live in sin and unrighteousness. Scripture bears this out. "If I had not confessed the sin in my heart, the LORD would not have listened. But God did listen! He paid attention to my prayer." (Psalm 66:18–19 NLT)

God will not hear our prayers if we have unconfessed sin in our lives. The Bible talks about this in the book of Isaiah:

When you lift your hands in prayer, I will not look.

Though you offer many prayers, I will not listen, for your hands are covered with the blood of innocent victims.

Wash yourselves and be clean! Get your sins out of my sight. Give up your evil ways. (Isaiah 1:15–16 NLT)

And as Jesus taught,

I tell you, you can pray for anything and if you believe that you've received it, it will be yours. But when you are praying, first forgive anyone you are holding a grudge against, so that your Father in heaven will forgive your sins too. (Mark 11:24–25 NLT)

Again, in the words of the apostle Peter, "The eyes of the LORD watch over those who do right, and His ears are open to their prayers. But the LORD turns His face against those who do evil" (1 Peter 3:12 NLT).

There are numerous scriptures that underscore the importance of righteousness when we approach God in prayer. The message is clear. If we want our prayers to be effective, then we must confess every sin and turn away from any form of wickedness in our hearts. God is always ready to forgive our sins and answer our prayers.

God wants us to arise and shine for His glory, but the starting point is holiness and righteousness! Let's hear the heart of God in 2 Chronicles.

At times I might shut up the heavens so that no rain falls, or command grasshoppers to devour your crops, or send plagues among you.

Then if my people who are called by my name will humble themselves and pray and seek my face and turn

239

from their wicked ways, I will hear from heaven and will forgive their sins and restore their land.

My eyes will be open and attentive to every prayer made in this place.

For I have chosen this Temple and set it apart to be holy—a place where my name will be honored forever.

I will always watch over it, for it is dear to my heart. (2 Chronicles 7:13–16 NLT)

The temple God was referring to was Solomon's magnificent temple. But now you and I are the temple of God, and God is saying if we repent from our sins, His ear will be attentive to the prayers that come from us—His New Temple in which His Spirit now resides. He will hear from heaven and heal our land because we are dear to Him.

The blessings associated with living in holiness in relation to answered prayers are mind-boggling. If you and I would take God at His Word and repent from every sin and call upon Him with righteous hearts, He will answer our audacious prayers. Heaven will answer when we call because the prayer of a righteous person is powerful and effective. So the first key to effective prayer is to pray from a righteous heart.

There is a strong correlation between righteousness and the effectiveness of our prayers. Read what the Bible says concerning the prayers of Jesus Himself and its connection to righteousness.

While Jesus was here on earth, He offered prayers and pleadings, with a loud cry and tears to the one who could rescue him from death and God heard His prayers because of His deep reverence for God. (Hebrews 5:7 NLT)

God answered the prayers of Jesus not just because Jesus was the Son of God or prayed loudly with tears but because Jesus had a deep reverence for God. A person who has a deep reverence for God is someone who lives in righteous obedience to God. Jesus Himself said in Matthew 5:6 (NIV), "Blessed are those who hunger and thirst for righteousness, for they will be filled." That is a blank check from God. They will be filled with answered prayers, divine favor and protection, blessings beyond their imagination, resources to fulfill their destinies, and God-given vision.

Our righteousness or reverence for God shows in the way we conduct ourselves on a daily basis. We reverence God by the things we think about, the conversations we hold, the things we view on the screen, the purity of our bodies (the temple of God), the choices we make every day, and our attitude toward the work of God. Our righteousness is not measured by our church attendance, the volume of our prayers, or even our knowledge of God's Word, even though these are all important. True righteousness is measured by the condition of our hearts.

The heart of a righteous person is always broken by the things that break the heart of God. The prayers of a righteous person receive attention in heaven because God can trust that individual with the privilege to do things that are dear to God.

God distinguishes the kind of fasting and prayer that gets His attention from that which He totally ignores as shown in this passage from Isaiah:

> "Shout with the voice of a trumpet blast.
>
> Shout aloud! Don't be timid.
>
> Tell my people Israel of their sins!
>
> Yet they act so pious!
>
> They come to the temple every day and seem delighted
> to learn all about me.

They act like a righteous nation that would never abandon the laws of its God.

They ask me to take action on their behalf, pretending they want to be near me.

'We have fasted before you!' they say.

'Why aren't you impressed?

We have been very hard on ourselves, and you don't even notice it.'

"I will tell you why!" I respond.

"It's because you are fasting to please yourselves. Even while you fast, you keep oppressing your workers. What good is fasting when you keep on fighting and quarrelling? ...

Is this what you call fasting? Do you really think this will please the LORD?

"No, this is the kind of fasting I want: Free those who are wrongly imprisoned; lighten the burden of those who work for you. Let the oppressed go free and remove the chains that bind people. Share your food with the hungry, and give shelter to the homeless.

Give clothes to those who need them; and do not hide from your relatives who need your help. "Then your salvation will come like the dawn, and your wounds will quickly heal.

Your godliness will lead you forward, and the glory of the LORD will protect you from behind.

Then when you call, the LORD will answer. 'Yes, I am here,' He will quickly reply. (Isaiah 58:1–9 NLT)

When we cleanse our lives from sin and allow our hearts to be broken by the things that break the heart of God, we position ourselves effectively for God to answer our audacious prayers because God is big on righteousness.

David, the man after God's own heart, understood the power of righteousness, so he cried out to God,

> Search me, O God, and know my heart; test me and know my anxious thoughts. Point out anything in me that offends you, and lead me along the path of everlasting life. (Psalm 139:23–24 NLT).

> **There is a powerful link between righteousness and answered prayers.**

If we want our prayers to be effective, then we must desire and hunger for righteousness. We must humble ourselves and ask God to forgive our sins. We must forgive those who offend us and ask for forgiveness from those we offend. Our hearts must be righteous. There is a powerful link between righteousness and answered prayers. All the people who prayed and received amazing answers to their prayers were people who recognized their sins and asked for forgiveness from God.

Before Nehemiah received favor to rebuild the wall of Jerusalem, He repented and asked God for forgiveness. Scripture records his words as follows:

> Let your ear be attentive and your eyes open to hear the prayer your servant is praying before you day and night for your servants, the people of Israel. I confess the sins we Israelites, including myself and my father's family, have committed against you. We have

acted wickedly toward you. We have not obeyed the commands, decrees, and laws you gave your servant Moses. (Nehemiah 1:6–7 NIV)

Nehemiah did not exclude himself. He acknowledged his own sins. Daniel did the same thing.

I prayed to the LORD my God and confessed:

"Lord, the great and awesome God, who keeps His covenant of love with those who love Him and keep His commandments. We have sinned and done wrong. We have been wicked and have rebelled; we have turned away from your commands and laws." (Daniel 9:4–5 NIV)

If we want our prayers to be effective, then we must pray from righteous hearts.

Key 2: Pray in the Name of Jesus

The surest way to receive anything from God the Father is to approach Him through the person of Jesus Christ His Son. The Bible says in John 14:6 (NIV), "I am the way, the truth and the life. No one comes to the Father except through me." If you want to receive from the Father, you must go through His Son. Jesus attests to this in John 14:13–14 (NIV). "And I will do whatever you ask in my name, so that the Son may bring glory to the Father. You may ask for anything in my name, and I will do it." Jesus underscores this further in John 15:16 (NIV). "Whatever you ask in my name the Father will give you."

Praying in the name of Jesus means we pray on the basis of who Jesus is and what He has done.

What exactly does the Bible mean by praying in the name of Jesus? Does this simply mean adding the phrase "in Jesus's name" as a formula at the end of our prayers? No! It means much more than that. Praying in the name of Jesus means we pray on the basis of who Jesus is and what He has done. It means we approach God on the basis of Christ's righteousness and atoning blood and our relationship with Him. Jesus is our High Priest. Jesus is the only true mediator between God and man.

Scripture makes it clear that "there is one God and one mediator between God and mankind, the man Christ Jesus, who gave Himself as a ransom for all people" (1 Timothy 2:5–6 NIV). This means humans are helpless outside the mediative role of Jesus before our heavenly Father. Our prayers will receive no hearing in the court of heaven unless we depend on Jesus, who is our advocate. The voice of Jesus, the Son, immediately secures the attention of the Father. We must therefore go to the Father through Jesus our Redeemer.

I liken this to the concept of applying for a car loan from the bank when your credit is bad. You need a cosigner! When Bill Gates cosigns for you, you know you have no problem. He has billions of dollars in assets! Similarly, Jesus is our cosigner on every prayer we send to heaven. No questions are asked in heaven when His signature is appended to our prayers. Adam and Eve ruined our credit, but Jesus cleaned it up and restored it. Jesus carries weight as the only recognized mediator between people and God. The Bible says of Jesus in Colossians 1:17 (NIV), "He is before all things and by Him all things hold together."

So how did Jesus earn this remarkable credit in heaven so that no check will be honored and no prayer answered except that He cosigns? We find the answer in the scriptures.

> Though He was God, He did not think of equality with God as something to cling to. Instead, He gave up His divine privileges; He took the humble position of a slave and was born as a human being. When He appeared in human form, he humbled Himself in obedience to God and died a criminal's death on the cross. Therefore, God elevated Him to the place of highest honor and

gave Him the name above all other names, that at the
name of Jesus every knee should bow, in heaven and
on earth and under the earth, and every tongue declare
that Jesus Christ is Lord, to the glory of God the Father.
(Philippians 2:6–11 NIV)

This is the treasure we have in the name of Jesus. This is why we
pray in the name of Jesus. God the Father has given Jesus the unique
privilege and authority to possess the name above all names. Jesus and
God are a package deal. You cannot access the power of God without
going through Jesus. There are power and authority in the name of
Jesus. That is why captives are set free in His name, sicknesses and
diseases are healed in His name, bondages are broken in His name, and
demons flee at the mention of His name.

In Luke 10:17–19 (NIV), the disciples said,

'Lord, even the demons are subject to us in your name.'
He replied, 'I saw Satan fall like lightning from Heaven.
I have given you authority to trample on snakes and
scorpions and to overcome all the power of the enemy;
nothing will harm you.'

We have power and authority in the name of Jesus. That is why
Peter looked at the blind man at the Beautiful Gate and said, "I don't
have any silver or gold for you. But I'll give you what I have. In the
name of Jesus Christ, the Nazarene, get up and walk" (Acts 3:6 NLT).

You may not have silver or gold, political power, or social influence,
but in the mighty name of Jesus, you have the power and authority to
bring freedom and healing to broken lives. This power is far better than
silver or gold. The only name God recognizes in heaven is the name of
Jesus. There is no other name! The Bible says in Hebrews 10:19 (NIV),
"We have confidence to enter the Most Holy Place by the Blood of
Jesus. By a new and living way, opened for us through the curtain, that
is through his body."

Approaching God through Jesus means we approach Him on the

246

basis of our personal relationship with Jesus. The only reason God listens to your prayers is because of your special relationship with Jesus. You can't approach God on the basis of someone else's relationship with Him. It is an individual issue! The Bible gives an interesting illustration in Acts.

> God did extraordinary miracles through Paul so that even handkerchiefs and aprons that had touched him were taken to the sick and their illnesses were cured and the evil spirits left them. Some Jews who went around driving out evil spirits tried to invoke the name of the Lord Jesus over those who were demon-possessed. They would say, 'In the name of Jesus whom Paul preaches, I command you to come out.' Seven sons of Sceva, a Jewish Chief Priest, were doing this.

> One day, the evil spirit answered them, 'Jesus I know and Paul I know but who are you?' The man who had the evil spirit jumped on them and overpowered them all. He gave them such a beating that they ran out of the house naked and bleeding. (Acts 19:11–16 NIV)

The seven sons of Sceva invoked the name of Jesus without a personal relationship with Him, but you and I have the unique privilege of coming to God the Father because of our relationship with Christ. God has given us access to His throne of grace, but it is only on the basis of our personal relationship with Jesus Christ!

When you come before the throne of grace, remind God of your special relationship with Him through Jesus Christ. Remind Him of His promises in His Word. Remind Him of this: "Father, You have said in Ephesians 1:3 (NIV), 'You have blessed me with all

> When you come before the throne of grace, remind God of your special relationship with Him through Jesus Christ.

spiritual blessings in heavenly places through Christ Jesus my Lord and Savior.'" Remind Him of Romans 8:32 (NIV). "He who did not spare His own Son but gave Him up for us all—how will He not along with Him, freely give us all things?" Remind Him of Jesus's words in John 15:16 (NIV). "My Father will give you whatever you ask in My Name." In order to pray effectively, we must pray in the name of Jesus.

Jesus made an astonishing statement in John 15:16 (NIV). "You did not choose me, but I chose you and appointed you to go and bear fruit—fruit that will last. Then the Father will give you whatever you ask for in my name." We have been chosen and appointed to be fruitful in our lives. Jesus expects us to bear fruit in whatever He has assigned to us. In fact, the Bible tells us in Ephesians 2:10 (NIV), "We are God's handiwork, created in Christ Jesus to do good works, which God prepared in advance for us to do." In order to do those good works and be fruitful, we need all kinds of resources. We need health, wisdom, money, favor from people, doors to be opened, protection, and many other things.

Jesus is saying that when we approach the Father in His name, God will give us whatever we need to accomplish the things He has chosen and appointed us to do! Because of your relationship with Jesus, God will give you whatever you ask for in His name so that you can be fruitful as a mother, father, student, lawyer, teacher, nurse, businessman, doctor, or whatever mode of employment or responsibility you have.

Why is Jesus able to do whatever we ask for in His name? Again, scripture provides the answer.

> Long ago God spoke many times and in many ways to our ancestors through the prophets. And now in these final days, He has spoken to us through His Son. God promised everything to the Son as an inheritance, and through the Son, He created the universe. (Hebrews 1:1–2 NLT)

Note this carefully: If Jesus has inherited everything in the universe, then He can give you anything you need in this universe, including wisdom to live a productive life, anointing to do His work, food, shelter, clothing, money to pay your bills, good health, a husband or wife, a house, joy, peace, children, and the most audacious requests you can ever present to Him! This is possible because Jesus has inherited everything in the universe! That is why Jesus says in Matthew 6:31–33 (NIV),

> So do not worry, saying, 'What shall we eat' or 'What shall we drink?' or 'What shall we wear?' For the pagans run after these things, and your heavenly Father knows you need them. But seek first His Kingdom and His righteousness, and all these things will be given to you as well.

Because Jesus has inherited everything, He can give us anything. If we understand these important keys to prayer, our prayer lives will never be the same again. Don't be afraid to seek help from Jesus because He has been appointed by God to help you. The Bible says,

> We also know that the Son did not come to help angels; He came to help the descendants of Abraham. Therefore, it was necessary for him to be made in every respect like us, his brothers and sisters, so that he could be our merciful and faithful High Priest before God. (Hebrews 2:16; 14–18 NLT)

Key 3: Pray according to God's Will

If God is to answer our prayers, then we must pray according to His will. That is a powerful key to effective prayer. The Bible says in 1 John 5:14–15 (NIV),

> This is the confidence we have in approaching God: that if we ask anything according to His will, He hears us. And if we know that He hears us—whatever we ask—we know that we have what we asked of Him.

This is a very profound promise.

First, the Bible says that if we pray according to God's will, we can be confident that God will hear our prayer. The word used in the Greek for *hear* (*akouo*) refers to more than audible hearing. It means to listen attentively and favorably. This means that God listens attentively and favorably to our prayers. He understands and grants our requests.

Second, the Bible says that if we pray according to God's will, we can be confident that God will grant us whatever we ask. When we pray according to God's will, we must have the confident assurance that He hears us the very moment we call and that He has already granted our requests, even if it takes time to materialize.

In Matthew 6:9–10 (NIV), Jesus taught the disciples to pray for God's will to be done on earth.

> "This, then, is how you should pray:
>
> "Our Father in heaven,
>
> Hallowed be your name,
>
> Your Kingdom come,
>
> Your will be done on earth as it is in heaven."

So what does it mean to pray according to God's will? What is God's will? God's will simply refers to what God wants to be done on this earth, in His church, or in our lives. Praying according to God's will means that we ask according to what God desires for our lives—a particular situation or His overall kingdom agenda. Praying according to God's will means that we don't just petition God about our needs but also use our prayer time to yield our lives to the will and work of God. The reason such prayers are effective is because we are seeking for God's will to be done and for His intentions for humanity to be accomplished. Praying according to God's will means we don't just ask for His will to be done on earth but also release our own will to God. Effective prayer is the kind of prayer that unites our will with the will of God.

The reason Elijah's prayer was effective was because he prayed according to the will of God. God had warned the Israelites that if they turned their backs on Him and sinned, the rain would stop. The warning is found in Deuteronomy 11:16–17 (NIV).

> Be careful, or you will be enticed to turn away and worship other gods and bow down to them. Then the Lord's anger will burn against you, and He will shut up the heavens so that it will not rain and the ground will yield no produce, and you will soon perish from the good land the Lord is giving you.

Elijah's prayer was not an arbitrary exercise of power. Elijah prayed according to God's will.

We must understand that God doesn't answer prayers just because we have knelt down to spout some words or scream into His ears. Our prayers are effective when we are in righteous fellowship with the Father, when we ask in Jesus's name, and when we ask according to His will. This is important because we don't want to waste our time when we pray. We want God to act when we pray. We want our prayers to be effective. God has a specific path outlined for each of His children as part of His overall kingdom agenda. This means that the most effective prayers we can ever pray, and the ones God will answer joyfully, are the prayers that tie directly into His plan and will for our lives, His church, and His kingdom.

Each of us has a God-ordained plan for our lives. Scripture tells us in Psalm 25:12 (NIV), "Who, then, is the man that fears the Lord? He will instruct him in the way chosen for him." God has a way chosen for you; therefore, the most effective prayer you will ever pray is the prayer that lines up with God's will for your life—the way He has chosen for you.

That is why the Bible says in Proverbs 3:5–6 (NKJV),

> Trust in the Lord with all your heart and lean not to your own understanding. In all your ways acknowledge Him and He will direct your paths.

God hears and grants our petitions when we pray in accordance with His will. This is a very important key to receiving answers to our audacious prayers.

Sometimes, we struggle between our personal will and God's will. We see this in the prayer of Jesus for God's will to be done and not His personal desires. It can be a real struggle. The issue of our personal will versus the will of God comes into sharp focus, especially during moments of crisis when we find ourselves in difficulties. Sometimes we pray for God to take us out of situations because the storms are too severe. We don't think it is God's will for us to experience any pain at all.

> Life is always preceded by death in both the natural and spiritual realms. Don't pray your way out of what God may be allowing to die in your life.

So just like the disciples, even with Jesus in the boat with us, we ask, "Lord, don't You care if we perish?" [Mark 4:38 NIV]. "I don't think this is Your will; otherwise, I will not be experiencing this pain!" We want to pray our way out of the pain and suffering we might be experiencing. But listen. God may want to teach you some new things out of that painful trial! That is why the psalmist says, "God is our refuge and strength, an ever-present help in trouble … Be still and know that I am God" (Psalm 46:1, 10 NIV). Just be still and know that God is with you in your situation. Don't be afraid when you run into some turbulence in life or if God allows some things to die out of your life! The Bible says in 1 Corinthians 15:36 (NIV), "What you sow does not come to life unless it dies." Life is always preceded by death in both the natural and spiritual realms. Don't pray your way out of what God may be allowing to die in your life: the death of that job, the death of that relationship, the closing of a particular door, etc. That may be God's will for your life, designed to lead you to abundant fruit in the days ahead. So don't pray your way out. Pray and believe for God's will to be done in the situation. Pray for God to give you strength through it.

Submitting to the will of God tells God that it is all about Him and what He wants and not about us. It tells God that we want Him to get the glory and not us! It tells Jesus that we acknowledge Him as the true Lord of our lives!

Key 4: Pray with Passion, Persistence, and Perseverance

If our prayers are to be heard, then we must learn to persevere in prayer. We must learn to pray our situations through. We must learn to pray until something happens. We must pray until we hear clearly from God.

There are times when the answers to our prayers may seem long in coming. The temptation to give up might be strong, but it is important that we persevere until we receive the answer. Perseverance is what makes the difference. There is a saying that success is 10 percent effort and 90 percent perseverance. It is not enough to make the effort; it is important to persevere until you see results. Never lose your fighting spirit.

> The story is told of two frogs who fell into a bowl of cream. The sides of the bowl were shiny and steep, and the cream was cold. One of the frogs, after failing a few times to climb out, gave up and started drinking the milk until it died. To him, the situation was hopeless.
>
> There was no point in trying anymore. The other frog did not give up. It paddled persistently, kicking, and swimming and trying to jump out.
>
> An interesting thing started happening: The more it kicked and paddled for freedom, the thicker the cream became. The kicking had a whipping effect until the cream became as thick as butter, and the frog was able to jump out—using the butter as a jumping pad![7]

Perseverance can turn your unfavorable circumstances into a jumping pad to victory.

In all things, God works together for our good. If you persevere like Joseph, God will use what the enemy meant for evil as a blessing. Your setback can become a stepping-stone to victory!

What happens to you is not as important as your response to the situation. You may have no choice over the situation and circumstances that life brings you, but you have a choice over how to respond. What happens to you is not as important as what happens within you.

Your internal dialogue—what you say to yourself—is more important than anything else you hear. How you process the experiences of life will either elevate you or sink you. You can either give up or choose to persevere tenaciously until the victory is won.

Always tell yourself, "I am a child of God. I can do all things through Christ, who strengthens me" (Philippians 4:13 NKJV). Never give up your fighting spirit.

Some years ago, I attended a graduation ceremony at the University of Maryland. As I watched the graduates receiving their diplomas and saw the cheers of friends and relatives in the crowd, one family had a sign. "Mom, you finally made it." It struck me that as a mother, the woman had probably gone through some incredible odds to graduate. A single parent perhaps? Some financial difficulties along the way? Sleepless nights to do her homework after the kids had gone to bed? A full-time job and school at the same time? What could the woman's real story be? I found myself speculating! Many things came flooding into my mind. I also thought about the fact that perhaps there were some who started the class with her but never graduated because they faced the same problems that this graduate faced and gave up. So what was the difference? Perseverance! Hence the sign "Mom, you finally made it."

I remember when I was studying for my doctorate, planting a church, raising our toddler twins, and caring for my wife who was very sick for over a year. One of my closest friends asked me to drop out from the doctoral program. I almost gave up, but I didn't. I persevered! Sometimes we give up too soon. Persistence in prayer is essential to victory!

James tells us that Elijah was a man just like us, yet he was able to pray and stop the rain for three and a half years. Look at the passage again. "Elijah was a human being even as we are. He prayed earnestly that it would not rain, and it did not rain on the land for three and a half years" (James 5:17 NIV). Earnest prayer is the type of blood and sweat prayer that Jesus prayed in the Garden of Gethsemane. Earnest prayer has passion and persistence. Earnest prayer desires to see results! Earnest prayer does not give up! Elijah was a man just like you and me. This tells me that God is no respecter of persons. God will hear you and me just as He heard Elijah if we pray passionately and earnestly. Let's go into the prayer room with Elijah and see what happened as he prayed.

> And Elijah said to Ahab, "Go eat and drink for there is a sound of heavy rain." So Ahab went off to eat and drink, but Elijah climbed up to the top of Carmel, bent down to the ground, and put his face between his knees. "Go and look toward the sea," he told his servant. And he went up and looked. "There is nothing there," he said. Seven times Elijah said, "Go back." The seventh time, the servant reported, "A cloud as small as a man's fist is rising from the sea." So Elijah said, "Go and tell Ahab, hitch up your chariot and go down before the rain stops you.'" Meanwhile, the sky grew black with clouds, the winds rose, a heavy rain came on and Ahab rode off to Jezreel. (1 Kings 18:41–46 NIV)

The only evidence that Elijah saw after he had prayed seven times was a cloud that was as small as a man's fist, but he persevered in prayer until the clouds started forming. Don't be discouraged because all you see on the horizon after so much prayer is just a small discouraging cloud. That cloud could be the sign of an abundant rain that God is about to send your way! Don't give up! The showers of blessing may be about to fall, even though the cloud is small!

The evidence may not be very encouraging, but don't give up the first time. Don't give up the second time. Don't give up the third time. Don't give up the fourth time. Don't give up the fifth time. Don't give up the sixth time. Don't give up the seventh time. Persevere in prayer until you see the small fist of cloud. It is the sign of abundant rain. It is a sign that things are turning around.

Sometimes the waiting period may be long.
It could even be years of praying and waiting,
but a divine delay is never a denial. God
will come through at the right time.

Sometimes the waiting period may be long. It could even be years of praying and waiting, but a divine delay is never a denial. God will come through at the right time. Every divinely ordained vision is for an appointed time; though it delays, wait for it. It will surely come.

Learning to persevere in prayer is critical. You and I have been blessed with all spiritual blessings in the heavenly places in Christ Jesus, but God moves on our behalf when we call upon Him in prayer. Prayer moves the hand of God on our behalf. Again, the words of Isaiah are instructive.

> I have posted watchmen on your walls, O Jerusalem,
> they will never be silent day or night ... You who call
> on the LORD, give yourselves no rest and give Him no
> rest till He establishes Jerusalem and makes her the
> praise of the earth. (Isaiah 62:6–7 NIV)

This is a profound revelation from the Bible! God is saying by way of application to our own situations,

> I have many blessings in store for you. I want you to be
> a crown of splendor in My hand. I want the nations to
> see your glory. I want you to come out of desolation.
> I want you to be called Hephzibah—the delight of the
> Lord. I want to delight over your success. I want you to
> become everything I have created you to be! I have all

these blessings in store for you, so give yourself no rest and give Me no rest until these promises are fulfilled.

Keep calling persistently in prayer until you see the manifestation of these promises. Persistence in prayer is essential to victory.

Blind Bartimaeus is an example. He called out persistently until Jesus stopped and healed him. He persisted until he got his healing. Persist passionately in prayer until you hear from God. Persist until Jesus calls your name. Don't stop believing. Don't stop fasting. Don't stop coming to the altar. Persevere until Jesus stops for you.

There are times when you might grow weak and tired, but don't give up. One day, your perseverance will pay off. One day, you will have a testimony to give. One day, Jehovah Jireh will provide. One day, Jehovah Nissi will give you your victory banner. One day, Jehovah Raphael will heal you. One day, Jehovah El Shaddai will rise up on your behalf. Don't give up! Persevere in prayer because the prayer of a righteous person is powerful and effective! Heaven will answer.

Key 5: Pray in Faith

In order for our prayers to be effective, we must pray in faith. The Bible says in Mark 9:23 (NIV), "Everything is possible for the one who believes." A person who has faith should expect all things to be possible. Faith is simply the belief—deep down in your soul—that God has the ability to supply the need you have placed before Him even though the circumstances may seem impossible and the evidence is not there to back you up!

My son used to have severe eczema, which usually kept him crying through the night as a baby. One Saturday night it was so bad that it kept us up till the early hours of Sunday morning. I barely slept that night, and I had to preach in the morning. No medication seemed to be working. I knew I had to cry out in faith. I took him to my study, anointed him with oil, and cried out to God in faith for about twenty minutes until he went to sleep. That was the end of our sleepless nights.

God healed him.

This is how the Bible defines faith in Hebrews 11:1 (NLT): "Faith is the confidence that what we hope for will actually happen; it gives us assurance about things we cannot see." Faith believes without seeing the evidence.

The Bible also says in Matthew 21:22 (NIV), "If you believe, you will receive whatever you ask for in prayer." In other words, you must believe to receive. In fact, the Bible says in James 1:6–7 (NIV) that when a person asks anything from God,

> he must believe and not doubt because he who doubts is like a wave of the sea blown and tossed by the wind. That man should not think that he will receive anything from the Lord.

Without faith, our prayers will not be effective. A faithless prayer is a useless prayer. It will not accomplish anything. Without faith, our prayers cannot penetrate the courts of heaven for answers to be released. What happens in the invisible realm of faith determines what happens in the visible physical realm where we live. There is a connection between the invisible spiritual realm where God has blessed us with all spiritual blessings through Christ Jesus and the visible, physical realm where those blessings are needed. That connecting bridge is called "faith." The prayer of faith is what causes the invisible blessings in heaven to become visible blessings on earth.

On numerous occasions, Jesus said to people that their faith had made them well. Blind Bartimaeus shouted persistently in faith until Jesus called him and said to him, "Go, your faith has healed you" (Mark 10:52 NIV). The woman with the issue of blood received her healing because she exercised her faith by touching the hem of Jesus's garment and He said, "Daughter, your faith has healed you" (Mark 5:34 NIV).

When Jesus told the story about the persistent widow who did not give up until she received her answer, He concluded with these words:

> Will not God bring about justice for His chosen ones who cry out to Him day and night? Will He keep putting them off? I tell you He will see that they get justice, and

quickly. However, when the Son of Man comes, will He find faith on the earth? (Luke 18:7–8 NIV)

Another powerful story of faith occurred during Paul's preaching in Lystra. Scripture says,

In Lystra, there sat a man crippled in his feet, who was lame from birth and had never walked. He listened to Paul as he was speaking. Paul looked directly at him, saw that he had faith to be healed and called out, 'Stand up on your feet!' At that, the man jumped up and began to walk. (Acts 14:8–10 NIV)

This is a notable example of how our faith can cause our situation to experience direct divine intervention. If our prayers are to be effective, then we must pray with the confident and unwavering expectation that God will answer our prayer! When you go to the altar to be prayed for, believe that you will not go back empty-handed! Believe that you will receive something from God.

The psalmist says in Psalm 5:3 (NIV), "In the morning, LORD, you hear my voice; in the morning, I lay my requests before you and wait expectantly." I don't wait in doubt; I wait in expectation because I am confident that my God will answer my prayer! Faith believes before it experiences the reality.

Faith is what caused us to believe that we would possess those twenty-three acres of property for our future church campus, and faith is what caused us to pray until it became a reality. Faith is what caused the Israelites to step into the Jordan River before it parted (Joshua 3:13). Faith is what caused the Israelites to take those seemingly senseless marches around the wall of Jericho until it came crashing down (Joshua 6:5). Faith says,

> Faith says, "Lord, the situation seems very hopeless right now, but I will not give up. I will continue to trust in you because I know you are able."

"Lord, the situation seems very hopeless right now, but I will not give up. I will continue to trust in you because I know you are able."

Job was a well-respected person until he lost all his wealth and influence. He found himself sitting in ashes, sick and rejected by everyone. Even his wife said to him, "Are you still holding on to your integrity? Curse God and die" (Job 2:9 NIV). But Job still held on to his faith in God. He said, "I know that my Redeemer lives" (Job 19:25 NIV). Like Job, faith is when people walk away from you laughing because they think you have failed but you continue to believe God and persevere because you are walking by faith and not by sight. In spite of the circumstances, you continue to believe that God will come through for you just like He came through for Job.

Moses is one of the people listed in the Bible's "Hall of Faith". Hebrews 11:27 (NIV) says, "By faith he left Egypt, not fearing the King's anger; he persevered because he saw Him who is invisible." Faith helps you to see the invisible One and helps you persevere. Moses was in that wilderness for forty years after he left Egypt, but because he had seen the Invisible One, he persevered in his faith until the Invisible One made Himself visible to him in that burning bush (Exodus 3:4).

As you call upon God in faith, believe that one day He will show up visibly in your situation and all will see that the Invisible One who you had believed in all along is not a figment of the imagination. He is real in His presence and assurance.

Let me point out three things about faith.

1: God expects us to walk by faith and not by sight.
Paul says in 2 Corinthians 5:7 (NKJV), "For we walk by faith and not by sight." We see an example of this in how Jesus trained His ministry workers. Jesus sent out His disciples on ministry assignments in a way that was designed for them to live out their faith in God on a daily basis. This is what He said to them in Mark 6:8–9 (NIV):

> Take nothing for the journey except a staff—no bread, no bag, no money in your belts. Wear sandals but not an extra tunic.

Jesus was teaching the disciples to depend upon God by faith for their daily provision. Life is not always easy.

There will be times when you have no idea when the next provision for you and your family will come. The same God who took care of the disciples will take care of you if you are living in His will. The best place to eat from is the palm of God's hand.

2: Our faith grows as we feed on God's Word.
The Bible says in Romans 10:17 (NIV) that faith comes by hearing the Word of God. This is why reading God's Word, making time for Bible studies, and being in church to hear the preaching and teaching of God's Word are so important. Frankly, that is why pastors should take time to preach God's Word and not just give emotional whip-ups with clever stories. I can't tell you the number of times over the years when people have said, "Pastor, that sermon answered my questions and gave me strength and faith to go on." The Word of God builds our faith. Satan will do everything and give you every excuse to stay away from church because you lose an opportunity to increase your faith and strengthen yourself for the journey of life.

3: Faith increases with use.
When Jesus rose from the dead, one of the disciples, Thomas, said he would not believe it until he saw the nail marks in His hands, put his fingers in those marks, and put his hand into his side. Jesus appeared to the disciples when Thomas was present and said to him, "Stop doubting and believe" (John 20:27 NIV). The literal translation of that statement is "Thomas, stop becoming unbelieving and get on with believing." Believing and unbelieving are not static. Your faith will either increase or decrease. Similarly, your unbelief will either increase or decrease. This saying is true: "What you feed grows; what you starve dies." If you feed your faith, your faith will grow; if you feed your doubts, your doubts will grow. That is why Jesus told Thomas to stop doubting and believe. Stop becoming unbelieving and believe.

If you keep hearing the Word of God yet keep doubting and going back to the same old attitude of stressing yourself about whether God will supply the money you need, whether He will give you a new job, or whether there will be food on the table, you are only feeding your doubts and destroying your faith. Don't sit down and fold your hands while claiming you have faith. Get on with the business of life and trust God to supply your needs without stressing yourself over every penny that you will need for tomorrow.

I remember an interesting experience I had one day. I had an expense that was coming due for payment. The amount was about $500. That week, I decided to bless someone who was in a difficult financial situation with an amount of $500. It wasn't exactly an easy decision to make since the money was for a budgeted expense, but I went ahead and did it. That very Sunday, someone handed me an envelope after service. Guess what was in it. Five hundred dollars in cash! That was definitely a faith builder. I exercised my faith and blessed someone with an amount that I could have used, and God replaced it that same week. Faith grows with use!

Key 6: Pray with Thanksgiving

If we want our prayers to be effective, then we must pray with an attitude of gratitude. Meditate on these words from Philippians 4:6–7 (NLT):

> Don't worry about anything; instead, pray about everything. Tell God what you need, and thank Him for all He has done. Then, you will experience God's peace, which exceeds anything we can understand. His peace will guard your hearts and minds as you live in Christ Jesus.

The lyrics to one of my favorite hymns are an encouragement to count our blessings even in the face of severe challenges. A paraphrase of that songwriter's words says, "When life tosses you up and down and you think all is lost, count your blessings; name them one by one and it will surprise you what God has done!"[8]

When you kneel down in prayer, enter the presence of God with an attitude of worship and gratitude. Be grateful for what God has already done in your life—the life you have today, His protection over the years, and His provision over the years. Be grateful for the fact that you are in a good and caring church where you hear the truth of God's Word. Be grateful for your spiritual growth over the years. The truth is it is easy to look at what we do not have and develop a spirit of ingratitude or even bitterness. Even if what you have seems so small and inadequate, thank God because God is in the business of multiplication. There are some who don't even have what you have! Be grateful and content even as you believe for an increase!

When Jesus was faced with a crowd of five thousand hungry men (plus any women and children with them), all He had were five loaves of bread and two fish. The Bible says Jesus took the little He had, gave thanks to the Father, and started breaking it. He thanked the Father for the little He had in His hand and immediately everything started multiplying to the point where everyone was fed, and they had twelve basketfuls left over!

Thanking God in prayer tells Him,

> God, I acknowledge Your goodness to me over the years. I acknowledge the fact that You are a good and caring Father. I acknowledge the fact that Your plans for me are for my good and never for my evil. I acknowledge the fact that You are in control of my life.

An ungrateful heart never moves the hand of God, but a grateful heart will always move God's hand in prayer. When you pray about that difficult job situation or that difficult boss, don't forget to thank God for the fact that you have a job anyway. Thank God for your husband or wife instead of being critical and ungrateful. Thank God for your church and your pastor and pray instead of being critical and ungrateful.

> Thanksgiving is really the twin of faith.
> Thanksgiving is an important spiritual
> disposition that tells God, "Father, I know You
> have already met this need, so thank You."

Why does an attitude of thanksgiving make our prayers effective? You see, thanksgiving underscores the fact that God has the ability to take care of your needs. Thanksgiving is really the twin of faith. Thanksgiving is an important spiritual disposition that tells God, "Father, I know You have already met this need, so thank You." Praying with thanksgiving does not just refer to the words uttered as we verbalize our gratitude to God. Praying with thanksgiving refers more to the disposition of our hearts as we come before the Lord in prayer. Our hearts are filled with thanksgiving for all God has already done, so there is a verbal outpouring from our hearts as we petition God for the new things we are asking Him to do. We pray out of the abundance of our hearts.

As we approach God in prayer, our hearts are filled with the assurances in His Word. We kneel down with Matthew 7:11 (NIV) in our hearts. "If we, being evil, know how to give good gifts to our children, how much more will our Father in Heaven give good gifts to those who ask Him?" So thank God for that promise!

We kneel down with Jeremiah 29:11 (NIV) in our hearts. "For I know the plans I have for you declares the Lord; plans to prosper you and not to harm you; plans to give you hope and a future." So thank God for that.

We kneel down with Psalm 16:5–6 (NLT) in our hearts. "Lord, you alone are my inheritance, my cup of blessing. You guard all that is mine. The land you have given me is a pleasant land. What a wonderful inheritance." So thank God for that.

We kneel down in prayer with Psalm 27:1 (NIV) in mind. "The Lord is my light and my salvation whom shall I fear? The Lord is the stronghold of my life—of whom shall I be afraid?" So thank God for that.

We kneel down with Psalm 23:4 (NKJV) in our hearts. "Yea, though I walk through the valley of the shadow of death, I will fear no evil for You are with me, Your Rod and Your staff they comfort me." So thank Him for that.

Thanksgiving is a powerful point of entry into the throne of grace.

CHAPTER 23

TIME TO ACT: PRAY YOUR AUDACIOUS PRAYERS

IT IS EVIDENT FROM SCRIPTURE that God does answer prayer, no matter how audacious those prayers might seem.

God Himself throws us a daring invitation in Jeremiah 33:3 (NKJV). "Call to Me, and I will answer you, and show you great and mighty things, which you do not know." He wants to show us great and mighty things far beyond what we currently see or experience.

In fact, the words of Jesus in Mark 11:23–24 (NLT) are a further invitation for us to make bold requests from God.

> I tell you the truth, you can say to this mountain, 'May you be lifted up and thrown into the sea,' and it will happen. But you must really believe it will happen and have no doubt in your heart. I tell you, you can pray for anything, and if you believe that you have received it, it will be yours.

As Christians, the salvation we have received from God is a package deal that entails all kinds of blessings and promises. The apostle Peter reminds us,

By His divine power, God has given us everything we need for living a godly life. We have received all of this by coming to know Him, the one who called us to Himself by means of His marvelous glory and excellence. And because of His glory and excellence, He has given us great and precious promises. These are the promises that enable you to share His divine nature and escape the world's corruption caused by human desires. (2 Peter 1:3–4 NLT)

In essence, as part of our salvation package, we should not lack anything—either spiritual or material—that would enable us to live lives that will glorify God. Divine provision has been made to ensure that our needs are adequately catered for in a way that enables us to live godly lives.

The truth is God takes no delight in depriving His children of necessities that constitute the fullness of life that Christ promises. Jesus specifically stated, "The thief's purpose is to steal and kill and destroy. My purpose is to give them a rich and satisfying life" (John 10:10 NLT). Again, in Psalm 84:11 (NLT), the assurance from scripture is clear. "For the LORD God is a sun and shield; the LORD bestows favor and honor; no good thing does He withhold from those whose walk is blameless."

Given all the promises of God regarding His provision for His children, I often wonder whether we are actually utilizing the entire package entailed in our salvation.

- Are we truly believing and earnestly entreating God to heal us and our loved ones when stricken by sickness? (Isaiah 53:5 NIV)
- Do we truly show forth the fruit of the Spirit of God who dwells in us? (Galatians 5:22–25 NIV)
- Do we live in anxiety because there are unmet needs in our lives, or do we truly have the peace of God that surpasses all understanding? (Philippians 4:6–7 NIV)
- Do we truly believe that because God is for us, nothing can be against us? (Romans 8:31 NIV)

- Is it really a foundational belief for us that the God who did not spare His own Son but gave Him up for us will along with Him freely give us all things? (Romans 8:32 NIV)
- Do we truly believe that we are more than conquerors through Jesus Christ our Lord and Savior? (Romans 8:37 NIV)

All these promises and scriptural assertions are part of our salvation package. If that is the case, then we should each be emboldened to present our audacious requests before God and believe for answers.

I want to end this book with a personal challenge to you.

Present your audacious requests before God, and dare to believe that He will answer!

- If you are a married person, unite with your spouse. Seek the Lord concerning a list of audacious things you want to believe God for. Of course, there are some personal requests you may have outside what you desire together as a couple. Be encouraged to write those requests down for yourself as well. Put a date on it, and trust God to answer.
- If you are single, put down the audacious things you want God to do in your life; date it, and believe for an answer.
- If you are a pastor, challenge your church to come together and believe God to answer some corporate audacious prayers you have as a church.
- If you lead a ministry in the church, petition God audaciously about some needs you have in your particular area of responsibility.
- If you lead a small group in your church, galvanize your group to believe God for answers to some audacious prayers you agree on to petition God about.
- If you are a business owner, put some impossible requests before God, and believe Him to answer.

There is simply no limit to what God can do if His children petition Him audaciously. I invite you to meditate on this prayer of Paul as you write out your audacious prayers and believe God for answers:

> I pray that your hearts will be flooded with light so that you can understand the confident hope He has given to those He called—His holy people who are His rich and glorious inheritance.
>
> I also pray that you will understand the incredible greatness of God's power for us who believe Him. This is the same mighty power that raised Christ from the dead and seated Him in the place of honor at God's right hand in the heavenly realms.
>
> Now He is far above any ruler or authority or power or leader or anything else—not only in this world but also in the world to come.
>
> God has put all things under the authority of Christ and made Him head over all things for the benefit of the church. (Ephesians 1:18–22 NLT)

Jesus controls all things for the benefit of the church, which includes you. Cry out audaciously to Him, and watch Him answer beyond your expectations!

Prayer

> Father, I ask in the mighty name of Jesus that You grant spectacular answers to the audacious prayers that Your children will be presenting to You. Grant every reader of this book the faith to believe that You will do exceedingly abundantly above all they are asking or thinking, according to Your power that is at work within us. Amen.

Now get into your "prayer closet," and petition God for answers to your audacious prayers.

Notable victory always comes with faith and great toil in prayer. The promises of God do not materialize like manna from heaven; they must be wrestled into reality through audacious prayers. So give yourself no rest, and give God no rest until you see the manifestation of the answers to your prayers. Heaven will answer your prayers. As you pray, remember these words of Jesus, and remain expectant for God to answer:

> Keep on asking, and you will receive what you ask for. Keep on seeking, and you will find. Keep on knocking, and the door will be opened to you. For everyone who asks, receives. Everyone who seeks, finds. And to everyone who knocks, the door will be opened.

> You parents, if your child asks for a loaf of bread, do you give them a stone instead? Or if they ask for a fish, do you give them a snake? Of course not! So if you sinful people know how to give good gifts to your children, how much more will your heavenly Father give good gifts to those who ask him? (Matthew 7:7–11 NLT)

Amen! Don't hold back. Ask audaciously!

ABOUT THE AUTHOR

Albert B. K. Appiah earned a Master of Divinity degree and a Doctor of Ministry degree. He is the lead pastor of Renewal Christian Center in Upper Marlboro, Maryland, which he planted with his wife, Angela. A gifted and an astute teacher and preacher of God's word, Appiah's compassion for people is demonstrated through his concern for their well-being and spiritual growth. He resides in Brandywine, Maryland, with his wife and their twin children.

ENDNOTES

Preface

1   *Merriam-Webster Dictionary*, s.v. "audacious," accessed September 28, 2020, https://www.merriam-webster.com/dictionary/audacious.

2   All Scripture quotations, unless otherwise noted, are from the New Living Translation.

Chapter 6

3   Samuel R. Chand, *Leadership Pain: The Classroom for Growth* (Nashville: Thomas Nelson, 2015), 47.

Chapter 15

4   Gene Edwards, *A Tale of Three Kings* (Newnan, GA: Christian Books Publishing House, 1980), 15.

Chapter 16

5   David Mercker, Jennifer Franklin, and Larry Tankersley, "How Do Acorns Develop?" University of Tennessee Institute of Agriculture, accessed November 14, 2020, https://extension.tennessee.edu/publications/Documents/W126.pdf.

Chapter 17

6   Charles Spurgeon, "'Whenever God ...' Quote," AZ Quotes, accessed October 4, 2020, https://www.azquotes.com/quote/874474.

7   B. Roy Zuck, *The Speaker's Quote Book* (Grand Rapids, MI: Kregel Publications, 1997), 286.

8   Johnson Oatman Jr., "Count Your Blessings," 1987, accessed October 5, 2020, https://library.timelesstruths.org/music/Count_Your_Blessings/.

The Story of Summer
Buttercups and Daisies

Rosie McCormick

HODDER
Wayland

an imprint of Hodder Children's Books

Text copyright © Rosie McCormick 2005

Design: Proof Books
Editor: Kirsty Hamilton

Published in Great Britain in 2005
by Hodder Wayland, an imprint of
Hodder Children's Books

The publishers would like to thank the following for allowing us to
reproduce their pictures in this book: Corbis: Adam Woolfitt title page;
Milt & Patti Putnam 2; Craig Tuttle 4; Mark Gibson 5; Craig
Hammell 6; David Muench 7; 8; Clay Perry 11; Tom Brakefield 12;
David Aubrey 13; Angela Hampton, Ecoscene 14; Australian Picture
Library 15; Ed Bock Photography, Inc 16; Rolf Bruderer 17; Martin
Harvey 19; Richard Klune 20; Robert Maass 21; Charles & Josette
Lenars 22; Stock Photos 23 / Getty Images: Howard Grey, Stone 9;
Stuart Redler, Taxi 18

British Library Cataloguing in Publication Data
McCormick, Rosie
Buttercups and daisies: the story of summer. - (The story
of the seasons)
1. Summer - Juvenile literature
I. Title
508.2

ISBN 07502 46227

Printed in China

Hodder Children's Books
A division of Hodder Headline Limited
338 Euston Road, London NW1 3BH

Contents

Warmer days

Summer rarely arrives suddenly. Instead, each day, tiny changes occur. The sun shines a little more brightly and late spring showers and cool winds are gradually replaced by warm breezes and clear blue skies.

4

Then, slowly, tempted by the changes taking place in the earth and in the sky, we start to spend more time outdoors. Until at last we realise that summer has arrived!

5

Buttercups and daisies

Summer is the warmest, and as far as nature is concerned, the busiest time of the year. With increased warmth and sunshine, plants of every kind can once again begin to grow and flourish. Flowers, trees and shrubs bloom and blossom in abundance. Food crops, nurtured by the earth and warmed by the sun, start to grow.

Gardens, parks, hedgerows and meadows become awash with vibrant colour. And the sweet, fragrant smell of summer is carried along by gentle breezes.

Eventually, tired and hungry, she fell down. Her ancestor spirits took pity on her and lifted her gently up into the sky world where she slept for a long time.

When she woke she found food and water and a fire. She was content. But as she looked down on her people she saw how sad they were that she had gone and how cold they were. So she built up her fire so that it was big enough to warm her people on earth. And she is there still, tending to the fire that we see burning in the sky each morning.

Glossary

Ancient – something from a long time ago

Blossom – flowers on hedges and trees

Cereal – grain that is used for food

Crops – plants grown by people for food

Flourish – when a plant grows healthy and strong

Nature – plants, animals and the earth

Nectar – sugars made by flowers to attract insects

Nurture – to help something to grow

Pollen – tiny grains found in flowers, which make seeds

Ripe – when fruit is ready to be picked

Seeds – the things that new plants grow from

Index